LIMITED NUCLEAR WAR

To Janice

LIMITED NUCLEAR WAR

Political Theory and War Conventions

Ian Clark

Princeton University Press

Published by Princeton University Press,
41 William Street, Princeton, New Jersey 08540

Library of Congress Cataloging in Publication Data

Clark, Ian, 1949-
    Limited nuclear war.
    Bibliography: p.
    Includes index.
    1. Atomic warfare.   2. Limited war.   I. Title.
UF767.C515   355'.0217   82-47623
ISBN 0-691-07644-8   AACR2

Printed and bound in Great Britain

Contents

Acknowledgments

This book was written in 1980–1 during a year's study leave spent in Cambridge, as Visiting Fellow in the Centre of International Studies. I am indebted to the University of Western Australia for its provision of this leave. I am also deeply grateful to Professor F. H. Hinsley, Master of St. John's and to the Centre of International Studies, University of Cambridge, for hosting my leave and making it such a pleasant and profitable one.

Some of the ideas contained in the book were first aired at a number of seminars: in the Department of International Relations, University of Keele; in the Department of International Politics, University College of Wales, Aberystwyth; in the Department of Politics, University of Glasgow; and in the Seminar on the History of International Relations, University of Cambridge. I would like to convey my sincere thanks to all those who organized the seminars and to those who contributed their thoughts and critical ideas.

Finally, I am indebted to Janice, my wife, for converting numerous illegible drafts into typescripts.

Introduction

At least one of the world's present superpowers, the United States, officially adheres to a strategic doctrine in accordance with which a future nuclear war could be conducted in a limited manner: the other power, the Soviet Union, officially denounces such a posture but is thought, by some analysts, to be likely to limit its own operations if once it found itself in a nuclear exchange with the United States. Whereas once we were assured of mutual destruction in a nuclear war, officialdom now encourages us to believe in the possibility of limited nuclear survival: the war that was deemed to be the ultimate form of total war is increasingly presented as a rational and controllable instrument of national policy. What has made it seem such is the growing belief that wars, even intercontinental nuclear ones, might be fought within tacitly agreed limits.

This perspective has emerged as a major one in the 1970s and appears set to dominate strategic thinking in the 1980s. It entails a substantial change of emphasis. As against the realist attitude, which regards war's only problem to be that of discovering how best to win it, and as against the utopian attitude which conceives of war's problem as being one of effective abolition, the limitationist occupies the middle ground: he shares the realist assumption that wars will occur and that they have a purpose, while going part-way with the utopian denial of egoistic national self-assertion and hence accepting the need for restraint in war, if not its prohibition. All the fundamental paradoxes of war-limitation derive from this initial position because the limitationist is, in a sense, attempting to square the circle. The realist describes war in zero-sum terms whereas the utopian insists on a harmony of

1

human interests, in the context of which war can be no more than an absurdity: the limitationist has the unenviable task of explaining why belligerents have interests in common at that very moment when they attempt, by violent means, to prevail over each other. It is this uneasy juxtaposition, of a sophisticated perception of mutuality with the crass physical realities of combat, which provides the teasing paradoxes and contradictions in which the limitation of warfare abounds, especially when it is recalled that limitation requires a level of co-operation with the enemy in war that proved unattainable in averting recourse to hostilities.

It is also apparent what has prompted the re-orientation of nuclear strategic theory towards concepts of limited usage. Given the attainment of some degree of strategic parity between the superpowers by the early 1970s, and given the consequent diminution in the credibility of massive nuclear exchanges, and of the deterrence based thereon, theorists were driven once again to the task of constructing an intellectual framework within which nuclear force and political ends might be brought into meaningful relationship. In the most general terms, the recent attraction of strategic theory to the creation of limited nuclear options has been stimulated by the perceived erosion of the Clausewitzian paradigm of politically-instrumental war. Limitation has been the chosen means by which strategists have sought to put the policy back into the usage of nuclear weapons.

At no time in history has a proper understanding of limits to war been more pressing than it is now. We live in an age of uncomfortable choices and even when the alternative seems to be one of all-out nuclear holocaust, there is nothing like a consensus in favour of opting for the path of limited war. As *The Economist* was to express the view a quarter of a century ago, but in words as germane today: 'logic says that the most unutterably horrible war that does not happen is preferable to the most humane war that does' (Groom 1974, p. 74). There are those, therefore, who regard the adoption of limited nuclear alternatives with the utmost trepidation. But for these same people, insensate Armageddon is no more attractive a prospect. Neither side in this strategic debate has a monopoly on virtue and it is this fact which lends the issue its special poignancy.

It is in the shadow of these painful choices that this study finds its justification and its particular perspective. The author's intellectual point of departure is from the confluence of the disciplines of international relations, of strategic studies and of political philosophy. Such philosophical enquiry as there has been into the nature of international relations has been mostly preoccupied with the great issues of war and peace and with what they tell us about the existence, or workings, of an international society. This is not to be wondered at because, if we accept the Clausewitzian contention that war (or, at least, battle) is simply what cash settlement is to the market, then war must be understood as an integral and highly revealing element of the social whole. It follows also from this analogy that the form of settlement can scarcely be suppressed without provoking dislocations in the workings of the entire system. Political theorists who have turned their minds to the study of international relations have, in turn, been forced to come to terms with the institution of war.

At the risk of doing violence to a complex area of intellectual history, it may be said that political theory has traditionally explored three aspects pertaining to war and its place in the modern nation-state system. Firstly, it has periodically attempted to define the nature of war itself by providing an insight into its essential characteristics — viewed variously as a socio-political institution, as an expression of human predispositions in the natural state, as a pathological condition of international society, or as some form of natural cataclysm, to mention but some of the profferred conceptions. Secondly, and deriving from the particular definition of the nature of war, theorists have dwelt upon the possibilities of establishing perpetual peace and upon the difficulties attendant thereon. Thirdly, political theory provides us with a rich, if less familiar, body of ideas about the reasons for resorting to war, and about the appropriate limits within which it might be conducted. However, while there have been these three distinct and well-established strands of political thought on war, it is no exaggeration to say that what has been missing is a systematic endeavour to integrate them. The nature of war, its permanence or otherwise, and war's intrinsic or extrinsic limits — these are all important areas of speculation, but none can be convincingly explored without reference to the others. To put it as unequivocally as possible, no theory of limits to war that is not located within an overarching theory of war itself can hope to be persuasive.

Approached from this angle, the idea of introducing limits into warfare becomes much more than a problem of military strategy. Unfortunately, it is as a problem of military strategy that most of the post-1945 discussion of limits to war has been conducted. While not denying the military dimensions of any consideration of limits to war the underlying theme of this study is, therefore, that its full importance is lost unless it is seen as a problem in the theory of international relations, and, by extension, in the realm of political philosophy. The debate about limits to war is too vital to be left in the hands of the strategists alone.

A study of limits to war raises questions of politics and of philosophy of the greatest magnitude. We have to face the issue of whether limiting war is, in principle, desirable and if so, whether it is a goal that is capable of achievement; we are compelled to face the vexing question as to whether, by limiting the horrors of war, we make its onset more likely or, by alternative reasoning, whether a limited war is a more credible deterrent and thence an inhibition on resort to it? On a more elevated philosophical plane, but no less fraught with practical consequences for that, we have to ask ourselves what, morally and politically, does the introduction of limits into war tell us about the nature of war itself? What is the point of war, and how is that point affected by constraining the war's conduct to less than its full military potential? Does the acceptance of conventions of war depend upon prior acceptance of a particular conception of international society and of war's function within that society? How is that function changing in the light of rapid technological advance and, in particular, how has the acquisition of vast nuclear arsenals impinged upon the need for, or the possibility of, limitation in war? It is around questions of this kind, questions which take us far beyond the purely military dimensions of limits in warfare, that the present study is constructed.

Historically, the limitation of war has assumed many forms

and been undertaken for a range of differing reasons. The most tangible form of limitation may be found, perhaps, in the positive conventions and international law of modern warfare and the person interested in limits to war should, as Best (1980) has done, review the development and implementation of this legal code of conduct. Alternatively, it might be contended that the most impressive intellectual tradition of speculation about limits to war is to be found in that body of just war theorizing which stretches back into the medieval period. We might then, as with Walzer (1977) or with Paskins and Dockrill (1979), seek for limits in war by distinguishing between just and unjust modes of combat and by constructing a contemporary variant of the classical *ius in bello*. Yet again, we might concede that wars have been limited for a variety of prudential, technological, political and humanitarian reasons, and seek for enlightenment on limits to war by reviewing past efforts to mitigate it, the forms such limitation has taken, the implications of such efforts and the historical factors which facilitated, or undermined, these attempts. In such a case, Howard (ed.) (1979) is an indispensable source.

It is arbitrary to single out these recent studies from the rich store of writing that is available to the student interested in a fuller understanding of limits to war. Likewise, it is not to call into question the excellence which each of these studies achieves in its own area if it be said that the present book is different in conception from any of the aforementioned. In this study, we are concerned not only with the modern law of warfare, nor with just war reasoning, nor with the historical practice of limited warfare, but with all of these and more. This is at once an academic impertinence and at the same time absolutely fundamental to the nature of the task: only by encompassing all of these various perspectives and by combining them with historical illustrations of limits to war, as well as with the history of ideas about limits in its widest possible sense, can we hope to ask the really important questions about warfare limitation — let alone be in a position to offer even tentative answers. It is the intention of this study that it review in wide-ranging terms the evolution of thinking on limits to war, starting from a conviction that political philosophy should have something to offer on the great questions confronting us. If this is deemed too ambitious a task, the retort must be that, in the prevailing militaristic climes, political theory should aspire to nothing less. It is surely now commonplace that political philosophy cannot artificially restrict itself to contemplation of the *polis* alone but must shed some light on the relationship between one *polis* and another. In no area is this need more urgent than in the study of war's means and ends, and of how the introduction of a principle of limitation into warfare affects the interrelationship between the two. As Fairbanks (1976, p. 165) has remarked: 'if war-limiting is in its broadest sense a problem of the relation between ends and means, it is of great interest to the political theorist'.

Both the scope and the timeless depth of the approach require further justification. It might be thought fanciful that limits to war should be treated in such a general and cavalier fashion as is to be found in these pages: surely, to regard a single combat between David and Goliath, the medieval Peace of God, a prohibition on the use of poisons, an attempt to distinguish between combatants and noncombatants and the development of doctrines of selective nuclear options — to regard all of these as constituting equally instances of war-limitation is to conceal much more than it reveals? Wars are fought in their individual social, cultural and technological settings, and what is a viable and effective form of limitation in one context becomes an anachronism or absurdity in another: a convention of war in one culture, if transposed to a radically different context, would change war into a game or an essentially apolitical form of chivalric display. We, therefore, should not treat limits to war in such an ahistoric manner.

The argument is not without substance. Political scientists are notorious for their raids upon history, both ancient and modern, from which these latter-day Vikings bring back their pillaged and plundered data. It is not in this spirit that the following study is offered. Rather it is in these very historical and cultural differences amongst the limited war practices reviewed in this study that the value of such a survey is to be found. The stylized and gentlemanly warfare of the eighteenth century could, within a generation, be lampooned by no less a figure than von Clausewitz, because the military practices appropriate to the age of dynastic or commercial wars were deemed by him to be inappropriate in the emerging age of nationalist wars. What this illustrates is that the intellectual stock-in-trade of one generation can become the fantasies or the frivolities of another. There is the danger, then, that we become the prisoners of our own preconceptions and of prevailing cultural orthodoxies. In contemplating limits to war, we may conclude in such a restricted framework that too much, or too little, can be done. In this sense, a mere recapitulation of the diversity of human experience of war is a mind-stretching exercise.

There is a special reason why it is important to compare and to contrast past writings on limits to war with the contemporary body of speculation on limits in nuclear warfare. At heart, it is the theorists of limited nuclear war themselves who are assuming, if only by implication, that it is meaningful to discourse about limited nuclear war, in much the same way that it has been meaningful to discourse about limits to war in the past. The theme of continuity, of a persisting concept of war and of a persisting concept of its limitation, is a prominent feature of the recent strategic ruminations. To place the current analyses of limited nuclear war in the context of traditional speculation on the subject of limits to war is, from their own perspective, merely to take things to their logical conclusion. Accordingly, it is only appropriate that their philosophy of limitation be examined in juxtaposition to its more traditional formulations. It is, then, the brief of this study to outline the contours of past speculation on the subject of limits to war, and to make some judgment as to how contemporary theories have been accommodated to traditional moulds.

The point can be made with even greater insistence. If, at the heart of the various theories of limited nuclear warfare, there lies a unifying assumption as to the persistence of a politically-instrumental conception of warfare, then we might legitimately ask that there be continuity also in the assumption as to the place of, and the point of, limitation in such war. On their own admission, the theorists of limited nuclear war seek to deny the revolutionary interpretations of war in the nuclear age: to be consistent, they must also deny the revolutionary interpretations of the limitations that are practicable within such a context of warfare. It is the task of the analyst to investigate the precise continuities and discontinuities in the discussion of war's limitation, especially when legitimacy is sought for the new theories, by making appeal to the venerable traditions of thought that have preceded them.

That there should have been this prominent reversion to limited-war thinking in the nuclear age is in itself a revealing, if unsurprising, development. It provides testimony to the endurance of traditional concepts of warfare, even in the most inhospitable of technological environments. In the dialectic occurring between modes of thought about war and the technological parameters of the present day, the former seems to be proving the more tenacious. Such is the hold that traditional concepts of the usage of military power have retained, even in the nuclear age, that it is our persisting concepts of war, and of limitation in war, that appear to be shaping the physical realities, rather than the physical realities modifying our traditional concepts. When Kissinger (1979, pp. 217–8) writes of the crucial importance adhering to the development of a discriminating nuclear strategy, in the absence of which strategy and foreign policy will be paralysed, he is implicitly arguing that whatever yields in the nuclear age, it cannot be the exercise of military power in support of national strategy.

Morgenthau (1977) is a powerful critic of such reasoning and demonstrates well the ideological presuppositions that have been carried forward into the discussion of warfare, and of limited warfare, in the nuclear age. In doing so, he attacks the fundamental conservatism of a pattern of thought that has not adjusted to new realities, regardless of the lip-service that it might pay to them:

> From the clean H-bomb through graduated deterrence, to the counter-force strategy of ex-Secretary of Defense, James Schlesinger, there is one impulse tying these different strategies together: to find a way by which a nuclear war can be fought in a conventional way, that is, to conventionalize nuclear war in order to be

able to come out of it alive. In other words, there is what I would regard as an absurd attempt, not to adapt our modes of thought and action to the new objective conditions of the nuclear age but to transform those objective conditions in the light of the pre-nuclear modes of thought and action (Morgenthau 1977, p. 256).

Equally, such a perspective provides us with a sense of direction. One book which surveyed the development of war practices found evidence of gross moral decline as reflected in its revealing, if tendentious, title *Advance to Barbarism* (Veale 1968). To notice that what is acceptable now, say as regards treatment of noncombatants, is dramatically different from what would have been regarded as acceptable a genera-tion ago, or a century ago, does not permit us to conclude that modern warfare is *ipso facto* unjust; but the evolution of these attitudes should not be lost to sight. We cannot expect to treat the subject of limits to war adequately without having before our eyes the multiform practices of the past, and the various options which cultures have allowed them-selves because of their own conception of the nature of war. Conceptions of war may be changed in accordance with the limitations actually practised within it: more fundamentally, however, it is changing conceptions of war which have dictated the nature and the provenance of its acceptable limits. To some extent, then, the nature of war, and the form that it takes, is dependent upon our social conception of what is its point.

A similar comment can be made in support of the rather ahistoric history of ideas about war-limitation which follows in these pages. The attempt to present Plato and ex-US Secre-tary of Defense, James Schlesinger, as participating in a time-less dialogue about the possibilities of restraint in war may test the reader's credulity beyond endurance. But there is value in such eclecticism. Granted that the purposes for which the two sought limits to war, and that the contexts in which it was to take place were as remote from each other as could conceivably be, the fact remains that each, in his own way, contributed an important perspective upon the limita-tion of warfare which enriches our understanding of what can, and what cannot, be achieved by way of restraint. If it is accepted that there is a continuing tradition of thought on the 'good society' or on 'individual rights', it is no less plausible, even if much sparser in noted contributions, that we think in terms of a tradition of thought on 'the good international society', on 'national rights' and, not far removed, on the proper or rational conduct of hostilities between states.

As will become clear in the course of the study, there are two principal issues with which the student of limits to war has to come to terms. These are, firstly, what do we limit when war is limited? The second concerns the effect which the introduction of limitations has upon our understanding of the nature of war and, more specifically, revolves around the extent to which war can be limited, while still remaining the social institution that we recognize war to be.

Two main devices will be employed to shed light on these questions, if not to offer complete answers to them. In response to the former question, two alternative answers will be provided, in terms of what I have called convention A and convention B. The first, convention A, is a description of limitation in war which argues that war can be limited by defining the actual process of war, by outlining the ground rules in terms of which war is a recognizable procedure. The second, convention B, is a description of limitation in war which argues that it can be limited by stipulating substantive limitations within the process itself: more or less of such limitations, while greatly affecting the amount of suffering experienced in war, do not call into question the essential nature of the activity itself.

A simple analogy might clarify this point. The process of withdrawing money from a bank account is readily distinguishable, to a person knowing the normal procedures, from the process of taking money from a bank at gunpoint. Not only are the two discrete activities, but we make the additional judgment that the former is a legally-permissible activity while the latter is not.

Contrast the foregoing with the following situation. A gunman who demands that the bankteller give him $100 can be distinguished from the gunman who demands $100,000. However, in this second instance, the money is obtained by the identical process in either case, the only substantial difference being in terms of the quantity of cash thus extracted.

It is the argument of this study, to be elaborated below, that war-limitation can be analysed on the basis of a similar distinction: limitation by modifying the nature of the process of war (convention A) and limitation by diminishing the quantum of damage inflicted in war (convention B).

The second device employed in the study is the construction of three alternative models of war-limitation. These are, for the purposes of the study, labelled as the champion, the charity and (for want of more exact alliteration) the city-swapping models. Each in turn describes a model of limits to war and seeks to analyse, in abstract terms, the structural properties possessed by the respective models. Some of these differing properties can be captured by employing the convention A/convention B distinction, but other points of difference between the three models will be described in turn. To anyone who reads the literature on limits to war, both past and present, it soon becomes apparent that limits are perceived in radically different ways as between writers, and as fulfilling quite disparate functions. The presentation of these three ideal-types of limitation should provide us with a basis upon which to recognize some salient differences between strategies of limitation and to know what can, and what cannot, be expected to result from the types of limitation that have been proposed. Like all good consumers, as we are being invited to buy a strategic package with the brand name of limited nuclear options, we should insist on finding out what the package contains and what guarantees come with the purchase.

1

On War and its Limitation

ON WAR AND THE DESIRABILITY OF LIMITATION

The desirability of limitation in war is not self-evident nor universally recognized. As Brodie (1959, p. 314) remarked more than twenty years ago: 'all of us assume almost without question that peace is better than war, but it is curious and interesting that we do not have the same consensus that limited war is preferable to total war'. Whether it be because a war worth fighting at all is considered worth fighting hard to win or because co-operation, in any form, with an armed adversary is deemed inappropriate, many people believe that warfare is one area of social activity in which a principle of moderation is not to be applied unthinkingly.

There are many, and complex, reasons why this should be so: we need explore them only in so far as they shed light on the concept of limitation by elucidating some of its consequences. Accordingly, it is possible to illustrate the issues surrounding the desirability, or otherwise, of limitation in warfare by reviewing the historical interplay and development of the two components of the just war doctrine, namely the *ius ad bellum* and the *ius in bello*. Put crudely, the classical *ad bellum* doctrine specified the just ends of war whereas the *in bello* doctrine specified the just means. However, the two notions have been variously interrelated. In terms of a history of ideas, it might be said that the limits upon war tended originally to derive from the *ad bellum* ends, in the sense that the means adopted by the party fighting for a just cause were *ipso facto* permissible, whilst the unjust party had no legitimate rights in war. This was the prevalent position throughout the Middle Ages. As Hartigan (1967, p. 210) has observed:

12

'when their work is closely examined, one finds a consistent lack of attention paid to the means employed in a just war. This was as true of St. Thomas in the thirteenth century as it was of St. Augustine in the fifth century'. In other words, the only restrictions upon the conduct of warfare were the authority, cause and intention of the just party.

Subsequently, and certainly by the eighteenth century, the *ius in bello* broke free of the *ius ad bellum*: the conduct of the parties in warfare could be judged on its merits, jointly and severally, and not in the shadow of the reasons for which war had been undertaken. Under the sway of positive international law, both parties enjoyed equal rights according to the rules of war, and each was subject to the identical prohibitions: the justice of the cause, as distinct from the means, of warfare was *ultra vires* as far as international law was concerned. Vattel (1916, p. 305) offers us a concise analysis of this development in the Law of Nations:

> The first rule of that law ... is that regular war, as regards its effects, must be accounted just on both sides. This principle ... is absolutely necessary if any law or order is to be introduced into a method of redress as violent as that of war, if any bounds are to be set to the disasters it occasions ... Thus the rights founded upon the state of war ... do not depend, externally and in the sight of men, upon the justice of the cause, but upon the legality of the means as such ...

The logical corollary of this was that any regulation or limitation that might be introduced into warfare could be inserted only by way of a *ius in bello*. It is not, perhaps, surprising that since the eighteenth century the primary concern of legalists and moralists alike has been the nature, and the justice, of the means of warfare. As Osgood and Tucker (1967, p. 302) were to argue: 'if we are to find a distinctive quality in *bellum justum,* a quality that sets clear and meaningful limits to the necessities of the state ... it must be in the restraints placed on the conduct or means of war'.

In fact, in the twentieth century, and especially since 1945, the relationship between *ius ad bellum* and *ius in bello* has undergone a further, and radical, transformation. It is now common for the justice of war to be adjudged in accordance with the means employed, and for this judgment to insinuate itself into the analysis of the merits of the cause of war. What this means is that the prohibition upon certain forms of warfare can be so severe as to outlaw wars fought by these means, whatever the objective justice of the ends pursued.

This turnabout in the relationship between an ends-derived justice of warfare and a means-derived justice of warfare has been summarized as follows:

> ... just war doctrine ... is until the end of the Middle Ages focused foremost on the question of whether Christians may ever in the first place take up arms, not on the related question of what they may legitimately do after war is begun. Today the situation is reversed: principal focus, in both Christian thought and international law, is upon what weapons may be used and against whom they may legitimately be employed. Where it is assumed that modern war necessarily implies thermonuclear war, the moral prohibition of such weapons is read back to prohibit war itself. Thus today the tendency is to derive a *ius ad bellum* (or rather, as Paul Ramsey has called it, a *ius contra bellum*) from *ius in bello* limitations. In the Middle Ages exactly the opposite obtains (Johnson 1975, p. 41).

What emerges from the preceding summary history of just war doctrine is that the limitation of the means of warfare cannot be, and has not been, regarded as a universal good. For it to be considered so, there must be no overriding end which will be stultified by adherence to conventions of limitation. Moreover, as is clearly revealed in our historical narrative of the just war, it was thought iniquitous that the righteous party, fighting for a just cause, should be bound by the same rules of warfare as the delinquent state. Rules of war-limitation, in as much as they are mutual and reciprocal, do not possess a uniform attraction.

Additionally, while limitation in war may be overridden by the compelling ends of a just war, so likewise may these limitations be countermanded from the opposite end by a conception of just war which prohibits any resort to certain forms of warfare that are deemed to be intrinsically unjust. We thus have the paradoxical situation in the history of ideas, that limits to war have been rendered inoperative by the need to prosecute successfully a just war, while at other periods these limits have been rendered irrelevant by a conception of just war which regards even such minimal use of an unjust force to be unacceptable. While just war theorizing has been an historically important source of thinking on limits to war, it has also provided intellectual ammunition for the arsenal of the opponents of limitation.

The arguments surrounding the desirability of limitation run even deeper than this and tend to take two distinct, though structurally similar, forms. They are, firstly, that anything which diminishes the horrors of war will tend to protract war's agonies and, secondly, that anything which dampens war's ardour will make it more likely: no matter how good the intention underlying the attempt to restrain war, the outcome of these efforts will tend to be detrimental in the extreme. These arguments may be briefly outlined in turn.

The notion that a generously-fought war will long outlast a brutal one has been around for some time. Pufendorf (1934, p. 1317) notes the argument in passing, even if he is not fully persuaded by it:

> But since war is allowable for this end, namely, that we may defend or assert our rights when that is impossible by peaceful methods, it should be agreed that the shortest way by which that can be attained is the most agreeable to nature. And so when those pacts which only temper the use of force in war do but increase and nourish war, it is manifest that they are repugnant to nature.

Or, as in the opinion of one British peer: 'the most insidious way of prolonging war as a means of settlement between nations is to endeavour to make it a gentlemanly occupation' (Quester 1966, p. 79). Put simply, this amounts to an argument that a little humanity in the short run, to the extent that it thwarts war's business, may entail a lot of inhumanity in the long run. An address, delivered in 1903 in honour of Robert E. Lee, by the great-grandson of John Adams, developed the same theme in relation to the rules of warfare:

> On this point two views, I am well aware, have been taken from the beginning, and still are advocated. On the one side, it is contended that warfare should be strictly confined to combatants, and its horrors and devastations brought within the narrowest limits . . . But, on the other hand, it is insisted that such a method of procedure is mere cruelty in disguise; that war at best is Hell, and that true humanity lies in exaggerating that Hell to such an

extent as to make it unendurable. By so doing it is forced to a
speedy end.

The speaker, Charles Francis Adams, went on to deliver his
own counter-argument:

> That war is Hell at best, then make it Hell indeed, that cry is not
> original with us: far from it; it echoes down the ages ... What
> was the result? Hell was indeed let loose; but so was Hate. Was
> the war made shorter? No! Not by an hour! It was simply made
> needlessly bitter, brutal, and barbarous ... (Friedman 1972,
> p. xx).

The second argument against limitation echoes the first.
To many minds, nothing short of the abolition of war can
serve humanity's needs, especially in the nuclear age. Anything less is too little and will probably be too late. To other
minds, such a diagnosis is unrealistic: there is no substitute
for war as the *ultima ratio* of international politics, and we
should consequently be trying to tame the beast rather than
vainly attempting to exterminate it. This second perspective,
therefore, focuses attention on possible areas of restraint or
limitation in war.

The two attitudes may, but need not, be in conflict. Some
would say that both avenues should be explored simultaneously, that we can seek to alleviate the symptoms of a
disease while maintaining faith in a long-term cure. Others
would have it that the dilution of war's ill-effects may sap the
will to extirpate it − that, in order to confront the enormity
of the threat which war poses to humanity, we must gaze
upon it, warts and all, and not pretend that war is more palat-
able than it is in reality. According to this latter perspective,
fear of war is the only possible salvation and this fear should
be nurtured, not assuaged. If war is amenable to restraint and
limitation, then it may yet have a purpose. In this sense, the
abolitionists and the limitationists, kindred spirits in many
ways, are engaged in a moral, and perhaps deadly, tug-of-war.

This anti-limitationist argument is frequently deployed. It
finds unsubtle expression in the view that 'far-reaching regulation of military methods and instruments, if rigorously
enforced, might do away with many of the evils of war, but
such a result would tend to reduce the reluctance to resort to

war and so make war more frequent' (Wright 1942, p. 330). Likewise, Tucker (1960, p. 78) notes the belief that 'freedom from war is . . . made dependent upon the appreciation of the necessity of war's unlimited effects' and Walzer (1977, p. 45) highlights the limitationist-abolitionist controversy when he says of the war convention that 'it is often described as a program for the toleration of war, when what is needed is a program for its abolition'. On the other hand, there have been those who have denied that there is any relationship between the limitation of war and its frequency. Halperin (1963, p. 100), recalling the view that nuclear war could occur only as a result of accident, suggests that from this perspective 'the discussion of how an emphasis on controlled counterforce affects the likelihood of war misses the point that such activity does not influence the probability of central war'.

The arguments are, of course, virtually identical to those surrounding the strategic debates of the 1960s and early 1970s — whether we should aim to deter wars or, alternatively, plan to fight them sensibly should they occur? The one view echoes the posture of mutual assured destruction, to ensure that war will not occur, and the other calls for damage — limiting measures in the event that it does. Once again, assured destruction may be regarded as an insane policy for fighting a war, but its supporters denounce the damage-limitationists for making the war more likely.

We can now move on to set out various distinctions which are important in the analysis of the role and nature of limitation in war. In the first place, we ought to distinguish between limitation in war as fact and limitation as policy. For various technological, social or economic reasons, there may be inbuilt constraints upon the practice of war: historically this has been so (*see* Nef 1950). It has accordingly been suggested that:

> . . . we are differentiating modern limited war from anything that has happened in the past. We are talking about something quite new. If wars were limited in ages past, the reasons why they were so have little relevance for us today . . . wars were kept limited by the small margin of the national economic resources available for mobilization and by the small capability for destruction that could be purchased with that narrow margin (Brodie 1959, p. 311).

Limitation becomes policy, as opposed to fact, when it is not necessary that limitations be observed. In this sense, the political character of war-limitation reveals itself with special clarity in the present age. As Martin (1979b, p. 103) has written:

> In previous ages the urge to limit destruction for moral reasons, or to bring sacrifice into some reasonable proportion to the issues at stake, was reinforced to some degree by the sheer physical limits on military capabilities. The industrialization of total war in this century had already weakened this restraint, but nuclear technology has wholly eliminated it. Henceforth, if the destruction wrought in war is to be curbed, it will have to be by policies of deliberate restraint.

Artifice must take up where nature has left off. It is largely with conventions of the latter kind, deriving from policy choices, that this study is concerned.

Secondly, we might make a broad distinction in terms of the source of the impulse to limit war. Limits upon war might be fostered either in consequence of the nature of the ends sought by war or, alternatively, in consequence of the nature of the available means of warfare. Both the ends and the means of war may be conceived as ranging from the limited to the unlimited and, given such permutations, the interesting cases are to be found where unlimited war is a physical option and any constraints derive from policy choices. But in these situations is it likely that the ends will contaminate the means or vice-versa? Conceptually, there are various possibilities. Given limited ends, but unlimited means, holocaust is possible and limited war can result only from rigorous political control of the means, to ensure that they are not disproportionate to the desired ends. The greatest potential for disaster lies in the situation where the ends of the conflict are as unlimited as the means available for its prosecution. In this instance, we cannot expect constraints to derive from the objectives of war: if there are to be restraints, they must have their source elsewhere and this must be on account of the very nature of the means. Many analyses of conflict in nuclear conditions see the means as the source of restraint:

> ... in the nuclear age belligerents may exercise restraint in their conduct of war, not because they have limited objectives, but

because they acknowledge that lack of restraint on their part may destroy them both, whatever their objectives. Bernard Brodie had emphasized this point that nuclear states do not fight limited wars because they have limited objectives, but they sometimes settle for limited objectives because on sensible, prudential grounds they are only prepared to expend a limited amount of military effort in attaining them. In other words, it is restraint on means rather than ends which is critical to the notion of 'limited war' (Garnett 1979, p. 80).

As can be seen from the above, discussion of limits to war in the nuclear age has tended to centre upon the nature of the available military means. But, we might ask, if there is a feeling that the use of such weapons is inappropriate, on what grounds, moral or political, do the weapons fall under question? If we take as an example the massive retaliation doctrine of the 1950s, it is possible to distinguish two general strands of argument against the adoption of such a strategy. The first is the overtly moral or humanitarian stance that to obliterate centres of population is evil and therefore to threaten such an action is equally evil. Massive nuclear strikes against the enemy's citizenry were accordingly objected to on ostensibly moral grounds. It was, perhaps, even more common to come across a second argument which emphasized not the morality, or otherwise, of such nuclear threats, but rather their lack of credibility: a strategy of massive retaliation was not so much evil as ineffective. Clearly, in this second case, the critique derives from political assessments about which kinds of coercive threats will be instrumental and which will not.

This illustration makes the more general point that conventions of war-limitation may have various motivations or sources of inspiration. Moreover, moral and political considerations may well reinforce each other and strengthen the case for limitation: but we should not expect such a happy coincidence in all circumstances. As Bull (1979, p. 589) has remarked: 'although the search for ways of limiting war may be in part a response to the feeling that wars that are limited are morally preferable to wars that are not, that search is not necessarily connected with any such feeling, and derives as much or more from the fear of unlimited war and the desire to limit war so that it can serve as an instrument of policy'.

How, then, might we categorize the possible motivations for limitation of warfare? The standard dichotomies tend to be some variation upon the theme of moral versus political considerations. The literature offers, for example, the suggestions of categorical imperative versus prudence (Howard (ed.) 1979, p. 4), humanitarianism versus pragmatism (Trooboff (ed.) 1975, p. 6) and absolutism versus utilitarianism (Nagel 1974, Brandt 1974). Clearly, one could produce a longer list referring to religious, moral, humanitarian, political, pragmatic, chivalric and military motivations for limitation of war, but most of the central issues are embraced within the standard dichotomies already mentioned. Moreover, no matter how confidently we can enumerate these disparate motivations, it can be said with equal confidence that, at the edges (and the edges are frequently very thick), these motivations tend to merge with each other.

We may rapidly survey the historically most important motivations for limits to war and denote the principal areas of overlap between them. Firstly, we can readily delineate the main characteristics of the religious – moral – humanitarian stance, regardless of the specific metaphysical or philosophical foundations which may be called upon to support it: this case, stated simplistically, is that there are restrictions upon the extent and manner of violence, even in a situation of warfare. These restrictions may derive from religious, moral or natural law sources. As Wolff (1934) was to express it: 'nature herself is opposed to the right of absolutely limitless slaughter of enemies'. The primary concern of this motivation is, therefore, that lives should be spared where possible and suffering diminished in order to 'humanize' the activity of warfare.

It may be difficult to define the moral–humanitarian motivation more precisely than this, and it is even more difficult to assess the historical impact of such motivation. But that it exists, even if only as a residual category, many commentators seem in no doubt. In this context, Friedman (ed.) (1972, p. 4) has contended of the rules of warfare that it is easy to consider them 'as nothing more than strategic military wisdom . . . But many of the historical restraints on war cannot be explained solely by such strategic pragmatism'.

What is left when the pragmatism is stripped away is an irreducible ideological inspiration for the mitigation of war's extremes.

If the parties to a war will not limit it in accordance with some external system of values (moral, religious etc.), then it remains only that limits to war be sought out of self-interest, or where the restraints are reciprocal, out of mutual self-interest. Such considerations are explicitly avowed in situations of deterrence where restraint is induced, not by some exterior code of conduct, but by the dynamics of the relationship itself and its intrinsic threat of reprisal. Schelling (1966, p. 24), as other deterrence theorists, suggests 'that belligerents might, out of self-interest, attempt to limit the war's destructiveness'.

The appeal to pragmatism and self-interest forms part of a venerable tradition. It manifests itself in the advice of Diodotus that Athens extend clemency in its treatment of Mytilene:

> ... if Cleon's method is adopted, can you not see that every city will not only make much more careful preparations for revolt, but will also hold out against siege to the very end, since to surrender early or late means just the same thing? This is, unquestionably, against our interests (Thucydides 1954, p. 188).

Here we have the argument for unilateral restraint: the restraint becomes reciprocal and may embody itself in conventions of limitation when both parties are in a position to do massive damage to each other. It was a relationship, and a motivation for limitation, recognized by the international lawyers of the seventeenth and eighteenth centuries. Grotius, for instance, claimed that the law of nations prohibited the killing of an enemy by means of poison. His account of the reason why such a law came to be adopted is instructive: 'agreement upon this matter arose from a consideration of the common advantage, in order that the dangers of war, which had begun to be frequent, might not be too widely extended' (Grotius 1925, p. 652). Likewise, another jurist argued against the poisoning of weapons because 'if you poison your weapons, your enemy will do the same, and thus without gaining any advantage over him, you will merely have added to the cruelties and horrors of war' (Vattel 1916, p. 289). Finally, we may note that the argument of utility and mutual advantage was one deployed by Pufendorf (1934, p. 228) when he advised that a party fighting a just war need not observe rules of mitigation 'unless he prefers to observe them for some advantage to himself, in that he may find his enemy less cruel to him and his troops' and later observed that: 'the uncertainty of the outcome of a war leads us to temper its licence, for fear the examples we have set may by the hand of fortune be turned against us' (p. 1299).

Finally, in this section, mention must be made of instances of war-limitation which are ambivalent in their motivation, deriving from, or having the appearance of deriving from, both morality and prudence. In some cases, the apparent application of a principle of humanity turns out to be little more than a veneer for tangible interests. For instance, it is well documented that the institutions of slavery and of ransom had a 'humanizing' effect on the treatment of prisoners of war. Likewise, to the extent that Roman warfare was more humane than that of ancient Greece, the difference can be attributed largely to the political aspirations of an Empire, *vis-à-vis* those of the *polis,* and to the kinds of wars, and war aims, engendered by each respectively. In yet other instances, the tangible interest, though less visible, is nonetheless present. For example, an historian of the laws of war in ancient Greece analyses one 'humane' practice in the following terms:

> It is worthy of note that occasionally in open engagement in the field it was forbidden to pursue the enemy beyond the field of battle after the victory was gained . . . This prohibition was due . . . not so much to deliberate moderation and magnanimity as . . . to prudence — it being anticipated that the enemy, aware that his pursuit was not followed up, would thus seize the opportunity of leaving the field entirely (Phillipson 1911, p. 242).

The topic of chivalry might also be broached from this perspective. Was chivalry a motivation for placing limits on warfare and, if so, how are we to understand its nature? Chivalry, as a source for the conduct of warfare, is open to contradictory interpretations and can be seen, in its medieval European manifestation, as the expression of a quasi-moral sense of fair play and honour in combat, but equally as the pragmatic expression of a class or military caste self-interest. Traditionally, there have been historians who have subscribed to both of these interpretations. One study of ancient Chinese warfare in fact discovers in it a 'kind of chivalry obviously rooted in a moral order, but just as obviously contrary to any kind of military pragmatism' (Kierman 1974, p. 43). However, much of the debate concerning chivalry seems to hinge precisely on its moral content, or lack of it, and upon the relationship between honour and morality. Huizinga (1954, p. 105) clearly differentiates between the two when he argues in his discussion of chivalry in the late Middle Ages that 'if a little clemency was slowly introduced into political and military practice, this was due rather to the sentiment of honour than to convictions based on legal and moral principles'.

Other writers implicitly assume a moral quality in the codes of chivalry to the extent that they were influenced by, and closely connected with, the canon law of the Church and its pronouncements on just war. Mattingly (1962, p. 23), for instance, concedes the influence of Church teachings, even if the practice of chivalry modified such teachings and Verbruggen (1977, p. 299) maintains that 'the ideology of Knightly conventions and customs was indeed penetrated by Christian doctrine and this did lead to a more humane type of warfare'.

The final group of writers bring into prominence the element of caste self-interest which underpinned chivalric warfare and, in doing so, make it difficult to maintain that chivalry had any moral inspiration. The harshness of the judgment varies from writer to writer. Keen (1965, p. 242) is content to point out that the medieval law of arms 'was the law of a hereditary noble class'. Many have noted that moderation in fighting served the general interest of this class and also that its purely pragmatic nature is revealed by its exclusiveness, since outsiders and inferiors did not benefit from the application of the chivalric code: 'in a real sense chivalry comprised a system of values effective only in terms of a military elite' (Barnie 1974, p. 70).

There is a harsher judgment still. According to it, chivalry not only cloaked self-interest, but this self-interest was little short of venal:

> The rules were to be observed not from fear of punishment but from a desire not to be excluded from a share in the profits of war. It was a law similar to that of the joint-stock company, evolved in the interests of its members and administered by those who shared the same trade (Wright 1976, p. 21).

There are, therefore, certain persistent themes in the history of recorded attitudes towards the application of principles of limitation in warfare. At core, there has been an ongoing and unresolved debate, as to whether limitation is desirable, with the proponents of humane warfare consistently being opposed by a variety of philosophic arguments ranging from the superior rights of the just party, through the case for making war short by making it nasty and brutish, and to the argument for abolition that regards moderate war as tolerable war. At the same time, the argument about the desirability of limitation in war has been caught up in the diversity of opinions as to why, if at all, it should be considered a worthwhile goal and appeal, on this score, has been made to a broad spectrum of ideological and pragmatic principles. What is striking about our contemporary debates is the extent to which the arguments for and against the adoption of limited nuclear strategies have accommodated themselves to the traditional patterns.

ON WAR AND THE POSSIBILITY OF LIMITATION

There is a fundamental problem involved in any discussion of the possibility of limits to war: this is whether, in principle, warfare is an activity that it makes sense to limit? Alternatively, does not the attempt to limit the degree and impact of force in warfare involve a basic contradiction, an undermining of war's very purpose?

The nature of this dilemma was outlined in Clausewitz's classic analysis of the concept of war. In that work, Clausewitz indicated the two positions which might be adopted in relation to war and its limitation. On the one hand, he started by maintaining that war, in essence, is limitless:

> The maximum use of force is in no way incompatible with the simultaneous use of the intellect. If one side uses force without

compunction, undeterred by the bloodshed it involves, while the other side refrains, the first will gain the upper hand. That side will force the other to follow suit; each will drive its opponent toward extremes, and the only limiting factors are the counterpoises inherent in war . . . To introduce the principle of moderation into the theory of war itself would always lead to logical absurdity (1976, pp. 75–6).

And yet, he concedes, war in essence is not like war in reality. In practice, there is restraint on the application of the utmost degree of force and that restraint is exercised by the nature of the political objective:

> The smaller the penalty you demand from your opponent, the less you can expect him to try and deny it to you; the smaller the effort he makes, the less you need make yourself. Moreover, the more modest your own political aim, the less importance you attach to it and the less reluctantly you will abandon it if you must . . . The political object — the original motive for the war — will thus determine both the military objective to be reached and the amount of effort it requires (1976, p. 81).

The essential question to be answered in any discussion of limitation in war derives from the nature of the relationship of war itself: does war entail the termination of all the rules, conventions or constraints which characterize the relations of states in peacetime? In other words, how are we to define the condition of war and the rules, if any, which govern it? As Vattel (1916, p. 322) was to express it: 'war would become too cruel and too destructive if all intercourse with the enemy were absolutely broken off'.

But what is the nature of this continuing intercourse and how may it prevent war from becoming 'too cruel' and 'too destructive'? Briefly, we might outline three standard responses to this question. They are, respectively, that war is a political, a legal or a moral condition and, as such, is subject to various intrinsic restraints.

The first position, that war remains a political condition and not one of indiscriminate violence, has already been mentioned in connection with Clausewitz. It insists that the nature and degree of force employed be subject to the political ends of the war and it follows that if the political objectives of both parties are limited, there is no absurdity in the creation of conventions which might restrict the cruelty or destructiveness of war for both sides. Such restraints are, however, essentially political in nature and derive from the fundamentally political condition of the war.

A second response is that war can be defined as a legal condition and is subject, accordingly, to legal restraints. In fact, the description of war as a state of law has been a pervasive one in the history of ideas. Sturzo (1929, p. 89) provides a representative example of this style of thinking when he maintains that 'the concept of war is thus restricted to its function and aspect as a lawful institution'. Although war is an extraordinary legal condition, it is yet a legal condition. As one study has commented: 'war is an exceptional state of law in which destruction and killing are permitted, although not without restrictions' (SIPRI 1976b, p. 292).

Thirdly, there is the view that however abhorrent war may be, it persists as a moral condition and is subject to moral restraints. The most cogent and eloquent recent defence of this position can be found in Walzer and in his recurrent theme that war is 'a world of permissions and prohibitions — a moral world, therefore, in the midst of hell' (1977, p. 36). Walzer's position was, however, by no means original and forms part of a much older tradition. The words of Grotius might have been those of Walzer when the former insisted that 'those who are enemies do not in fact cease to be men' (1925, p. 792) and it is upon this premise that the moral rules of warfare are based.

The conception of war as a continuing moral condition can, perhaps, be best understood by comparing it with the opposite view which is that war is a condition of military necessity to which moral judgments are inappropriate. Tucker, although he does not himself subscribe to this view, provides a concise statement of it:

> If war must follow a necessity of its own, then it is useless to indulge in moral judgments on the manner in which hostilities are conducted. If war has no limitations save those imposed 'by the limitations of force itself' then the attempt to distinguish among the weapons and methods of warfare, let alone to observe such distinctions, is little more than a futile gesture. Moral distinctions, and moral judgments based on these distinctions, are largely irrelevant once men have decided to make force the arbiter of their differences (Tucker 1960, p. 76).

The general issue underlying both the assertions and denials of war as a political, legal or moral condition is whether it is legitimate to regard war as a rule-governed activity at all? In its broadest terms the question is whether, if we assume that limits imply the introduction of rules or conventions of behaviour, war may appropriately be considered as a rule-governed activity or whether the notion of limits in war entails a fundamental contradiction?

There have, of course, been opinions ranged on both sides, each trying to provide an answer to the paradoxical question 'why have rules governing the conduct of war if, by definition, war is a total effort to destroy the enemy?' (Trooboff (ed.) 1975, p. 6). On the one side, there is to be found the argument that there are no rules in warfare except the rules of military efficiency and that the attempt to introduce extrinsic rules is self-contradictory. The view has been outlined by Howard (ed.) (1979, pp. 6−7) as follows:

> A strong case can indeed be made for the argument that if war *can* be limited, if the belligerents can be reasonable enough to accept extraneous limitations on its conduct and regard the enemy almost as a *frère adversaire,* they should be reasonable enough to avoid fighting altogether ... Agreed limitations on warfare imply rational understanding with an enemy who, if he can be reasoned with, should not be an enemy.

Pufendorf had earlier commented in the same quizzical fashion upon the possibility of concluding pacts with the enemy during warfare and had cast doubt on the appropriateness of such pacts, based on faith:

> And yet it implies a confusion for me to demand that another keep faith with me, and at the same time avow that I intend to remain his enemy, that is, to remain a person who would injure him in every way possible. For a state of hostility of itself grants one the licence to do another injury without limit. Therefore, the promise that I will not exercise the licence of hostility against another seems opposed to actual conditions, so long as I proclaim that I will continue in a full state of war (Pufendorf 1934, p. 1316).

We have already encountered the opposing view that war is rule-governed in the brief outline of the political, legal and moral rules of warfare. It is a view which is implicit in the many attempts to distinguish the nature of warfare from other forms of killing, such as the distinction between 'war and murder' (Anscombe 1970) and 'war and massacre' (Nagel 1974). Commentators may differ about the nature of the rules of war, but most are agreed that it is the existence of such rules which sets war apart from indiscriminate violence or killing. As Gentili (1933, p. 251) was to express it, quoting Livy: 'war, like peace, has its laws'. For Walzer, these rules of warfare derive from a moral theory of human rights. For Vattel, they derive both from a law of nature and from common prudence, but they are no less essential to the notion of war for being prudential:

> It would be an error equally abhorrent and disastrous to imagine that all duties cease and all ties of humanity are broken when two Nations go to war ... They are still subject to the Laws of Nature; otherwise there would be no laws of war ... There are a thousand occasions during the actual course of war when, for the sake of setting bounds to its fury and to the disasters which accompany it, the common interest and the welfare of both belligerents require that they be able to agree together on certain things ... War would degenerate into cruel and unrestrained acts of violence, and there would be no limit to its calamities (Vattel 1916, p. 296).

Clearly, then, 'cruel and unrestrained acts of violence' are not a part of war: they occur only when warfare has degenerated and become something else; when, in other words, the rules of warfare have been broken.

However, it might fairly be objected that to ask simply whether war is, or is not, a rule-governed activity is to ask an overly-crude question. To ascertain whether it is appropriate to speak of conventions limiting warfare, we need to know not only whether warfare is rule-governed, but also what kind of rules may be thought to apply to it. In other words, are there various types of rules only some of which are applicable to warfare? If so, what is their nature? More fundamentally, indeed, we might ask whether some rules, if applied to warfare, might not change the very essence of warfare and make it into something it is not? What kind of rules can be applied to war, and to what extent can it be regulated, while retaining the essential characteristics of war *as war*?

Not all rules are of a similar nature. Various social practices are rule-governed, but the nature of the rules may be different in kind as between one practice and another: the rules of successful cookery are, in principle, not the same as the rules of cricket; nor are the rules of cricket, in principle, the same as the rules of judicial evidence. It follows, therefore, that if various practices require different types of rules, then by making a fundamental change in the rules we may change basically the nature of the practice. Clearly, for our purposes, the crucial question is the extent to which war may be governed by rules of limitation, while leaving it as recognizably the practice of warfare.

Part of the problem stems from the fact that 'war' may be a generic term which covers a variety of related, but discrete, practices, rather than a description of one single practice. Just as Rapoport (1960) had demonstrated that there may be various forms of conflict (analysed by him, in terms of fights, games and debates), so it might be supposed that there are various forms of war, each entailing its own distinctive rules. In fact, Schelling (1966, p. 166) has argued that there are, in terms of objectives and means, at least three variant forms of war, which he describes as 'wars of the battlefield', 'wars of risk' and 'wars of pain and destruction'. Each can be a form of limited war but the nature of the limits varies from case to case.

Wright (1942, p. 76) provided actual evidence of distinctive forms of war in his discussion of primitive types:

> Primitive peoples often distinguish different types of war. Among the Melanesians there is a very mild form of war between related clans seldom resulting in casualties, fought with clubs only, in the spirit of a game. With more habitual enemies there is a form of pitched battle which, while resulting in casualties, is surrounded by elaborate formalities and rules limiting its destructiveness and distinguishing it from the most serious type of war — ambushes or early-morning raids with the object of annihilating the village.

Evidently, rules of limitation appropriate to one of these forms of war would be absurd in the context of another. However, the basic problem remains of whether, in Wright's categorization, we are being invited to consider one activity with various sets of rules, or various discrete activities, one of which may be war but the others not.

Certainly, Wright was not alone in believing that there were various manifestations of war, each with a different form and each characterized by different rules. Gentili (1933, p. 276) provides an excellent illustration of this approach in quoting Cicero:

> Those wars which have for their aim the glory of supremacy must be waged with less bitterness. For just as when we contend at law, the contest is of one kind with an enemy and of another with a competitor, with the latter for honour and position, with the former for life and reputation; thus with the Celtiberians and Cimbri war was waged as with enemies, to decide, not which of us should rule, but which should survive; but with the Latins, Sabines, Samnites, Carthaginians and Pyrrhus it was a struggle for empire.

In any discussion of the appropriateness of applying rules to warfare, and of the nature of the rules which might be applied, one inevitably comes up against the game analogy: this asks whether war can, or should, be regarded as a game and asks also what are the implications of doing so? The close connection between limits to war and rules of war invites this kind of comparison.

Huizinga is, of course, the notorious exponent of the ludic functions of warfare and best establishes the parameters of the game analogy: 'all fighting that is bound by rules bears the formal characteristics of play by that very limitation' (1949, p. 89). The number of descriptions of warfare, couched in game terminology, is legion. For instance, it has been claimed that war, in the ancient Indian epics, 'was treated as a manly sport and it was considered to be a test for valour and skill of the heroes. The war was fought on a battlefield previously settled – the two armies met on the battlefield like two rival teams in a game' (Mukherjee 1967, p. 56). Likewise, it is customary to refer to eighteenth century warfare as a royal game or princely sport and one eminent international lawyer invokes the analogy, in connection with the Cuban missile crisis, when he remarks that even 'poker is not played without rules' (O'Connell 1975, p. 62). The attraction to the game analogy, and to game terminology, has therefore been persistent.

But is this mere analogy or are we entitled to equate the

rules of warfare with the rules of a game? It has been said, for instance, that there is a form of agonistic war in terms of which 'war is interpreted as a game or a play that may confer glory on the victor and reveal his side as just, only if he complies with the rules that form an integral part of the contest. Violations of the rules governing war not only deprive victory of its meaning, or worth, but dishonour the victor' (Osgood and Tucker 1967, p. 214). However, two antagonistic conclusions could be drawn from this: the first is that there have been instances of wars fought as if they were genuinely games; secondly, or alternatively, if wars cannot be understood in terms of game-like rules, then agonistic war is not a form of war at all but rather an instance of some other social function.

It has, consequently, been as common for the game analogy to be denied. Tolstoy's Prince Andrei may be regarded as Huizinga's most vehement protagonist:

> War is not a polite recreation but the vilest thing in life, and we ought to understand that and not play at war. Our attitude towards the fearful necessity of war ought to be stern and serious. It boils down to this: we should have done with humbug and let war be war and not a game (quoted in Howard (ed.) 1979, p. 7).

A more limited variant of the game analogy, but one structurally similar, is the tendency to regard war as equivalent to a duel, which is, of course, a highly formal and rule-governed procedure. Thus even Clausewitz, who certainly regarded war as a deadly serious business, was to write that 'war is nothing but a duel on a larger scale' (1976, p. 75). Indeed, it has been claimed that historically there are strong reasons for the application of the duel analogy:

> While the medieval customs by which princes had sometimes actually settled international controversies by a personal duel, and usually instituted war by sending a defiance by herald in the manner of a challenge, had fallen into abeyance in the Renaissance, these practices showed that modern war and the duel were one and the same in origin, though the two institutions had diverged (Wright 1942, p. 880).

So seriously was this analogy taken that some peace supporters believed that war could be eliminated on an international scale just as duelling had been suppressed at the national level (Clark 1958, p. 30).

However, just as some have thought that the point of war is not the same as the point of a game, so there have been those who have denied that the point of war is equivalent to that of a duel. Gentili (1933, p. 142) provides an incisive indictment of both the game and the duel analogies during a discussion of the use of stratagems in war:

> In the imitations of war (I mean sports and games) they are not permitted ... And the reason is clear; namely, because the laws of games are such that the contest is directed to the purpose of the game. Therefore those who have to contend in running have nothing to do but run; or if they do something else, they no longer contend in running ...
> There is the same difference between war and the duel, and for duellists the conditions ought to be equal, since theirs is a contest of personal courage. That, however, is not the case in wars, where the test is the valour of kingdoms. In war, therefore, there is no strict law of that kind, but victory is sought in no prescribed fashion.

There are crucial issues, of both a semantic and a policy-prescriptive nature, at stake here: they concern the place, if any, of rules in warfare and the nature of these rules. They raise policy issues also, in the sense that, if we dislike the notion of 'playing' at war, should we assuage our moral sensibilities by extending the cruelty and carnage of warfare as a demonstration of the seriousness of our intent?

Suffice it for the moment to comment that the game analogy has historically fostered two distinct, and antagonistic, attitudes towards war. Toynbee (1951, pp. 16–17) has given a vivid description of this episode in the history of ideas about warfare:

> Both reactions proceeded from the common postulate that to fight for fun was shocking, but, while one school of reformers took the line that an evil which had been turned into a sport both could and should be abolished altogether, the other took the line that the evil could not be borne if it were not to be endured for a serious purpose.

This leads to a contest between the pacifist 'who seeks to abolish "the sport of Kings" and the militarist who seeks to reconvert it into a serious business of the peoples'. The limitationist finds himself in the middle of this struggle fighting, as it were, a war on two fronts. As against the pacifist, he argues that enough rationality and mutual self-interest to limit war does not mean that these are a sufficiently-solid foundation for eliminating warfare altogether; as against the militarist, he argues that while war is not a game played for fun, it is a curious inversion of moral priorities to maintain that the honour and seriousness of combat can be proven only by fighting without any restraints whatsoever.

ON WAR AND THE NATURE OF LIMITATION

This study is an extended treatment of various conceptions of war-limitation, the full philosophical implications of which have not been adequately explored. Thinking along these lines should help us to clarify the nature of war-limitation and its relevance to the analysis of war in a nuclear context.

Accordingly, this section will investigate further the very notion of limitation and its implications. Firstly, however, we should perhaps distinguish between conventions of war-limitation, on the one hand, and conventions of war-fighting on the other. By this is meant that there can be ways of regulating warfare such that the resulting war, although fought according to rules, cannot meaningfully be said to be limited. A brief example will suffice to make this point. To the extent that the ABM treaty in SALT 1 underwrote a deterrent posture of mutual assured destruction, it could be said that the agreement enshrined a convention about future war-fighting in which centres of population would be held as defenceless targets. In the event of nuclear war, this would entail maximum civilian loss of life. In other words, the ABM treaty can be regarded as an instance of war-regulation but can scarcely, in the accepted understanding of the term, be seen as a form of war-limitation. Likewise, when Halperin (1963, p. 95) maintains that central war might be 'limited' by the agreement of both sides to engage 'purely in counter-population attacks', he goes beyond accepted understanding of the term.

The major distinction around which this study is constructed pertains to the very concept of limitation in relation to war. When we speak of limits to war, what precisely do we have in mind that is being limited? The literature provides a range of answers – restrictions on targets, restriction on weapons, rights for the injured or captured, acceptance of less than total victory, anything less than total nuclear warfare, and so on.

There is nothing unsatisfactory about these instances of war-limitation. All are, indeed, examples of ways in which the competing states experience less than the full potential impact of war. For that reason, it is proper to speak of all these ideas, practices or theories as contributing to a general notion of war-limitation. Nonetheless, there is a sleight of hand involved in this recounting of war-limitation, a sleight which can be detected only by asking, and answering more rigorously, *what is being limited when war is limited*?

It appears on reflection that at least two different things might be limited by conventions of war-limitation, although the distinction has not been adequately brought out in the existing literature. The closest that commentators have come to appreciating this distinction, and its significance, is in the works of Schelling and of Tucker who sense the complexity of the notion of limitation, even if they do not fully succeed in analysing this complexity.

We may start with a discussion of Schelling's contribution to this point. Schelling displays repeatedly his awareness that the notion of limitation is a complex one and attempts on three different occasions to explain what is limited when war is limited. On the first occasion, Schelling contrasts the limits of the two World Wars with the limits of the Korean war in the following manner:

> The striking characteristic of both world wars is that they were unstinting in the use of force, and the restraint . . . (was) mainly in the method of termination . . . Contrast the Korean war. It was *fought* with restraint, conscious restraint, and the restraint was on both sides (1966, p. 129).

Schelling is hinting, however vaguely, that there may be limits both to the manner of terminating the war and to the manner of fighting during the war. He briefly returns to this theme on a second occasion when he remarks: 'and in limited warfare, two things are being bargained over, the outcome of the war, and the mode of conducting the war itself' (1966,

p. 135). Schelling's third, and fullest, statement of this point takes the following form:

> What is the bargaining about? First there is bargaining about the conduct of the war itself ... What weapons are used, what nationalities are involved, what targets are sanctuaries and what are legitimate, what forms participation can take without being counted as 'combat', what codes of reprisal or hot pursuit and what treatment of prisoners are to be recognized ...
> Second, there would be bargaining about the cease fire, truce, armistice, surrender, disarmament, or whatever it is that brings the war to a close — about the way to halt the war and the military requirements for stopping it (p. 135).

Once again, and however imprecisely described, Schelling's recurrent distinction is between limitation as a form of conduct and limitation as a form of termination.

As far as I am aware, the only other writer to explore seriously the question of what is limited when war is limited is R. W. Tucker. He likewise draws a distinction although it is not clear that it is the same one referred to by Schelling. Tucker's views can be presented only by lengthy quotation:

> In the history of the attempts to impose limitations on the conduct of war two views have vied with one another. The one, and much the older, view has placed primary emphasis upon the regulation and direction of actual hostilities. It assumes that war is not, or at least need not and should not be, the negation of all order ... War may be a very grim and tragic 'game' but it must nevertheless remain a game, in the sense that the participants accept limitations upon their behaviour ... The principal purpose for restraining the manner in which hostilities are conducted is not to protect human rights or to mitigate suffering but to ensure that the minimum foundations of order will be preserved even in war ... The other and more modern view implicitly rejects the contention that war can or should be regarded as an institution compatible with some form of order. In this view, the essence of war is that it signifies the breakdown of all order. The restraints that are applicable during a period of hostilities can only have as their purpose the mitigation of human suffering and the protection of those fundamental human rights which survive even in war. It is not their purpose to regulate the manner in which a game may be played ... (Tucker 1960, pp. 81–2).

Schelling's distinction and Tucker's are by no means identical: Schelling separates out *conduct* from *termination*, whilst Tucker seems to be concerned with two motivations for regulating the *conduct* of war. Even so, both of these writers hint at elements in the distinction which I should now like to introduce. To our question, what is limited when war is limited, we might provide two alternative answers: conventions of war-limitation can be understood as either

    A)   conventions about *how conflict may be resolved* while limiting the impact of the conflict

or B)   conventions about *how the impact of conflict* may be limited while the conflict is resolved

What does this distinction mean and is it tenable? The distinction, which is a partial rather than an absolute one, will be elaborated in the course of this study. However, to prepare the ground, some preliminary observations can be made. There are some closely-related distinctions which foreshadow the general tendency of the subsequent analysis. We can, for instance, accept a general distinction between process and substance and suggest that limitation can be understood as pertaining either to the definition of the process of war or, alternatively, to the mode of its substantive conduct.

While, at the poles, these are distinguishable, there is inevitably a grey-area, a range across which the two categories overlap. A process cannot be totally devoid of content or of substantive implications, and to this extent the distinction loses clarity. For instance, imagine the following stylized situation. Two prehistoric men are in competition over possession of a cave, they fight bare-handed and they are evenly-matched. Neither wins. Next time they meet, possession of the cave is still in dispute but one of the protagonists has a deadly bow and arrow with him which guarantees him the capacity to kill the other at distance. If the two contestants agree that bows and arrows will be banned in the resolution of their conflict, would we say that they have established a convention defining the process of resolution, or one limiting the impact of the process of resolution. Clearly, in this case, the convention does both things simultaneously and we cannot meaningfully say that one objective is more clearly enshrined in the convention than is the other. Presumably the reason for this is that the process of resolution which has been prohibited, if allowed to go unchecked, would have had the necessary effect of causing death and therefore the limitation has the necessary effect of saving life. The rule of procedure — bare-hands only — is practically inseparable from the substantive principle — no loss of life. What we understand by resolution of the conflict is indistinguishable from the quantum damage done: resolution of the conflict is merely a transcription of the body-count. Or to put it in other words, the damage is the necessary and the sufficient cause of the resolution of the conflict and the resolution of the conflict is the necessary and sufficient cause of the damage. In this case, then, we cannot conceive of any application of convention A which would not also entail application of convention B, and vice-versa.

We might approach the same issue from a different angle. When we impose limitations upon war, should this be construed as setting limits to the bargaining or as permitting bargaining to certain limits? In the former case, the limits pre-exist the bargaining; in the latter, the limits are an outcome of the bargaining itself. Taking limited strategic war to mean strategic city interchange, Ramsey (1963, pp. 23—4) has described the essentials of the latter limits in the following way:

> Even the understandings reached during the fighting will be arbitrary ones, maintained only by encounters of resolve. The bargaining is not only over survival or prevailing. It is also over the criteria of behavior permissible in the nuclear age; such war is a contest to define the rules of the game while the game is being played. The teachers must themselves be learning what they are going to will this war to be.

The problem can be perceived as a chronological one, whether the rules embodying the limitations ante-date or post-date the playing of the game. But this chronological dimension to the problem is a superficial one and conceals a more important and underlying issue: this is the relationship between the rules defining a process and the process which establishes the rules. We might wish to speak in this case of a distinction between meta-rules (limits to the process) and rules (process to certain limits).

So far we have argued that the distinction between conventions A and B relates in some manner to the distinction between limits of a procedural and of a substantive nature and also to the distinction between meta-rules and rules. It might also be the case that the specific modalities of war-limitation have some bearing upon the distinction. For purposes of preliminary exposition, we shall argue that the modalities of war-limitation can best be conceived under two headings, limitation by immunity and limitation by withholding of forces-in-being. The two are interrelated, but can be distinguished in accordance with the perspective from which they are viewed. Just as rights and duties are intertwined, any right imposing corresponding duties, so we can say that war can be limited by conventions of immunity, on the one hand, and by conventions to withhold forces-in-being, on the other. One side's immunities conventionally depend upon the other side's withholding. But just as heads and tails are two sides of the same coin, there is no difficulty in telling them apart.

All of these categories and sets of distinctions are crucial to the ongoing argument of this study. In order to help us think about these issues, to help us to unpack the concept of war-limitation, we will eventually describe and analyse three models of war-limitation – limitation by champion, limitation by charity and limitation by city-swapping. Each is a highly stylized and abstract model of a conflict situation and each presents an ideal-type in terms of which war might be limited. It is the intention of this study that by setting out in a systematic fashion the premises of war-limitation, the modalities of war-limitation and the consequences of war-limitation, we might be better placed to think through the momentous political issues raised by warfare in the nuclear age.

2

Historical Forms of War-Limitation

FORMS OF WAR-LIMITATION

There would be little point in providing a random selection of historical instances of war-limitation. What is essential both to the philosophical understanding of war-limitation and to its political practice, is that we should be able to order these various forms of limitation in such a way that their essential nature is clarified and their implications appreciated. In other words, the task confronting us is basically one of devising a heuristically-useful system of categorization — not to botanize for its own sake, but to increase understanding by comparison and contrast between different forms of limitation.

There are many ways in which this might be achieved and there is no compelling reason for preferring one classificatory scheme to another. For instance, Falk (1975, p. 40) has argued that the laws of war are underpinned by four primary principles which he specifies as:

> a prohibition upon methods, tactics, and weapons calculated to inflict unnecessary suffering (principle of necessity)

> a requirement that methods, tactics, and weapons generally discriminate between military and nonmilitary targets and between combatants and civilians (principle of discrimination)

> a requirement that the military means used bear a proportional relationship to the military end pursued (principle of proportionality); and

> an absolute prohibition upon methods, tactics, and weapons that are inherently cruel in their effects and violate minimal notions of humanity (principle of humanity)

39

There is no doubt that most of the historical forms of war-limitation could be seen to be associated with one or other of these four principles. However, as a means of thinking about war-limitation, they do not meet the present need. In as much as our central question in this study is: 'what is limited when war is limited?' we would have to discard Falk's classification on the grounds that it obscures distinctions which it is necessary for us to make.

How, then, might we begin to devise a satisfactory scheme? The general pattern of historical forms of war-limitation is fairly familiar and has tended to revolve around such things as restrictions on targets, on weapons, on times and locations for fighting, and the etiquette or formality of warfare. As Wright (1942, p. 98) reported, in his exhaustive study, about the forms of limitation in primitive war:

> ... illustration can be found in the war practices of primitive peoples of the various types of international rules of war known at the present time: rules distinguishing types of enemies; rules defining the circumstances, formalities and authority for beginning and ending war; rules describing limitations of persons, time, place, and methods of its conduct . . .

It would be possible to organize some of the principal forms of limitation around a particular axis. For instance, as regards the late medieval theory of *ius in bello* and the emerging positivist theories of laws of warfare, it might be said that the major limitation was upon the character of the human targets who might legitimately be attacked in war, the discussion centring on notions of innocence and noncombatancy. However, over time, such conceptions have changed and it might be said of the twentieth century that, as the combatant/noncombatant distinction has blurred, the focus of debate has moved to how any human target might legitimately be attacked. This transformation is referred to in one writer's description of the contribution of the 1949 Geneva Convention which, he says, 'extend[ed] to civilians the rights which previous conventions had recognized as inhering in members of the armed forces with respect to humane treatment at the hands of belligerents' (Howard (ed.) 1979, p. 12). It is perhaps ironic that the category considered by just war theorists as the first beneficiaries of *ius in bello* restrictions, namely noncombatants, should have been the last category to have its rights legally underwritten and codified: the rules of the battlefield had to be extended *pari passu* with the extension of the battlefield itself. Moreover, as a consequence of this, the principal axis of limitation has been transformed and this presents a further difficulty for any schematic representation of forms of war-limitation.

It is the argument of this study that the forms of limitation may be usefully considered under the categories of convention A and convention B, introduced in Chapter 1. Additionally, various other useful distinctions can be accommodated under these major headings. While, as has been previously conceded, the distinction between the two types of convention is not absolute, it does nonetheless point to kinds of limitation which, to a greater or lesser degree, differ on the basis of their principal intent. The main organizational distinction to be employed in this chapter is, therefore, between limitations more or less enshrining the rationale of convention A and those more or less enshrining the rationale of convention B.

Other distinctions will be subsumed under those general headings. For instance, as already argued, limitations which are predominantly of a procedural nature will be grouped under A and those of a substantive nature under B. Likewise, both Schelling's and Tucker's distinctions can be accommodated giving us the following general categorization:

Convention A	Convention B
procedural	substantive
termination	conduct
political	humanitarian

Schelling's limitations of termination and of conduct are a rough approximation to the distinction between conventions A and B, but are not coterminous with them: termination is an important part of a procedure but is not, in itself, a complete definition of a procedure; initiation is equally important. Likewise, although Tucker's dichotomy between political and humanitarian reasons for limiting the conduct of war is not identical to conventions A and B respectively, it can nonetheless be subsumed under these headings without doing undue violence to Tucker's intent. This becomes evident in Tucker's own elaboration of the two views of limitation:

> The former view is predominantly political in character, in that its first concern is with the task of attempting to preserve at least some semblance of international order even in war. Consequently, the distinctly humanitarian purpose of the restraints introduced in war forms a secondary consideration.

(c.f. my formulation: 'conventions about how conflict may be resolved while limiting the impact of the conflict'.) Tucker continues:

> The latter view, in concentrating its attention almost exclusively on the humanitarian purpose of these restraints, is necessarily unconcerned with the distinctly political problem. War may prove completely destructive of the political order existing at the time of the initiation of hostilities, but the requirements of humanity are alleged to remain as imperative and as unyielding in a war fought to unconditional surrender and the complete destruction of the 'aggressor' as in a war fought to adjust a frontier (Tucker 1960, p. 83).

(c.f. my formulation: 'conventions about how the impact of the conflict may be limited while the conflict is resolved'.)

Once again, we have returned to the problem previously encountered of untangling the nature of the relationship between rules and the processes of which they are a part and the distinction between sets of rules within a recognized process (convention B) and types of rules which turn one process into another (convention A). We can take a concrete demonstration of this dilemma. Commenting upon anthropological studies of primitive warfare, Turney-High (1949, p. 49) provides the following analysis of 'war' amongst the New Hebridean Melanesians:

> The two masses met and indulged in a series of individual combats . . . When one man was killed the action stopped so that all might feast and praise the successful warrior, his tribe, and their allies. The next day the enemy sought to get a score in the same way. Casualties were rare in such general skirmishes. *Of course such mass duelling, or individual combat of champions is not war at all, any more than duelling is war.* It is merely an athletic event, hardly more effective or lethal than football as played a few decades ago [emphasis added].

According to this argument, the conventions of limitation referred to were of convention A type and, consequently, turned the procedure of war into some other procedure. But would Turney-High's observation be valid if these limitations were understood to be of convention B type?

We may now move on from the general categories of limitation to the individual forms of limitation that are to be considered under them. As already mentioned, there have been many different practices of war-limitation relating to virtually every aspect of warfare. Accordingly, however crude it might seem, we can classify limitations in warfare under five categories — rules pertaining to the what, who, how, when and where of warfare: what may be done to the enemy? To whom it may be done? How it may be done? When it may be done? And where it may be done?

Several points of clarification have to be made in connection with such a classification. The first is that there are inherent ambiguities in some of these questions and these ambiguities may be crucial in any discussion of the philosophy of war. For instance, 'who?' might mean 'which categories of people?'; alternatively, it might mean 'who within any given category?' Likewise, 'how?' might mean 'by what instrument or technique?' Alternatively, it might mean 'by what process?'

Secondly, although we can distinguish these five categories in theory, we should not be at all surprised if, in practice, specific forms of limitation overlap two or more of these categories. Again, a simple illustration should clarify the point. The rules of surrender have traditionally constituted a major form of war-limitation. But from which category does the practice of surrender derive? It might be thought to be an instance of a 'who?' rule in the sense that a person who has laid down arms then falls into an immune category. However, surrender has traditionally also encompassed 'what?' and 'when?' rules. Even if those who surrender are in a different category from those who fight on, 'what?' can be done to those who surrender still needs to be specified. Are they to be made slaves? branded? ransomed? set free? Likewise, surrender has often entailed such 'when?' rules as the time up to which an act of surrender can be considered the basis of a claim for immunity. In Roman sieges, for instance, it was common for the treatment of a city which capitulated to be different from the treatment of a city which capitulated only after the battering-ram had first struck the walls.

Thirdly, and most fundamentally, it has to be re-iterated that the distinction between limitation as process and limitation as substance is far from absolute. For instance, in the earlier example of the cavemen and their use, or non-use, of bows and arrows, we encountered an instance where the application of a single principle of conduct was sufficient to revolutionize the process itself and so undermine any meaningful distinction between conventions A and B.

There is one important theme in some of the literature which illustrates this point that the nature of the process can depend crucially upon the application of a single substantive principle of conduct: this is the contention that significant limitation can be derived only from 'who?' rules. This is best demonstrated in the case of Walzer (1977). It is his position, as already noted, that war is a 'moral universe' even if located in Hell. Additionally, Walzer argues, what lends war its moral attributes is the application, not of rules of behaviour in general, but of 'who?' rules in particular. Walzer is insistent on this point, that war as a moral process derives from the application of such rules; without these rules, even if there were other forms of limitation, war's moral universe would disappear. In this sense, 'who?' rules are conspicuous by their moral primacy. Walzer makes his point in distinguishing between two sets of rules of warfare. Of the first set, he says:

> Rules specifying how and when soldiers can be killed are by no means unimportant, and yet the morality of war would not be radically transformed were they to be abolished altogether ... Any rule that limits the intensity and duration of combat or the suffering of soldiers is to be welcomed, but none of these restraints seem crucial to the idea of war as a moral condition.

By way of contrast, he says of the second set that they are:

> more closely connected to universal notions of right and wrong. Their tendency is to set certain classes of people outside the permissible range of warfare, so that killing any of their members is not a legitimate act of war but a crime ... (1977, p. 42).

Were Walzer's argument acceptable, it would demonstrate that the very nature of warfare itself can take its character from one set of prohibitons; indeed, it would show that the moral dimension of war hinges exclusively on its application of 'who?' rules. And yet there are reasons for thinking that Walzer's arguments are not fully persuasive. At the very least, his assertion of the moral primacy of 'who?' rules is not universally admitted. That seems to be the implicit significance of Nagel's (1974, p. 13) comment that 'absolutist restrictions in warfare appear to be of two types: restrictions on the class of persons at whom aggression or violence may be directed and restrictions on the manner of attack'. This must be understood as an assertion of the moral equivalence of 'who?' and 'how?' rules, a position which seems more defensible than that of Walzer.

Perhaps the issue can be clarified by reverting to that ambiguity, alluded to above, which is inherent in 'who?' rules — whether we mean by it a) which categories? or b) who within any given category? Clearly, 'who?' in the second case may be crucially dependent upon such other variables as 'how?', 'when?' and 'where?'. For instance, the use of poison arrows would assuredly lead to more deaths within the category of combatants than would the non-use of such weapons. In such a case, it is not at all clear why the 'who?' question touches on deeper issues of morality than the 'how?'. Walzer (1977, p. 42) seems to raise precisely this point when discussing the comparative non-lethality of arrows without feathers:

> It is clearly a good rule, then, that arrows not be feathered, and we may fairly condemn the warrior who first arms himself with the superior and forbidden weapon and hits his enemy. Yet the man he kills was liable to be killed in any case, and a collective (intertribal) decision to fight with feathered arrows would not violate any basic moral principle.

This is confusing. Even if a soldier is liable to be killed in any case, it may well be 'how?' rules which determine whether he is, in fact, killed. Again, even in purely quantitative terms, it is not inconceivable that a 'how?' rule may save more lives than a 'who?' rule, because it may save more lives within the category of combatants than does a rule setting aside separate categories of noncombatants. Which, one might ask, did the greater moral mischief, the millions of military lives lost in 1914–18, arguably in the absence of humane rules against inhuman means, or the civilian lives lost in Hiroshima and Nagasaki, arguably as a result of contravention of rules protecting noncombatants? Such a moral calculus is grizzly; but that it should not be dismissed reveals the moral seamless web interrelating many of the conventional limitations upon warfare: the fact that soldiers were likely to be killed in any case does not seem to invalidate the moral worth of other rules of warfare that may determine how many are *actually* killed.

Finally, it might be said that significant limitation of war derives from the acceptance of conventions about fundamental procedures rather than from any single substantive principle specifying who may be killed or how they may be killed. In other words, even though conventions of type B may individually prescribe morally desirable goals, it is in conventions of type A, which formulate the essential nature of the process itself, that the basis of war's limitation is to be discovered. The potential nature of war in the nuclear age reveals that this is so. Given nuclear conditions, Walzer's moral universe of war collapses not simply when 'who?' rules are transgressed, but when the rules defining the process of war so change as to turn that process into something else.

WAR-LIMITATION AND CONVENTION B

We can now begin to survey historical forms of war-limitation beginning with those considered to be instances of convention B and predominantly concerned with limiting the impact of war, with substantive principles of limitation, with the conduct of warfare rather than the process of settlement and with humanitarian considerations as opposed to fundamental political procedures.

'What?' conventions

There are many types of act that one can perform against an enemy. Consequently it is not surprising that a major manifestation of conventions of war-limitation has been a restriction upon what can be done to the opponent in war. This is irrespective of gradations in enemy character and of the various arguments about who, on the other side, constitutes the enemy or is deserving of punishment. This section then, deals with conventions which might limit what enemies do to each other, even in cases where there is no dispute about the combatant status of the other party. It also leaves aside the closely related question of how you may do what you are doing: you can kill an emeny but you can kill him in many ways. At this point, we are concerned with the nature of the act rather than the means of its execution.

Of the possible limitations upon what may be done to the enemy, some are more meaningful than others. Arguably, the taking of a scalp was a limitation upon the actual decapitation of the opponent. As Turney-High (1949, p. 200) tells us: 'the head is cumbersome to carry about, so it was to be expected that some tribes would be content with only the scalp'. Such a limitation is scarcely significant in any moral, humanitarian or political sense.

However, there have been historical instances of conventions, whereby it is agreed in advance what the two parties in a battle may do to each other. Such a situation is found in its most stylized form in the medieval signs of war. In many cases, such signs, the banners carried into battle by opposing armies, depicted the ground rules of the ensuing encounter. These signs are examined in some detail by Keen (1965) but have the general function of being 'used by soldiers to indicate to their opponents what rules they would observe in battle' (p. 103). Keen continues:

> There appear, in our period, to have been four possible conditions or states of war which could be signified. In the first place there was war to the death (*guerre mortelle*). This was what the lawyers called Roman war, fought by the rules which in antiquity had applied in the wars of the Roman people. There was no privilege of ransom, the conquered could be slain or enslaved. Secondly, there was public or open war (in legal Latin, a *bellum hostile*), that is the war of one sovereign Christian prince against another. In this men might take spoil, and captured enemies had the right to ransom themselves. Thirdly, there was feudal or covered war (*guerre couverte*), in which men would wound and kill without blame, but could not burn or take spoil . . . (p. 104).

The rules of battle derived, it can be seen, from the particular legal status of the war itself. These rules were conveyed by different flags or standards. 'The usual sign of war to the death,' Keen informs us 'was the carrying of a red flag or banner' (p. 105).

Most of the forms of capture, ransom, capitulation and surrender embody conventions about what it is permissible to do in warfare, and serve to limit the amount of bloodshed. They reveal a recurring theme in the history of warfare that the killing of members of the enemy is not always necessary, even in strictly military terms, or that even where it is, there may yet be some social stigma attached to that killing. Indeed, many societies have inflicted punishment upon their own warriors for killing in war even at the same time as they have recognized the legitimacy of the act. The medieval church in Europe imposed its various penances upon those who had spilled blood (Friedman 1972, p. 7) and many so-called primitive societies have subjected their warriors to deprivation and ostracism (Turney-High, 1949, p. 222).

Apart from those conventions that limit war by drawing some distinction between killing the enemy and variants upon capturing the enemy, there have also been efforts to try to implement a distinction between killing the enemy and stopping him. This issue is, for instance, involved in efforts to ban the use of poisoned weapons, a perennial concern to which we shall return in due course. However, many of the arguments against the use of poisoned weapons refer as much to 'what?' you may do to the enemy as to 'how?' you may do it and the implied distinction has generally been some variant on the theme of militarily incapacitating versus killing or mutilating: the prime object of war is to disable the enemy militarily, not to kill him, even if it is conceded that killing may often be the only way of achieving that objective. Such a distinction is considered fundamental by some writers. Vattel (1916, p. 289) provided reasons against using poisoned weapons in precisely these terms:

> . . . their use is none the less prohibited by the natural law, which forbids us to multiply the evils of war indefinitely. It is, indeed, necessary to strike down your enemy in order to overcome his designs; but once he is disabled, is there any need that he should inevitably die of his wounds?

Nagel has argued a similar case based on the twin distinctions between stopping and killing or maiming, and between attacking the soldier and attacking the man. He makes such 'what?' arguments the basis of a prohibition upon unnecessarily cruel weapons 'designed to maim or disfigure or torture the opponent rather than merely to stop him . . . The effect of dum-dum bullets, for example, is much more extended than necessary to cope with the combat situation in which they are used. They abandon any attempt to discriminate in their effects between the combatant and the human being' (Nagel 1974, p. 21).

'Who?' conventions

Conventions specifying whom might legitimately be attacked in war have, historically, constituted the most common form of war-limitation. They occur in virtually all societies at all historical periods. One can sympathize, on this basis, with Walzer's aforementioned feeling that 'who?' rules are distinctively related to universal human notions of right and wrong.

There have, of course, been many different manifestations of this general principle of limitation: however, its central theme, that certain categories are not to be directly attacked, remains constant. Whether adhered to or not, it has formed part of the formal or informal rules of war in many cultures.

The literature upon customs and rules of warfare in ancient India is pervaded by the immunity granted to various individuals or groups in society. Bhatia (ed.) (1977, pp. 103–4) provides a list of some seventeen categories of people who enjoyed immunity – ranging from those who are asleep, to those who are mad and to those who are skilled in some special art. Most, if not all, of these categories can be regarded as noncombatants. The most generally commented upon of these immunities was that accorded to farmers, as reported by the Greek Megasthenes. The agricultural husbandsman was, he observed, free of molestation even when the fighting raged close at hand (Spellman 1964, p. 160). It becomes clear, however, that the granting of immunities was not purely on the basis of noncombatancy. Mukherjee (1967, p. 59) reveals this when he asserts that 'a sharp difference was

made between combatants and noncombatants and it was a
sin to kill one not actively engaged in fight'. It is implied in
this statement that even a soldier was entitled to immunity if,
for various reasons, he was not *actively* in fight.

Additionally, ancient Hindu custom apparently extended
immunity to various camp-followers who were not strictly
noncombatants and who were manifestly active in assisting
the war effort. Such a point was made in the Mahabharata,
one of the most famous of the ancient epics:

> The Mahabharata recognized various grades in enemy character.
> Thus, according to the Mahabharata, men who go out of the
> camp to procure forage or fodder, men who set up camps, and
> camp-followers as well as those who wait at the gates of the King
> or his ministers or those who do menial service to the army-
> Chiefs, or those who are chiefs of such servants, shared the im-
> munities of the non-combatants (Bhatia (ed.) 1977, p. 100).

Immunities were recognized and practised in ancient
Greece. They were accorded principally to all types of religious functionary, but also to competitors and spectators at
the Panhellenic games. Suppliants, too, were to be spared the
sword (Phillipson 1911, Garlan 1975). Similarly, an authority
on the Islamic law of warfare notes that immunities were to
be granted: 'the jurists agreed that noncombatants who did
not take part in fighting, such as women, children, monks
and hermits, the aged, blind, and insane, were excluded from
molestation' (Khadduri 1955, pp. 103—4).

The whole issue of developing immunities in warfare has
loomed large in the Western tradition of *ius in bello* and in
the construction of an international law of war. The centrality of such traditional Western immunities is testified to by
the widespread uncertainty surrounding their applicability in
the conditions of contemporary warfare, both nuclear and
insurgent.

The medieval church attempted, with ecclesiastical sanctions, to institute a system of immunities through the Peace
of God, the aim of which was 'to protect ecclesiastical buildings, clerics, pilgrims, women and peasants from the ravages
of war' (Fuller 1946, p. 62). However, this practical effort
was not for some time followed through by the clerical
theorists of the *ius in bello* for whom the specification of

targets to be legitimately attacked would have been tauto-
logical. As one analyst of the medieval just war tradition has
explained:

> That the canonists paid scant attention to this medieval expres-
> sion of non-combatant immunity, the Peace of God, may seem
> puzzling at first ... In their view wars were usually waged by
> persons to whom fighting was licit, that is, soldiers, and all other
> were *hors de guerre*. For a just war to remain a just war, it had to
> be conducted properly, which meant that it could only be waged
> on other soldiers. And an unjust war should not be fought at all,
> so there was no need to specify that it should not attack non-
> combatants (Russell 1975, p. 186).

Such immunities, and the discussions of them, were not the
sole prerogative of the ecclesiastical authorities: they found
expression also in the more secular notions, either of chivalry,
or of the laws of war. Bouvet's *Tree of Battles*, for instance,
written in the late fourteenth century, stipulated a range of
immunities which, he hoped, would be enforced by the
sovereign prince: 'however terrible Bouvet may have felt the
punishment of excommunication to be, he was well aware
that ecclesiastical sanctions were not as effective as the more
tangible civil form' (Wright 1976, p. 17).

The whole question of the proper basis of any claim to
immunity will be returned to below (Chapter 3). For the
moment, it will suffice to outline the main formulations of
the principle of immunity in the modern Western tradition.
Grotius (1925, p. 736) had only a faltering conception of
what constituted immunity, but came closest to it when he
quoted Livy to the effect that 'by the law of war armed men
and those who offer resistance are killed'. The rest, by implication, might enjoy immunity from death. Vitoria had
spoken vaguely of 'guilt' and 'innocence' without giving
specific content to these terms. However, as with Grotius, the
most common approach was to extend some limited immunities to those not actually offering armed resistance. Such was
Vattel's position when he prohibited maltreatment and
violence against women, children, old men and the sick
because 'they are enemies who offer no resistance' (1916,
p. 282). Gentili (1933, p. 262) seemed to come to the heart
of the issue when he maintained that 'war is a contention of

arms and that therefore there can be no war with unarmed men'.

The issue of distinguishing legitimate objects of attack in war has lately re-emerged in the theoretical literature about possible nuclear wars. As the accuracy of nuclear missiles has been perfected, it appears that statesmen and strategists have some area of choice as to the targets to be struck and the debate focused upon counterforce targeting *vis-à-vis* counter-value targeting may be seen, at least in part, as the most recent manifestation of the age-old search for the proper targets of warfare. This debate, and its detailed rationales, will be presented in a later section of the book (Chapter 5).

'How?' conventions

The most common 'how?' conventions have related to the nature of the weaponry to be used in warfare. At the present time, strategists ruminate about the possibility of limiting war by restricting it to conventional weaponry; or perhaps to tactical nuclear weaponry. Again, the current search for prohibitions on certain forms of weaponry, and for conventions that might be mutually respected, is as old as the history of warfare itself.

One of the earliest, and most frequently cited, examples is that of the Amarynthion inscription, agreed to by Eretria and Chalkis, and reported by Strabo:

> In general, these cities were in accord with one another, and when differences arose concerning the Lelantine plain they did not so completely break off relations as to wage their wars in all respects according to the will of each, but they came to an agreement as to the conditions under which they were to conduct the fight. This is shown by a certain inscribed pillar which forbids the use of long-range missiles (Garlan 1975, p. 29).

Polybios was also to describe such conventions of ancient Greek warfare:

> For so far were they from plotting mischief against their friends, with the purpose of aggrandizing their own power, that they would not even consent to get the better of their enemies by fraud, regarding no success as brilliant or secure unless they crushed the spirit of their adversaries in open battle. For this

reason they entered into a convention among themselves to use against each other neither secret missiles nor those discharged from a distance, and considered that it was only a hand-to-hand battle at close quarters which was truly decisive . . . (Pritchett 1974, Vol. II, p. 251).

Similar instances, even if not formalized in an inscription but attested to by mutual observance, can be found in the anthropological accounts of primitive war. Turney-High (1949, p. 167) refers to the American Plains Indian at war:

These tribes knew how to make stone arrow points, for they used them in hunting. Yet with the full knowledge that stone-tipped arrows were the more dangerous, that they produced more nervous shock and bleeding than blunt shafts, they carried headless arrows to war.

Prohibitions on the use of certain forms of weaponry were certainly a part of the ancient Hindu code of warfare, although there is great uncertainty as to the extent to which such codes were observed. The Indian epics do, nonetheless, reiterate this theme: 'when a King fights with his foes . . . let him not strike with instruments concealed, with barbed or poisoned weapons, the points of which are blazing with fire' (Chakravarti, p. 185).

Conventions of this nature have not always emerged spontaneously. It thus became part of the Church's role in medieval Europe to enforce similar conventions by providing sanctions against the use of certain types of weaponry. The Second Lateran Council of 1139, for example, barred the use of crossbows, bows and arrows and siege machines (Russell 1975, pp. 70, 156). There does seem, nonetheless, to be reason for doubting the effectiveness of this, and similar, prohibitions.

One type of weapon that has perennially attracted scrutiny is poison, whether administered directly or via some other weapon. The legitimacy of it as a weapon troubled the ancients, and was again a point of focal attention for the early modern international lawyers: their various attitudes towards the use of poison and their reasons for or against its use are illustrative of general notions of the permissible means to be employed in warfare. Grotius (1925, p. 652) argues that 'if you take account only of the law of nature, in case it is permissible to kill a person, it makes no difference whether you kill him by the sword or by poison' but then goes on to claim that, for largely prudential reasons, poison is prohibited by the law of nations. Wolff (1934, p. 450) was later to adopt a more permissive position:

> An enemy is killed in order to diminish his strength, and diminution of his strength is sought, not his death. If then you use poisoned bullets or arrows, so that, if the enemy should not die from the wound, he nevertheless would die from the poison, consequently his destruction would become so much the more certain; that which makes the killing of the enemy allowable, also makes the use of poison allowable. Of course it is just the same whether you get rid of the enemy by a single or by a double mortal wound.

The attempt to restrain the use of certain classes of weaponry became embodied in sundry international agreements from the nineteenth century onwards. One of the first of these agreements was the Declaration of St. Petersburg of 1868 which stated that legitimate military objectives would be exceeded by the use of weapons 'which uselessly aggravate the sufferings of disabled men, or render their death inevitable' (Trooboff 1975, p. 14). These efforts were taken further by the Hague meetings at the turn of the century.

A discussion of 'how?' one may fight a war against the enemy probably needs to cover more than the single issue of weaponry. Arguably, the question of intention forms part of an extended notion of 'how?' wars are to be fought. These are large and complex issues which can receive only cursory treatment in this study.

At least one possible answer to the question of 'how?' one may attack the enemy is to differentiate between an intentional mode of attack and an accidental one. It is in this context of limitations upon the means of attack that there has evolved an enduring debate as to whether certain forms of attack might be legitimate if considered from the point of view of primary intent, even if they might not be so considered from the point of view of secondary effects. In other words, recurring attempts to restrain the means of warfare have touched upon the equally recurrent doctrine of double effect which stipulates both limits upon means of warfare and limits upon these limits. The central argument of the theory of double effect has been summarized as follows:

> The principle states that one is sometimes permitted knowingly to bring about as a side effect of one's actions something which it would be absolutely impermissible to bring about deliberately or as an end or as a means. In application to war or revolution, the law of double effect permits a certain amount of civilian carnage as a side effect of bombing munitions plants or attacking enemy soldiers (Nagel 1974, p. 10).

This principle has been appealed to at many times in the history of warfare and usually in connection with weapons which are, to varying degrees, indiscriminate in their destruction of targets. The principle has been invoked apropos of sieges and siege-guns, in connection with aerial bombardment, in connection with the cleaning-out of insurgent villages and, most prominently of all, in relation to nuclear deterrence and the types of damage that might be permissible in an actual nuclear war. This is not the place to consider these issues. We can, however, note that the doctrine of double effect has not been confined to Western Catholic thought. Islamic jurists have argued similar propositions. For instance, we are told that, as an aspect of siege warfare, 'Sufyán al-Thawri and Abù Hanifa permitted attack even if shooting by arrows or hurling machines would kill the believers, provided that the jihadists intend to shoot the unbelievers; the killing of believers (including women and children) would be regarded as killing by mistake' (Khadduri 1955, p. 107).

'When?' conventions

Wars can be limited in the sense of restricting the times at which they may be fought. It is, of course, open to question whether conventions of this kind actually limit the destruction or suffering of war — indeed, they may protract it — or whether they merely provide war with a decorous timetable?

Historically, there have been many instances of conventions of this kind. Many cultures have prohibited or discouraged fighting at night. Armour (1923, p. 77) notes the general aversion to night attacks in ancient India and argues that it embodied 'a wholesome instinct against treacherous attack, and a clear distinction between what was a regular act of war and what was murder'. Conversely, with the advent of aerial bombardment, one author was to suggest that bombing raids, against industrial areas, take place *only* at night when the buildings would be unoccupied (Spaight 1947, p. 18). There have been prohibitions against fighting on certain days of the week or at certain times of the year. In ancient China, for instance, war was prohibited during the planting and harvesting seasons (Friedman 1972, p. 3).

The most common form of such time restrictions has been the religious or holy truce which can be found in many cultures and at various periods. The Greeks notably had their holy truces, even if sometimes violated. Pritchett (1974, Vol. I, p. 125) accordingly argues that 'the weight of the evidence shows that the Greeks, especially those of the Peloponnesos, among whom the force of religious routine appears to have been strongest, could not bring themselves easily to forego observance of venerated solemnities'. Specific examples include the postponement of a Spartan attack on Argos in 419 B.C. because of a religious festival (Adcock and Mosley 1975, p. 200). Phillipson (1911, p. 284) remarks generally that 'the commencement of a festival was deemed *ipso facto* to suspend warlike operations; though usually there was also a formal proclamation of a truce . . . in order that all . . . might have unrestricted access to the common games and religious ceremonies'. The truces were sometimes violated and even abused. Pritchett (1974, Vol. I, p. 124) cites an example of the Argives tampering with their callendar in order to claim immunity, in accord with a holy truce, when attacked by the Lakedaimonians.

Such truces were also a part of Islamic tradition, again if not always enforced, and seem later to have been abrogated: 'the Muslims, following a pre-Islamic customary rule, were not allowed to go to war during the sacred months . . . these constituted the grace of God when all people should abstain from fighting' (Khadduri 1955, p. 105).

In Europe, the best known example of religious restraint upon the time of fighting is the Truce of God of the early eleventh century. Various canons were enunciated demanding the cessation of fighting during certain periods of the year (Brundage 1969, p. 12). In 1035, the Archbishop of Arles decreed:

> This is the peace or truce of God . . . that all Christians, friends and enemies, neighbours and strangers, should keep true and lasting peace one with another from vespers on Wednesday to sunrise on Monday, so that during these four days and five nights, all persons may have peace, and, trusting in this peace, may go about their business without fear of their enemies (Friedman 1972, p. 9).

Limitations upon the time for warfare could be, and have been, also of the obverse sort: conventions may not only specify when parties should not fight; they may also specify precisely when the parties should fight. Thus it has been common for opposing armies formally to invite each other to battle at a mutually agreed time. In ancient Greece, 'armies might be encamped opposite each other for several days, or longer. A challenge might be issued for a drawn battle, and such a challenge might be declined or accepted' (Pritchett 1974, Vol. II, p. 147).

Such conventions, relating to the timing of battle, were commonplace in medieval Europe, abounding, for instance, in the pages of Froissart's chronicles. One example will suffice, relating to King Edward of England's campaigns in France against King Philip:

> When the King of England had halted in the champaign country of Tierache . . . he was informed, that the King of France was within two leagues of him, and eager to give him battle . . . [A herald was sent] to offer him battle and to fix the day . . . [the herald] told them, that the King of England . . . demanded and required the combat of one army against the other. To this King Philip answered willingly, and appointed the Friday following for the day, this being Wednesday . . . The day being thus fixed, information of it was given to the captains of either army, and every one made his preparations accordingly (Froissart 1839, p. 55).

As a variation on this theme, there was an elaborate protocol surrounding the procedures for relieving a besieged town, a major part of which was that the relieving force should arrive by a specified date in order to do battle with the besiegers. If they failed to arrive by the agreed date, the town capitulated (Keen 1965, p. 129).

'Where?' conventions

As with the foregoing 'when?' rules, 'where?' conventions have generally been of two distinct kinds: firstly, conventions prohibiting fighting in certain locations or beyond certain boundaries; secondly, and conversely, conventions stipulating where, in fact, an encounter shall be fought.

The first set of conventions is predicated upon the notion of sanctuaries, that once certain geographic thresholds are crossed, the fighting will be discontinued. Frequently, the field of battle was itself the limit of hostilities and the very act of fleeing the field meant the attainment of sanctuary because there would be no pursuit beyond it. Schelling (1966) demonstrates convincingly how such conventions, if they are tacit, depend for their observance upon geographic saliencies in order that the parties should easily recognize when a threshold has been crossed.

A classical instance of such a convention can be found in a treaty signed between Sparta and Argos in 420 B.C. Thucydides (1954, p. 334) provided the following account: '. . . there should be a peace treaty for fifty years, but each side should have the right . . . to issue a challenge to the other and decide the question of the disputed land by battle . . . no pursuit to be allowed across the frontiers of Argos or of Sparta'.

In some cases, the negative injunction not to fight in certain places merely reiterates the positive injunction to fight in a specified location. However, the two need not be identical and we should, therefore, briefly mention conventions stipulating the arena of battle. Normally, the location was offered as part of the challenge to battle along with an agreed time: opposing armies contracted not only to meet at a certain time, but also at a certain place.

As regards some of these conventions, however, we can have legitimate doubts as to the extent to which they limited warfare in any meaningful sense, as opposed to simply regulating it. In fact, Oman (1953, pp. 62–3) contends that such invitations to battle were inspired by little more than a pragmatic concern to ensure that the opposing armies should find each other:

> Nothing could show the primitive state of the military art better than the fact that generals solemnly sent and accepted challenges

to meet in battle at a given place and on a given day. Without such precautions there was apparently a danger lest the armies should lose sight of each other and stray away in different directions.

However, it should not be thought that the practice of stipulating the arena of combat died out after the Middle Ages. Even if the formalities were not so politely observed, there might be good reason for regarding the Crimean War as a more recent example in the sense that the reasons for fighting the war, in that specific location alone, were by no means compelling and rested, in part, on a tacit convention not to extend the hostilities elsewhere.

WAR-LIMITATION AND CONVENTION A

In this section, we will introduce some of the conventions of war-limitation that appear to be preponderantly examples of convention A. That is to say that they are concerned, to a greater or lesser degree, with the procedures of war rather than its substantive limitation and with the political dimensions of such limitation rather than its humanitarian impulses, even though these impulses might be embraced within the conventions.

There are some forms of limitation that fully embody both convention A and convention B. The most perfect example of such a dual function is the agreement to settle a war by combat between single champions from both sides. However, the champion, as a form of war-limitation, will be examined in detail in a later chapter and requires no further discussion at this point. Accordingly, in this section, we will briefly outline the forms of limitation that are characteristically instances of convention A.

Pacta sunt servanda

The first convention that might be mentioned is so obvious that there is a danger of overlooking it. The question is whether, between enemies in war, the principle of *pacta sunt servanda* is to be applied? In other words, should one keep faith with the enemy or is fraud and treachery a legitimate means of securing the enemy's defeat? This strikes, of course, at the very heart of any convention for the limitation of warfare, because without assurance of reciprocity there can be little prospect for the observance of the conventions themselves: the convention that conventions will be respected therefore, forms a fundamental aspect of the process of war-limitation. It, in fact, helps to define the very nature of warfare itself and, as such, might be considered under the category of convention A. Sturzo (1929, p. 90) adheres to this position when he insists that there is no war without its elementary rules amongst which he cites 'the respect of pacts'.

Testimony to the centrality of this issue to a discussion of war-limitation is to be found in the widespread preoccupation with it on the part of the early international law theorists: they debated endlessly whether it was necessary to keep faith with the enemy and arrived at their varying conclusions.

The notion of keeping faith with the enemy is to be found in classical times and became a part of the European just war tradition via the teachings of Augustine. So essential was the observance of promises to the reciprocal nature of war-limitation that virtually all the international law theorists subscribed to the principle that, even between the bitterest of enemies, *pacta sunt servanda*. However, most also made some distinction between 'good faith' and the adoption of legitimate 'stratagems', as in Gentili (1933, p. 148) who declared that 'we approve of stratagems. But a stratagem is one thing, treachery another'. Grotius likewise insisted that a promise made to an enemy had to be fulfilled, and went further in applying this not only to 'expressed' promises, but also to those that were 'implied' (1925, p. 619). The rationale for the mutual observance of pacts and conventions between enemies, even when one party might gain an advantage through breach of the convention, was elaborated at length by Vattel (1916, p. 297):

> ... a belligerent is bound to observe whatever promises he may have made to the enemy during the course of the war, for in treating with the enemy while he is actually at war with him he necessarily, though tacitly, renounces the power to break the agreement as a means of indemnification and because of the war

... otherwise nothing would be gained by treating with the enemy and it would be absurd to make the attempt.

He goes on to demonstrate that this does not entail a prohibition upon other means of deceiving the enemy, provided no perfidy is involved: indeed, he suggests that such deceptions are commendable if they help avoid the slaughter of battle. Nonetheless, expediency remains circumscribed by the fundamental principle that the 'desire to avoid the shedding of blood never warrants us in resorting to perfidy, the use of which would be attended with too disastrous consequences, and would deprive sovereigns, when once at war, of all means of treating together and of restoring peace' (Vattel 1916, p. 297).

Formal initiation of war

There is a sense in which wars can be limited by having them formally initiated. Not only does this reduce the element of surprise, but it also regularizes war and demonstrates that war has a distinctive status which sets it apart from other resorts to violence. While not a universal practice, it has nonetheless been widespread for the parties about to embark on war to indicate their intentions by means of a formal document, heraldic proclamation or some similar symbolic enactment.

As far as modern Europe is concerned, the requirement of formal declaration was part of the process whereby the sovereign monarch obtained his monopoly over the legitimate resort to force in war: the monarch alone had the necessary authority to initiate the legal condition of warfare. In this requirement, we can see the confluence of the two elements of the just war doctrine, namely the *ius ad bellum* and the *ius in bello*. In so far as necessary authority became part of the just reasons for declaring war, it spilled over and exercised constraint upon the just conduct of the war. As Midgley (1975, pp. 245–6) has pointed out, 'some of these gross limitations upon the use of military violence to repair injustice are implicit in the conditions for just war itself. The competence to wage offensive war was limited to the sovereign authority which has had power to determine that some injustice should go unavenged, to make truces and to abolish all preceding marque in order to achieve a peace settlement.'

Thus formal initiation serves to give definition to the process of war and serves to limit war in various ways. It does so by restricting war to a condition initiated by socially-authorized persons, and it does so also by reducing the possibilities of surprise attack.

However, formal initiation does not by itself embody humanitarian purposes. Indeed, it is because such humanitarian effects are secondary to its main purpose, that we can consider formal initiation as an instance of convention A. The reason for saying so is that there are examples of formal initiation of war which, however much they might regulate warfare, do little or nothing to impose meaningful limitations upon the ensuing destruction: that formal initiation concerns the process of warfare, rather than the substantive saving of lives, is clearly indicated in this fact that it can regulate war without necessarily limiting the violence. Herodotos describes a case in point, from Greek warfare:

> When they have declared war against each other, they come down to the fairest and most level ground that they can find and there they fight, so that the victors come off without great harm; and of the vanquished I say not so much as a word, for they are utterly destroyed (Pritchett 1974, Vol. II, p. 252).

Conventions of equal advantage in warfare

There are many examples of societies which have insisted upon the observance of rules of equal advantage for the combatants upon both sides. Generally, we can assume that a convention of this kind would have the effect of reducing the number of violent deaths in war; and yet, we are entitled to see the primary significance of such conventions, not in their humanitarian effects, but rather in what they tell us about the very procedure of warfare because clearly, in such a situation, war is a very special form of rule-governed activity. In fact, nowhere does the activity of warfare more closely approximate the game analogy than in the situation where conventions of equal advantage are applied.

Such conventions have been widespread. Wright (1942, p. 94) tells us of the 'chivalric practice not infrequent among primitive people of insistence upon equal advantage in combat. The warrior will withhold his hand until the enemy is equally armed.' Specific examples include the following. One student of Maori warfare attests the observance of the convention of equal advantage, even when under attack from modern British troops: 'when British ammunition ran low they waited for them to bring up supplies, for why fight a man on uneven terms?' (Turney-High 1949, p. 225). The British, however, did not reciprocate.

A similar chivalric code emerges from accounts of warfare in ancient China, where the following tale is told:

> The chariots bearing Prince Ch'eng of Sung and Hua Pao, warden of Lü, meet, and Ch'eng's turns away. Hua Pao called out, 'Ch'eng!' and Ch'eng, angered, turned back again. As he was fitting arrow to string, Pao had already drawn his bow. Ch'eng said 'May the spirit of Duke P'ing yet support me!' Pao's arrow passed between him and his charioteer. When he was about to set arrow to string, Pao had again drawn; but Ch'eng said, 'Not to take turns is pusillanimous'. Pao took away his arrow, and Ch'eng shot him dead (Kierman 1974, p. 43).

Likewise, rules of equal advantage were laid out at length in the Hindu epics:

> Only equals should fight each other; elephants should oppose only elephants; and so the chariots, cavalry, and infantry should attack only their opposite numbers . . . No one should strike another who is confiding or unprepared or panic-stricken. A foe engaged with another should never be struck, as also one without armour, or whose weapon is rendered useless . . . (Singh 1965, p. 161).

The notion of equal advantage was also frequently embodied in the formal invitation to battle that has already been discussed. The location of the battle had to be mutually agreed and it was not unknown for the invitation to be declined if one of the parties felt at some disadvantage. Likewise, there are examples of one army allowing the other unhindered access to the field of combat even when, as in crossing a river, the other army would be highly vulnerable to attack. Oman (1953, p. 63) recounts the following episode from medieval European warfare:

... Béla IV of Hungary and Ottokar II of Bohemia were in arms in 1260 and both were equally bent on fighting; but when they sighted each other it was only to find that the river March was between them ... Accordingly, it was reckoned nothing strange when the Bohemian courteously invited his adversary either to cross the March unhindered and fight in due form on the west bank, or to give him the same opportunity and grant a free passage to the Hungarian side. Béla chose the former alternative, forded the river without molestation, and fought on the other side the disastrous battle of Kressenbrunn.

Conventions of this kind are intimately related to the essential nature of the process of war itself. Some would argue that it was absurd to incorporate such rules of courtesy in warfare: others that conventions of various kinds are an intrinsic part of warfare and that nothing could be more absurd than to have no conventions restraining permissible conduct. Whichever perspective is adopted, conventions of type A tell us much about how the participants view the process of war and what they deem to be essential to its proper conduct. For instance, the rules of equal advantage currently under consideration have been most stringently observed in situations in which it was thought that the function of war was to provide a verdict, either judicial or divine. In other words, the task of battle was to pronounce upon the justice of the contending causes, as in a judicial combat, or to give an indication of the wishes of God, as in other forms of divination. Elaborate rules of procedure became necessary to ensure a 'fair trial' for the plaintiffs in battle. Keen (1965, pp. 129–30) explains the conventions surrounding the relief of a besieged medieval town in precisely these terms:

> This exaggerated formality is revealing. The careful choice of a field of battle, the ban on the garrison's participation and the insistence that all be maintained in the precise order, as it stood when the treaty was signed, all had the same purpose, to secure absolutely fair conditions for a judicial duel. They are all thus part and parcel of the contemporary belief that battle was an appeal to the judgment of God. Every possible precaution had to be taken to thwart any attempt on the part of wicked men to weight the scales of divine justice.

Conventions of surrender

Schelling (1966), we have previously noted, considered that war could be limited in the form of its termination. It is the forms of termination that will be considered in this and in the final section. Arguably, there are two parts to the process of termination and they are closely interrelated but distinguishable: we can regard these as the conventions surrounding surrender (for the loser) and the conventions surrounding victory (for the winner). It is conceded, however, that in some situations, the two forms may be virtually identical.

The conventions of surrender tell us much about the process of warfare and are a crucial form of limitation. As Schelling (1966, p. 126) pointed out, we can contrast 'unconditioned surrender' with 'unconditional extermination' in as much as surrender implies an element of bargaining in warfare. It also tells us much about the objectives of warfare and about the price that a party is prepared to pay to attain these objectives. As has been said of ancient forms of warfare 'unless one of the adversaries deliberately decided to wage war until the opponent was totally exterminated, the conquered were always able, in the last resort, to avoid being wiped out, by appealing to the mercy of the victor, by capitulating' (Garlan 1975, p. 53). Such mercy need not be purely humanitarian; it can be founded upon self-interest, upon a calculation of the cost, to the victor, of exterminating the defeated opponent. Gentili (1933, p. 224) explains the rationale for sparing those who surrender in terms of an implicit bargain:

> ... if the captured are spared, how much the more ought those to be pardoned, who by continuing to fight either could not be taken or would give the enemy a bloody victory? Ought not at least their lives to be granted to those who left life to their enemies and made their victory a genuine one?

Conventions of surrender have been widespread both in ancient and in modern forms of warfare. It was common practice with the Romans, and Froissart provides numerous examples of its prevalence in medieval times. However, as previously noted, conventions of surrender are complex and may subsume various of our 'who?', 'what?' and 'when?' rules. Indeed, we may also regard them as instances of a 'where?' rule. Symbolically, surrender constitutes an escape route, an avenue available to the combatant who wishes to avoid being killed. But the symbolic function of surrender has, in fact, adopted quite literal forms whereby one side, in advance, allows an escape route to the other. Notably, Grotius (1925, pp. 739–40) mentions an old Jewish usage: 'the Jewish interpreters note that it was a custom among their ancestors that, when they were besieging a city, they would not completely encircle it, but would leave a sector open for those who wished to escape, in order that the issue might be determined with less bloodshed'. Functionally, the conventions of surrender and the above escape route are similar and there is, in consequence, a spatial element hidden deep within the forms of surrender. Taken as a package, therefore, these various elements combine to make the convention of surrender a crucial element in the process of warfare.

Conventions of victory

Victory is the other aspect of termination, and it likewise may be limited by conventions similar in purpose to those surrounding surrender. What has to be emphasized is that, in many situations of warfare, the very notion of victory and what it means is not at all clear and to that extent, victory is itself *conventional*. This becomes abundantly clear in specific forms of combat, such as that between single champions where, as we shall see, there is need for the constituents of victory to be agreed in advance and mutually understood. But it is not only in such limited forms of war that victory is conventional: in many full-scale battles, or in many protracted wars, the military outcome may be so indecisive that there is a need for conventions denoting victory and the rewards which will result from it.

The symbol of ancient victory was the erection of a trophy: 'if the retiring enemy acquiesced in the setting up of such trophies on the field of battle, his non-resistance implied an acknowledgment of defeat' (Phillipson 1911, p. 297). However, it was not uncommon for both sides to erect trophies and this makes us realize that trophies represented a claim of victory, but did not themselves constitute *prima facie* evidence of victory having been attained. How else, then, could victory be measured? Commonly, it was attributed on the basis of territorial possession. As one writer has commented:

Because victory could determine social and political standing it could not be equivocal. It was the result of a categorical judgment, of a quasi-divine nature, not open to dispute. Hence certain criteria of victory were required which would permit a firm decision even in the most doubtful situations, when neither side would admit defeat. The most generally used criterion was control of terrain, whether of the battlefield (on land or sea) or of the territory of the state (Garlan 1975, p. 60).

In the absence of such conventions, as with surrender, there could be no assurance of victory short of the enemy's physical elimination. In fact, it is a recognition of victory that permits the surrender of the defeated side. As mentioned, there are situations in which the conventions of victory are virtually synonymous with the conventions of surrender. Likewise, the standard was a symbol of continued resistance in medieval battles (Verbruggen 1977, p. 86). Its fall meant the end to that resistance, an act which both symbolized the surrender of one side and the simultaneous victory of the other

Victory is, accordingly, at least partially conventional. The convention, by allowing the winning party to secure its objectives short of eliminating the defeated, has the effect of limiting the damage resulting from warfare. But again, the convention tells us more about the very nature of the process of war as an activity in which winning has meaning, and in which the constituents of victory have to be stipulated. Victory is a convention which limits warfare both by saving lives but, more fundamentally, by demonstrating that warfare is a procedure which has a point to it.

3

Political Theorists and Limits to War

POLITICAL THEORISTS AND THE POSSIBILITY OF LIMITS TO WAR

The intention of this chapter is to locate our discussion of limits to war in the context of past philosophical treatment of the subject. It will review the forms and rationales of limitation in the history of political thought, for the reason that this study concentrates upon limits to war as a problem, not so much of military strategy, as of political theory. How, then, in the history of political thought have the problems associated with war-limitation been conceived and what answers have the classical political philosophers been able to advance in response to them?

Such an exercise provides an important perspective upon the present study. If asked to discuss past doctrines of limits to war, most people would readily make reference to two principal bodies of thought. These are, firstly, the medieval Catholic tradition of the just war and, secondly, the legal treatises of the sixteenth to eighteenth centuries which established a body of theory on the nature of international legal obligations. We associate names like Augustine and Aquinas with the former; names like Vitoria, Suarez, Grotius, Pufendorf and Vattel with the latter. And yet it has to be said that over and above these two specific intellectual traditions, there has also been a tradition of political philosophy which has concerned itself with discussion of the nature of limits to war. While I would not wish to see the just war doctrine, nor the early international legal treatises, as divorced from this other area of speculation, it is important for this study that we recognize the persistence and continuity of

68

political thought on this question, stretching back into the period of antiquity itself. The moral and political problems which flow from the topic of limits to war are by no means novel and have been debated by succeeding generations of political theorists, even if each has put its own gloss upon the issues and resolved them to its own varying satisfaction. In other words, many of the essential dilemmas of limitation in war were as familiar to the ancient Greeks as they are to the students of limited nuclear warfare. Stawell (1929, pp. 23–4) provides strong support for this perspective in his history of the development of international thought: 'to the Greek intellect . . . it would have seemed . . . sophistical to argue that because war was a resort to force it meant that the force must be unlimited. On the contrary, to find the right limit in war, as elsewhere, was to a thoughtful Greek the problem of problems'.

This is not, of course, to deny the deep divisions that have existed between various schools of thought. We might, for instance, distinguish between a broad natural law school which regards the observance of restraints in war as part of a natural moral order that men can intuitively appreciate, and a utilitarian school which regards the observance of limits in war to be conventional and based upon mutual interests. Historically, these two traditions have been prominent and influential and it would be useful to outline their contrasting accounts of the nature of the obligation to wage war in accordance with specific codes of conduct.

We can take Locke as representative of the former position. Without the assumption of a law of nature and of the rights which are provided in that natural condition, it would be impossible to understand these limits which Locke regards as inseparable from the proper conduct of war. As one commentator upon Locke has observed,

Locke's conception of international relations as a state of nature, in which commonwealths are subject only to the law of nature, follows directly from his two basic premises: that men are dissociated by nature, but that they also possess certain fundamental rights by nature. Thus, on the one hand, the absence of any common superior on earth means that there is no source of common positive laws, hence no source of a basis for sociability or community amongst independent commonwealths. But on the other hand, the explicit and severe restrictions on the right of conquest and the right to make war are rooted in the Lockeian conception of the consensual basis of political society and the natural right to property (Cox 1960, p. 162).

This contrasts markedly with utilitarian reasoning in support of limits to war, a position succinctly expressed by David Hume:

> The rage and violence of public war; what is it but a suspension of justice among the warring parties, who perceive, that this virtue is now no longer of any *use* or advantage to them? The laws of war, which then succeed to those of equity and justice, are rules calculated for the *advantage* and *utility* of that particular state, in which men are now placed. And were a civilized nation engaged with barbarians, who observed no rules even of war, the former must also suspend their observance of them, where they no longer serve to any purpose; and must render every action or encounter as bloody and pernicious as possible to the first aggressor (Wolfers and Martin (eds) 1956a, p. 70).

The various forms of limitation suggested in the works of notable political thinkers will be presented in due course. Initially, however, it is apposite to deal with the treatment, by the theorists, of the primary issue of the possibility of limitation. In other words, is there a serious tradition of political thought which would call into question the very possibility, or desirability, in principle, of establishing limits to war?

Most theorists have come down decisively on the side of striving for limitation. Erasmus, although he comes much closer to the pole of pacifism than most, can be cited as a typical demonstration of the proclivity to minimize the furies of war when he argues that 'the Prince's first care shall be to carry on the struggle with as little suffering for his people and as little shedding of Christian blood as may be, and to bring it to the speediest possible end' (Joyce (ed.) p. 57).

There are various possible exceptions to this general rule, thinkers who have questioned, or who have been interpreted as questioning, the very fundamentals of limits to war. We can consider Machiavelli, Kant and Clausewitz as possible writers of this *genre* and briefly review what these writers have said on the subject. It will become clear that in none of the authors cited do we find unequivocal denunciation of the possibility of restraint in war.

It is certainly true that Machiavelli's major work on military matters, *The Art of War,* contains not a mention of any conception of limited warfare. The reader will look in vain for enunciated principles of moderation in the conduct of warfare in this treatise and this lends support to the contention that, according to Machiavelli; 'no rules for the prosecution of war could be observed' and, again that 'his view of strategy thus emerges as the absolute opposite to the effort to achieve limited war' (Åkerman 1972, p. 39). On the strictest reading of the requirements for a philosophy of limits to war, this is no doubt a fair reflection of the general tendency of Machiavelli's thought and Gilbert (1944) provides further impressive evidence of his anti-limitationist dispositions. However, to leave the matter at this point would be to fail to give a rounded presentation of the position.

There are at least three areas, discussed by Machiavelli, that could be perceived as being related to a theory of limited warfare, although it is not suggested that Machiavelli himself articulated such a doctrine or that he would be at all sympathetic to many of the ideas associated with limits to war. The three areas explored by Machiavelli that have a bearing upon our discussion are as follows: firstly, he recommends a show of moderation for the utilitarian purpose of diminishing the enemy's resistance; secondly, he argues in favour of an economy of violence dictated by the need to preserve what is being militarily acquired; thirdly, and perhaps most importantly, Machiavelli urges the prince to tailor his political objectives in the light of the balance of forces with which he is confronted, and not to pursue military ventures that are hostages to fortune. A comment can be made on each of these areas in turn.

As to the first, Machiavelli thinks the military commander should use intelligence as much as brute force and that it may be militarily advantageous to show some moderation towards the enemy, although it is apparent that Machiavelli recommends such a policy for its instrumentality, rather than as an expression of humanitarianism in war. Accordingly, he proffers the following tactical advice:

... the captain who attacks a town should use what care he can, not to drive the defenders to extremities, lest he render them stubborn; but when they fear punishment should promise their pardon, and when they fear for their freedom should assure them that he has no designs against the common welfare, but only against a few ambitious men in their city; for such assurances have often smoothed the way to surrender of towns (Machiavelli 1883, p. 389).

On the second score, it is implicit in much of Machiavelli's writing, and explicit in some, that he adhered to a principle of economy of violence. As Wolin (1961, p. 222) has commented: 'one of the basic aims of *The Art of War* was to demonstrate that, while military action remained an unavoidable fact of the political condition, its costliness could be reduced by proper attention to strategy, discipline, and organization'. While this is not in itself a philosophy of limited war, it is by no means inconsistent with such and, indeed, could be considered an integral component of one. This becomes even clearer when Machiavelli counsels against despoliation of enemy territory that is to be acquired because such despoliation is contrary to the objectives of the campaign. Again, he insists that war be conducted with such a politico-economic calculus in mind. 'Whosoever makes war,' he instructs, 'whether from policy or ambition, means to acquire and to hold what he acquires, and to carry on the war he has undertaken in such a manner that it shall enrich and not impoverish his native country and state' (1883, p. 217).

This last principle in turn derives from the third and most important of Machiavelli's maxims on war. This is the crucial relationship which he posits between the resort to war and the extent of the war effort, on the one hand, and the state's political interests, on the other. In many respects, therefore, it is with Machiavelli that we find that nexus between war and politics, later given authoritative expression by Clausewitz, which constitutes an essential underpinning of most subsequent rationales for the limitation of warfare. The nexus is given physical expression in Machiavelli's admonition that only a civil militia can truly fight for the state and in such a manner as to secure the state's vital interests. As has been said of Machiavelli's argument: 'only a part-time soldier can be trusted to possess a full-time commitment to the war and its purposes' (Pocock 1975, p. 200). It follows from this integral link between war and the state's political independence that war should be entertained only with these interests firmly in sight, and that it should not be pursued beyond the point dictated by the prevailing balance of forces. It was for Machiavelli as great a sin that a prince aspire to too much as that he aspire to too little: overweaning ambition in war, as in politics, is but a princely folly. Wars therefore should not be undertaken, but political terms accepted, if military prudence so dictates. Likewise, war should not be pursued to the point where its outcome is wholly a matter of chance, but political objectives should be curtailed by a prudent calculation of the military prospects: 'a prince therefore, who is attacked by an enemy much more powerful than himself, can make no greater mistake than to refuse to treat, especially when overtures are made to him; for however poor the terms offered may be, they are sure to contain some conditions advantageous for him who accepts them . . .' Florence should, accordingly, have acceded to the political conditions offered to it, rather than attempt to improve its position by a rash and uncertain appeal to arms: '. . . nor ought they [Florentines], even with the possibility and almost certainty of greater advantages before them, to have left matters in any degree to the arbitration of Fortune, by pushing things to extremes, and incurring risks which no prudent man should incur, unless compelled by necessity' (Machiavelli 1883, pp. 304–5).

Machiavelli does not articulate a theory of limits to war as such and, in fact, in his requirement that military action be sharp and decisive, seems to argue against such a theory. Nonetheless, Machiavelli is fully cognizant of war's purpose in securing the state's interests. Hence, to the extent that theories of limited war are predicated on a notion of accepting less than total political results, but the best that prevailing circumstances will permit, Machiavelli may be seen as sharing intellectual links with later theorists of limited war: the prudential aspects of war-limitation could scarcely be alien to the man who more than most made prudence the touchstone of successful political action.

Those who have seen Machiavelli as opposed to certain

fundamental precepts of war-limitation have, to a greater or lesser extent, predicated their case on the primacy of the state in Machiavelli's political theory, and on the justness he thereby accords to military actions which are politically necessary: it is the antipathy between the necessities of political governance and universal codes of conduct that is thought to make Machiavelli inimical to the limits-to-war tradition. In the case of Kant, those who have placed him likewise outside the war-limitation tradition have done so for quite different reasons. If Kant was in any way unfavourably disposed towards the adoption of limits in war, he arrived at his position via philosophical premises that had little in common with those of Machiavelli. However, as we shall see, Kant much less than Machiavelli falls outside the limited-war tradition.

The most cogent expression of the argument that Kant was an anti-limitationist is to be found in an interpretative essay by Gallie (1978). Kant had, as is well known, denounced the early international lawyers such as Grotius, Pufendorf and Vattel as 'miserable comforters' thereby dismissing contemptuously their efforts to provide a legal basis for the resort to, and for the conduct of, war. Kant had commented bitterly that 'we may well wonder that the word right has not yet been entirely banished from the policy of war as pedantic' (Forsyth *et al.* (eds) 1970, p. 211). On this basis, Gallie (1978, p. 26) draws attention to the anti-limitationist elements in the Kantian approach to war and peace:

> Kant will have none of this insidiously 'comforting' approach to the problem of peace; and not, as one might expect, because of the great difficulty of keeping any war within proposed limits once it has begun, but because in Kant's reconstructed international law, everything depends upon — and also points towards — the thought that 'war is no way in which to pursue one's rights', since it amounts to the irrational acceptance of the role of the stronger . . .

What Kant is in effect saying is that, in as much as war is a moral affront, it remains so even if placed within a legal framework for its conduct. The emphasis in Kant is, therefore, upon the eradication of war, the creation of perpetual peace, rather than upon the institution of a code of conduct for what is a morally repugnant state of affairs.

It would, however, be incorrect to claim that Kant had set his face implacably against restraint in warfare. On the contrary, there are various instances in Kant's writings where he stipulates ground rules for the proper conduct of war and in doing so puts forward a conception of limited warfare. For instance, in his *The Metaphysics of Morals,* Kant sets limits to the means that may legitimately be employed in war and prohibits such things as employment of spies, poisoners or assassins on the general principle that 'the attacked state is allowed to use any means of defence except those whose use would render its subjects unfit to be citizens' (Reiss (ed.) 1971, p. 168). Moreover, it can be seen that Kant establishes gross limitations upon the conduct of war in accordance with its purpose as leading to a better peace and, with this end in mind, he insists that 'no state at war with another shall permit such acts of hostility as would make mutual confidence impossible during a future time of peace' (Reiss 1971, p. 96). It is on the basis of such recommendations that Best (1980, p. 37) is able to conclude that Kant was not far removed from the Enlightenment consensus upon the need for, and very real prospects of, securing agreed limitations and restrictions upon the activities of belligerents:

> Pending the stopping of war altogether, Kant was as desirous as anyone else of his generation to limit and mitigate it in the meantime, and he was, presumably, as pleased as any other reflective person to observe the extent to which war . . . was in fact a monster on a tighter rein than ever before.

By far the most difficult to assess of the theorists presently under review is Clausewitz. In part this is because Clausewitz was concerned principally with war itself and was not, as the others, a philosopher who only intermittently turned his attention to the topic: it is his very attempt to provide a comprehensive theoretical analysis of war that leads to the difficulties commentators have experienced in arriving at a consistent interpretation of the Clausewitzian position. At no point is the judgment of history more at variance than in the assessment of Clausewitz's attitudes towards limits in war.

The diversity of opinion can be easily demonstrated. While qualifying his judgment in various ways, Åkerman nonetheless remains convinced that there are fundamental differences between Clausewitz and the theorists of limited war in the nuclear age, in that the latter have a conception of the political disutility of total war that Clausewitz did not share. Thus Åkerman (1972, p. 45) claims that:

> Nowhere in his entire work, however, can we find what has been in the atomic age the most important argument for an increased emphasis on an alternative strategy, namely that the lower form of war is to be chosen not of necessity, not from weakness, but by free volition, based on an insight into the breadth of the higher form's irrationality.

Meanwhile, at the other end of the spectrum, Brodie punctures the inflated opinions of those who regard Clausewitz's main contribution to be in the realm of advancing a theory of total war. 'One remembers wryly' is Brodie's acid comment, 'that Clausewitz has often been called the "apostle of total war". This opinion is likely to be confined to those who have never touched the book' (Clausewitz 1976, p. 646).

Clausewitz's ambivalence on limits to war is accounted for by the apparent internal inconsistencies in his argument and it is necessary to outline the passages upon which various commentators have based their interpretations of the direction of Clausewitz's thought. What should cause least confusion is the distinction which Clausewitz draws between an absolute form of war, in which violence will tend toward the extreme, and war in reality, that is subject to various restraints which diminish the degree of violence exhibited within it: the confusion tends to creep in later in the argument.

Having moved beyond his depiction of war in its ideal state, Clausewitz enumerates the constraints to which real war is subject. On the basis of these passages, we might summarize the argument by saying that Clausewitz recognized three different sources of limitation in war — limitations of a social, practical and political nature. These passages clearly predispose one to regard Clausewitz as the foremost modern theorist of limits to warfare.

What, then, is the nature of the limits which Clausewitz envisages? Firstly, he describes those limits to the conduct of war that have their origin in fundamental social characteristics of the fighting states. These limits are not essential to war itself but are, as it were, historical accidents which will vary as between periods and with social conditions generally. Hence, says Clausewitz, 'if wars between civilized nations are far less cruel and destructive than wars between savages, the reason lies in the social conditions of the states themselves and in their relationships to one another. These are the forces that give rise to war; the same forces circumscribe and moderate it. They themselves however are not part of war . . .' (Clausewitz 1976, p. 76).

Secondly, and for a host of material, organizational and practical reasons, real war falls short of the extremities envisaged in its ideal conception: the metaphysician of war gives way to the hard-headed master of tactics, logistics, organization, discipline, morale and command. 'As soon as preparations for a war begin,' he suggests, 'the world of reality takes over from the world of abstract thought; material calculations take the place of hypothetical extremes and, if for no other reason, the interaction of the two sides tends to fall short of maximum effort' (p. 79).

Thirdly, and most memorably, war is to be limited in accordance with its political objectives. This will determine both the intensity of the effort to be made during the war and the point at which continuing hostilities no longer correspond with the objectives which are being sought. In this case, Clausewitz tells us, 'since war is not an act of senseless passion but is controlled by its political object, the value of this object must determine the sacrifices to be made for it in *magnitude* and also in *duration*. Once the expenditure of effort exceeds the value of the political object, the object must be renounced and peace must follow' (p. 92).

Moreover, with a view to explaining the different levels of expenditure of effort that may take place in war, and by implication the differing limits that may pertain in its conduct, Clausewitz comes closer to elaborating a theory of limited war by distinguishing between various types of war. In fact, Clausewitz presents us with forms of encounter which are virtually identical to what Schelling (1966) was later to label as 'wars of the battlefield' as contrasted with 'wars of pain and destruction'. The former is a physical contest whereas the latter, though expressed physically, has a pronounced psychological dimension to it. Moreover, both are subject to distinct forms of constraint since the limits appropriate to the former contest may not be appropriate to the latter. Clausewitz refines this distinction in two passages:

> When we attack the enemy, it is one thing if we mean our first operation to be followed by others until all resistance has been broken; it is quite another if our aim is only to obtain a single victory; in order to make the enemy insecure, to impress our greater strength upon him, and to give him doubts about his future (p. 92).

He subsequently elaborates in the following terms:

> Thus there are many reasons why the purpose of an engagement may not be the destruction of the enemy's forces, the forces immediately confronting us. Destruction may be merely a means to some other end. In such a case, total destruction has ceased to be the point; the engagement is nothing but a *trial of strength*. In itself it is of no value; its significance lies in the outcome of the trial (p. 96).

By very definition, therefore, the objectives of those two types of war are dissimilar and it is to be expected that each, in following its inner political logic, will conform to its own appropriate level of violence and be subject to its own principle of limitation.

Having given various indications as to how wars are, in fact, limited and further indications as to the principles which should govern their conduct, Clausewitz subsequently causes confusion by issuing a series of statements which, on their own, would read as a cogent expression of the argument against any limitation in war. A few such passages will be cited to convey the nature of the problem. Within them, two themes recur: the first is that slaughter and blood are an inevitable accompaniment of war and that there should be no shrinking from this aspect of it. There is, in short, no expression of humanitarian concern in the pages of Clausewitz; secondly, Clausewitz reiterates his advice that to pursue halfhearted or limited measures may be an act of folly, because it will give the advantage to the other side. In both these respects, and on either natural law or utilitarian counts, Clausewitz has the appearance of being a vocal anti-limitationist. Thus Clausewitz roundly denounced the staid and decorous limited wars of the eighteenth century:

In this type of war, where military action is reduced to insignificant time-killing flourishes, to skirmishes that are half in earnest and half in jest ... many theorists see the real, authentic art of war. In these feints, parries, and short lunges of earlier wars they find the true end of all theory and the triumph of mind over matter. More recent wars appear to them as crude brawls that can teach nothing and that are to be considered as relapses into barbarism. This view is as petty as its subject (p. 218).

It was also a dangerous point of view. Repeatedly, Clausewitz issued injunctions against such a military policy. 'Woe to the government', he admonished his readers 'which relying on half-hearted politics and a shackled military policy, meets a foe who, like the untamed elements, knows no law other than his own power! Any defect of action and effort will turn to the advantage of the enemy ...' (p. 219). There could be no place in military operations for idle sentimentality or notions of humanity. Thus we have the blunt assertion that 'we are not interested in generals who win victories without bloodshed. The fact that slaughter is a horrifying spectacle must make us take war more seriously, but not provide an excuse for gradually blunting our swords in the name of humanity. Sooner or later someone will come along with a sharp sword and hack off our arms' (p. 260).

In the latter stages of *On War,* we come across further tergiversations and changes of direction. The effects of the French Revolution and of the Napoleonic wars are presented by Clausewitz in such a way as to convey the impression that war was approximating increasingly to its absolute form. 'War, untrammeled by any conventional restraints,' he maintained, 'had broken loose in all its elemental fury' (p. 593). But even this 'elemental fury', we later learn, is capable of political control and, indeed, of moderation. In reverting to his theme that war is the servant of politics, Clausewitz assures us that 'the terrible two-handed sword that should be used with total strength to strike once and no more, becomes the lightest rapier — sometimes even a harmless foil fit only for thrusts and feints and parries' (p. 606).

In the light of the testimony of Book 1 of *On War,* with its fullest expression of war's instrumental function, and bearing in mind Clausewitz's indications as to the direction in which his revisions were taking him, we can accept Paret's conclusion that Clausewitz does offer us a description of war as an authentic form of limited violence, every bit as valid as the absolute concept which constitutes his point of departure:

> Limited wars might be a modification of the absolute, but need not be, if the purpose for which they were waged was also limited. Violence continued to be the essence, the regulative idea, even of limited wars fought for limited ends; but in such cases the essence did not require its fullest possible expression. The concept of absolute war had by no means become invalid, it continued to perform decisive analytic functions; but it was now joined by the concept of limited war (Clausewitz, 1976, pp. 21–2).

POLITICAL THEORISTS AND CONVENTION B

In the history of political thought, virtually all of the great issues pertaining to the limitation of war have been given consideration at one time or another — whether such limitation is desirable, whether it is practicable, what forms such limitation might take and what kind of reasoning should form its basis. The student who reads the works of political theory stretching back over the past two and a half millennia will be confronted by discussions of a multitude of issues that directly relate to the theme of limitation in war. The topics most frequently attended to by these theorists include the following: what it is permissible to do to the enemy during a war; to what extent the pursuit of a just end in war delimits the means for its attainment; on what ground belligerents might meaningfully distinguish between various human targets in war; whether faith should be kept even with an enemy; what rights victory confers on the conqueror in relation to the conquered? In fact, at various periods, theorists have devoted attention to all those possible forms of limitation that we have previously encompassed under the headings of convention A and convention B. As always, the core problem has been to reconcile the substantive limitations of convention B with the procedural forms of convention A in such a way that war might be meaningfully limited, while still preserving its functions as a means of protecting or extending tangible interests. Montesquieu (1949, p. 5) came as close as anyone to sensing the nexus between these two elements, but brought us little closer to understanding how they might be reconciled, when he urged as a general piece of advice that 'the law of nations is naturally founded on this principle that different nations ought . . . to do one another . . . in time of war as little injury as possible, without prejudicing their real interests'. How injuries can be minimized while real interests are safeguarded is the fundamental dilemma of limitation in warfare.

Accordingly, in the following review of some of the main issues of war-limitation, as they have been discussed by political theorists, we will again organize the presentation around the twin formulae of convention B and convention A. Most of the issues that are prominent in the intellectual history of war-limitation can be conveniently treated under one or another of these headings.

There is, however, one possible exception to this rule and its importance warrants special treatment at this stage. It is an instance of a form of substantive limitation that would appear to merit inclusion under the heading of convention B but which, on further study, has a good claim to be considered as an instance of convention A. The precise issue referred to is that of a 'who?' convention, that is an attempt to distinguish between categories of human targets. Moreover, just as we previously encountered Walzer's argument that war's moral character was uniquely dependent upon the application of 'who?' rules, so in this case the similar proposition is advanced that war is recognizably war only in circumstances where a specific 'who?' convention is implemented and observed. The view in question is that of Rousseau and it does seem to constitute a grey area in which conventions A and B are more than ever difficult to disentangle from each other.

What does Rousseau say that causes such a problem? Rousseau seeks to make a distinction between the *persona* of the soldier and the *persona* of the citizen and his rule of war that flows from this is that the soldier alone is a legitimate target of war. That this is so, Rousseau argues, derives from the very nature of war itself which is not a relationship existing between people but only between states. The full significance of Rousseau's point can be grasped only by following the development of his philosophical position. To start with Rousseau (1973, p. 170) demonstrates that war, in origin, cannot be a relationship between individual persons:

> Men, from the mere fact that, while they are living in their primitive independence, they have no mutual relations stable enough to constitute either the state of peace or the state or war, cannot be naturally enemies. War is constituted by a relation between things, and not between persons; and, as the state of war cannot arise out of simple personal relations, but only out of real relations, private war, or war of man with man, can exist neither in the state of nature, where there is no constant property, nor in the social state, where everything is under the authority of the laws.

Rousseau does not, however, leave the argument in the realm of philosophical abstraction. From this base, Rousseau draws concrete conclusions about the rights of war and what may, and may not, be done in the name of war:

> Even in real war, a just prince, while laying hands, in the enemy's country, on all that belongs to the public, respects the lives and goods of individuals ... The object of the war being the destruction of the hostile State, the other side has the right to kill its defenders, while they are bearing arms; but as soon as they lay them down and surrender, they cease to be enemies or instruments of the enemy, and become once more merely men, whose life no one has any right to take. Sometimes it is possible to kill the State without killing a single one of its members; and war gives no right which is not necessary to the gaining of its object (p. 171).

A superficial reading might suggest that Rousseau is doing no more than restating a theory of noncombatant immunity. But the argument runs much deeper than this. In Rousseau's analysis, discrimination between the soldier and the citizen is not simply a subsidiary rule of warfare (convention B) but a stipulation of the very nature of warfare itself. Rousseau, in telling us that civilians are not to be directly attacked, does not purport merely to set substantive limits to the conduct of war but is telling us what war is, in essence. From that perspective, as providing a definition of the process of war, Rousseau's principle of discrimination comes close to constituting an example of convention A, or, at the very least, is an instance which collapses useful distinction between the two types of convention.

The main difficulty for Rousseau's position was that the tide of political theory, and of actual political practice, was flowing in a direction contrary to the discrimination which he wished to institute. Whereas Rousseau sought to predicate the institution of war on a material distinction between man, the soldier, and man, the citizen, the major thrust of political theory, at least since Machiavelli, had been counter to any distinction on this basis. It is precisely in these terms that one historian of social thought sees Machiavelli's importance, as serving to forge unity between the notions of soldier and citizen:

> This is, I think, Machiavelli's greatest single contribution ... to modern thought: the firm uniting of the military to the political and the vivid sense that within the political order the military machine must be rooted, not in an obsolete guild of Knights, not in mere mercenaries who will fight to the limit of their wages and no more, but rather in a conscript army that will reflect the full manhood of the political order (Nisbet 1976, p. 70).

In the history of thought devoted to war and its limitations, the strand which dominates all others is the recurrent speculation on the possibility of meaningful discrimination between the human targets of war and on the proper philosophical bases of that discrimination. In summary, it can be argued that theorists have developed various categories of differentiation within the ranks of the enemy and have argued for various legitimate acts of war in accordance with the given category: for our purposes, it will be contended that, in terms of a history of ideas about the targets of war, four related pairs of categories have dominated the dialogue. Accordingly, we may describe the following philosophical solutions to the problem of distinguishing the proper targets of warfare: political discrimination (leaders and followers); institutional discrimination (state and society); moral discrimination (guilt and innocence); and finally, military discrimination (combatants and noncombatants). In some theories these categories overlap and become virtually inseparable. This is especially so in the case of the last mentioned because this is frequently used as a transcription, in objective terms, of the former three. In other theories, the categories are quite distinct and it is certainly true that each of the pairs has received special emphasis in one or more bodies of political writing. The essentials of each argument will be reviewed in turn and illustrated by reference to its main historical exponents.

Political discrimination — leaders and followers

According to this first position, it is proper to distinguish between those who are politically responsible for directing their state's enmity towards us, and the rest of the population who have no option but to follow this political lead. In consequence, military action ought properly be directed against those who have incited the war or, at least, who have made the political decisions from which the war results. Acts of reprisal, which would be appropriate against these political leaders, would be inappropriate if directed against the population at large or even at the state's armed defenders. In other words, according to this perspective, it is not at all self-evident that the state's military forces share, with the political leadership, responsibility for the war.

As will be seen shortly, this tradition can be traced at least to Plato but as there are some complications with Plato's treatment of the topic, his contribution is best reserved to the end of the section. Otherwise, this distinction appears in the works of many thinkers who have turned their minds to the scrutiny of moderation in war. More (1964, p. 122) for instance, has his Utopians observe a range of restrictions on their conduct of war and seems to do so on the general principle that 'the common folk do not go to war of their own accord but are driven to it by the madness of kings' and Rabelais was to observe similarly that retribution in war should not be directed against the whole people but only against 'the incendiaries or fomentors of the war' (quoted in Stawell 1929, p. 79).

John Locke gave detailed consideration to the rights of war and was to enunciate an impressive array of restrictions to be observed in and after war, even on the part of a just victor. Suffice it for the moment to notice that Locke's restrictions are associated with a principle of discrimination in enemy character. In the case of a victor who is successful in a just war, Locke (1963, p. 406) insists that the following limitation be observed:

> ... the Conquerour gets no Power but only over those, who have actually assisted, concurr'd, or consented to that unjust force, that is used against him. For the people having given to their Governours no Power to do an unjust thing, such as is to make an unjust War, (for they never had such a Power in themselves:) They ought not to be charged, as guilty of the Violence and Unjustice that is committed in an Unjust War, any farther, than they actually abet it.

There are, of course, difficulties with this formulation and with its implementation. The notions of 'assisting' and 'abetting' might be understood in the purely military sense, in which case Locke's principle would simply be a reiteration of noncombatant immunity. The notions of 'concurring' and 'consenting' are no less intractable, and if Locke's consent is understood in its tacit sense, which features prominently elsewhere in his philosophy, then it becomes difficult to see where the political line of division is to be drawn and where, in terms of political responsibility, the buck is to stop.

An even fuller statement of this political distinction is to be found in the writings of the eighteenth century jurist and publicist, Vattel. The distinction forms the basis of a principle of noncombatant immunity but, at base, is a principle related to the individual's function in society. Vattel's argument has been analysed in the following words:

> ... not all enemies are guilty, because not all function in such a way as to cause direct harm to oneself or one's friends. Here the criterion of function in society as regards war is linked to the concept that the sovereign alone is guilty in unjust war to produce Vattel's position on the definition and immunity of noncombatants. With the guilt associated with the sovereign, those who most clearly adhere to his unjust designs on others are to bear with him ... the punishment of war. Others in the enemy society, who to be sure are obeying their sovereign but who nevertheless are engaged in just pursuits having to do with the internal good of their society, are to be regarded as entirely innocent and treated accordingly (Johnson 1975, p. 247).

It should already be clear that in many cases the political categories of leaders and followers overlap with the moral categories of guilt and innocence. As in the case of Vattel, many theorists have equated moral culpability with political office and have thus collapsed the two categories into one. To some extent, this tendency was already apparent in Plato, who was certainly one of the earliest to develop this line of argument. In the case of Plato, one senses that he is really distinguishing between persons in political authority and all others, but instead he chooses to express himself in terms of the guilty and the innocent. At any rate, Plato suggests that the enemy is not amorphous in character and that not all should share in the same military retribution, at least in a war within the family of the Greeks. He is more indulgent in his prescriptions for a war against the barbarian:

> As Greeks they will not devastate the soil of Greece or burn the homesteads; nor will they allow that all the inhabitants of any state, men, women and children, are their enemies, but only the few who are responsible for the quarrel. The greater number are friends, whose land and houses, on all these accounts, they will not consent to lay waste and destroy. They will pursue the quarrel only until the guilty are compelled by the innocent sufferers to give satisfaction (Plato 1941, p. 170).

Several comments are in order on Plato's treatment of the problem. Firstly, it seems valid to include Plato as an expositor of political differentation as a basis for the conduct of war, in the light of his definition of an enemy as one who is 'responsible for the quarrel', even though he later muddies the water by usage of the broader terms of 'guilty' and 'innocent'. Secondly, however, it is clear that in Plato's presentation, although he does make this distinction, this does not ensure immunity for the politically innocent. He thinks they are deserving of less harsh treatment but provides no operative principles to guarantee that this can be accomplished. As Bainton (1960, p. 38) has noted: 'Plato was here verging on the distinction between the combatant and the noncombatant, but used rather the terminology of the guilty and the innocent and did not suggest that they could be segregated during the course of the conflict'. This is evidenced by Plato's reference to 'innocent sufferers'. Thirdly, and following from this, Plato's formulation, although generously intended as a restriction on over-zealous and indiscriminate military activity, is, as it stands, open to perversion and serious abuse.

His final injunction that the quarrel be pursued only until the guilty are compelled by the innocent sufferers to give satisfaction, could readily be made the basis of terror campaigns and of punitive expeditions. In this corrupt form, Plato has indirectly contributed to the notion of the political hostage, and his principle of moderation in war has been corrupted into campaigns of area bombing and into postures of nuclear deterrence, in order that the 'innocent sufferers' might secure the good behaviour of their political masters. It is this form of Platonic limitation which provided the rationale for a Dresden or a Hiroshima.

Institutional discrimination — state and society

This second tradition of thought we have already encountered in Rousseau's masterly exposition of it. It seeks to draw a clear line of demarcation between the institutional apparatus of the state and the persons who are its members, and maintains that it is the other state which is the legitimate enemy and only incidentally the human beings who are in association with it. This in turn becomes for Rousseau (1973, p. 171) the basis of proper moderation in the conduct of war:

> War then is a relation, not between man and man, but between State and State, and individuals are enemies only accidentally, not as men, nor even as citizens, but as soldiers; not as members of their country, but as its defenders. Finally, each State can have for enemies only other States, and not men; for between things disparate in nature there can be no real relation.

That this forms the basis of limitation in warfare by distinguishing between targets and non-targets is attested to by one editor of Rousseau's works. Thus, according to Vaughan (ed.) (1962, pp. 291–2): 'the state which adopts methods of barbarism in warfare stands convicted, quite apart from its moral guilt, of confounding the distinction between the body politic, which alone is the legitimate object of hostility, and the individuals who compose it'.

Rousseau's views influenced other writers and we can see this distinction echoed in the pages of other theorists. For instance, although there are many pronounced differences

between Rousseau's and Kant's attitudes towards international relations, and on the problem of war and peace
specifically (Clark 1980), on this point the two writers
appear to be in substantial agreement. This, at least, would
seem to be a fair conclusion to draw from Kant's prohibition
upon the plundering of the people of the enemy state which,
in Kant's view, would be an act of robbery 'since it was not
the conquered people who waged the war, but the state of
which they were subjects which waged it *through them*'
(Reiss (ed.) 1971, pp. 168–9).

A similar line of argument had also been advanced by
Montesquieu. In his concern to mitigate the ills of conquest,
he argues as follows against some contemporary international
lawyers:

> What has led them into this mistake is, that they imagined a con-
> queror had a right to destroy the state; whence they inferred that
> he had a right to destroy the men that compose it: a wrong con-
> sequence from a false principle. For from the destruction of the
> state it does not at all follow that the people who compose it
> ought to be also destroyed. The state is the association of men,
> and not the men themselves; the citizen may perish, and the man
> remain (Montesquieu 1949, p. 135).

Moral discrimination – guilt and innocence

To some theorists, the crucial factor in determining what can
be done to which categories of people in war, is the moral
guilt or innocence of sections of the population: the wrath of
war is to be directed against the guilty alone. In this section,
we consider the tradition which regards the guilt–innocence
dichotomy in moral terms although it is conceded that, in
many instances, the distinction between moral guilt, and
political responsibility as outlined above, is a very fine one
indeed. In fact, with some authors, there is no basis on which
to judge whether it is culpability in a moral sense or simply
political direction that the writer has in mind. Thus Cicero
(1913) in recommending limits to the pursuit of war, gives no
clear indication as to who the guilty parties are: 'as to
destroying and plundering cities, let me say that great care
should be taken that nothing be done in reckless cruelty or
wantonness. And it is a great man's duty in troublous times

to single out the guilty for punishment, to spare the many . . .'

It is with St. Augustine that the rights of war become inextricably bound up with moral notions of guilt and innocence. Surprisingly, however, although Augustine is painfully aware of these distinct categories in any belligerent country, he does not make it the basis of an operative principle in the actual conduct of warfare. Augustine does not guarantee special immunity to those whom he considers to be innocent.

In order to understand fully the tradition of thought which makes moral discrimination a basis for limiting the punitive force of war, and to understand Augustine's importance within this tradition, it is necessary perhaps to make mention of the distinction between guilt in its objective, and guilt in its subjective senses. According to the former, it is the tangible external act which constitutes the guilt; to the latter, it is the internal state of wrong that entails retribution. The former is the more readily recognizable condition and has, in the hands of some theorists, become equivalent to a principle of noncombatant immunity in as much as it is the act of bearing arms which is tantamount to objective guilt and, *ipso facto,* noncombatancy provides a claim to objective innocence. But when we enter the muddy waters of subjective guilt, any discrimination is imperfect, and the scope of enemy targets can be interpreted either restrictively or permissively in the light of this principle.

As far as St. Augustine is concerned, the balance of scholarly opinion favours the view that he did not make guilt and innocence the basis of an operative code of war-limitation, and that he tended to conflate the objective and subjective dimensions of moral guilt, or to let the latter render the former superfluous. Russell (1975, p. 19) argues in this vein when he claims that, in Augustine's philosophy, 'the subjective *culpa* or guilt of the enemy merited punishment of the enemy population without regard to the distinction between soldiers and civilians. Motivated by a righteous wrath, the just warriors could kill with impunity even those who were morally innocent. Objective determination of personal guilt was not only unnecessary but irrelevant.' A just war was for Augustine a divine retribution but, in the words of another commentator: 'the punishment can only be rough justice; the innocent will suffer with the guilty' (Deane 1963, p. 156). The fullest expression of this interpretation, that Augustine made token recognition of moral categories in war, but failed to predicate a *ius in bello* upon them, is to be found in Hartigan (1966, p. 199):

> Because there exists for Augustine such an intimate connection between the juridical and moral orders a *delict* which occurs in the former necessarily involves a sin in the latter as well. Hence, if one nation violates the legal rights of another, it has also broken the moral law. This is the essential fact which explains why for Augustine just war is action designed above all else to restore a violated moral order.

From this, Hartigan concludes that 'just war has become a crusade of retribution in which the enemy population's guilt may be presumed. The death of the "innocents" is an accidental consequence of the just act of war' (p. 204). To the extent that this is an accurate reflection of Augustine's thought, he may be taken to illustrate, by default rather than by observance, the distinction between guilt and innocence in war.

Military discrimination — combatants and noncombatants

The right to immunity for noncombatants in war may be derived from other, more fundamental, principles. Alternatively, it may be seen as a basic norm from which other principles are to be deduced. The combatant and noncombatant distinction has been treated in both these ways in the history of political thought. Noncombatant immunity may, accordingly, be predicated on a variety of other claims or may, in turn, give rise to a variety of claims. Theorists have arrived at a bewildering array of permutations as between these categories. Thus it would appear that Grotius deduces an innocent class both from political inertness and from noncombatancy itself. 'These classes of people are innocent in both respects regarding war' argues one discussion of Grotius, in that 'they have little or no say in the decision that takes the nation to war ... and they do not aid directly in its prosecution' (Johnson 1975, p. 227). In the case of Vitoria, the granting or withholding of immunity is based exclusively on a capacity for combatancy without reference to other associated principles. He accordingly asserts in his *De Indiis* the opinion that 'everyone able to bear arms should be considered dangerous and must be assumed to be defending the enemy king; they may therefore be killed unless the opposite is clearly true i.e. unless it is obvious that they are harmless' (quoted in Hamilton 1963, p. 152).

Finally, and as a most powerful demonstration of a theory which posits limits to war on the basis of discrimination between combatant and noncombatant, we can cite the work of Paul Ramsey. For Ramsey (1961, p. 135), respect for civilian immunity is an irreducible norm of warfare:

> ... what is said concerning civilian rights is not an attempt to bring upon an alien affair which in itself has no intrinsic limits a sentimental or extrinsic criterion. What is said concerning them constitutes the very law of conflict between peoples, the intrinsic, natural law for the conduct of war, so long as this human action remains, by the skin of its teeth, a rational activity at all. Statements about the immunity of civilians are at one and the same time statements about the only kind of warfare that can have any minimal rational or human meaning at all.

What is striking about Ramsey's position is that the only other principle upon which noncombatant immunity is dependent is the 'rationality' of warfare itself. Put in these terms, it is manifest that Ramsey, like Rousseau, sees a restriction in targets to be, not an extrinsic code imposed upon war, but a fundamental characteristic of the very process of warfare. From that perspective, Ramsey's noncombatancy, like Rousseau's state—society division, is a limit upon war that shares the features of convention A: its limits are more than incidental rules within a procedure, but part of the very definition of the procedure of war.

To round out this rapid review of principles of discrimination in the history of ideas about warfare, brief mention should be made of those theorists who have explicitly denied the applicability of any such principles to the conduct of war and to those who, while recognizing some basis of discrimination, have argued in such a way that the principle, in practice, is seriously eroded.

As to the former, Thomas Hobbes is the most redoubtable of champions. In the most concise form, he dispels any notion that the sovereign, defending his realm by military means, should be encumbered by codes of conduct in war or should distinguish between various grades of enemy character. Innocence can have no meaning in a context where an enemy is an enemy:

> But the infliction of what evil soever, on an innocent man, that is not a subject, if it be for the benefit of the commonwealth, and without violation of any former covenant, is no breach of the law of nature. For all men that are not subjects, are either enemies, or else they have ceased from being so by some precedent covenants. But against enemies, whom the commonwealth judgeth capable to do them hurt, it is lawful by the original right of nature to make war; wherein the sword judgeth not, nor doth the victor make distinction of nocent, and innocent, as to the time past nor has other respect of mercy, than as it conduceth to the good of his own people (Hobbes, pp. 207–8).

The history of political thought provides few more forthright disavowels of the relevance of discrimination to the conduct of war.

Other theorists have balked at such a stern condemnation of limits in war but, while more charitable in their general disposition, have so eroded the principle in practice as to take them no short distance along the road travelled by Hobbes. Adam Smith is a useful, if unexpected, case in point. Smith draws attention to the fact that not all sectors of the enemy population are equally guilty and that to inflict the same ravages of war upon them all indiscriminately is against normal notions of justice:

> ... suppose a subject of any government is injured, they who have injured him become natural objects of resentment, and also the government which protects him if it refuse satisfaction, but the greater part of the nation is perfectly innocent ... Upon what principle or foundation of justice therefore do we take their goods from them and distress them in all possible ways? (Schneider (ed.) 1948, p. 331).

Smith answers his question by an appeal to practical necessity which, in the situation, creates its own form of justice: 'it must be upon necessity, which, indeed, in this case, is a part of justice'. Since there is no other way of seeking retribution, action must perforce be taken against innocent parties, a situation which Smith appears to accept with considerable equanimity:

> ... it is often very difficult to get satisfaction from a subject or from a sovereign that may have offended. They are generally in the heart of the country, and perfectly well secured. If we could get at them, no doubt, they would be the first objects of our resentment, but as this is impossible, we must make reprisals some other way (Schneider (ed.) 1948, p. 332).

Some members of the early Spanish school of international law, such as Vitoria and Suarez, had already diluted the effects which recognition of discrimination was to have in the actual practice of warfare. They both write in terms of guilty and innocent sectors of the populace and make a case for differential treatment of the innocent in warfare. The argument, however, in both cases, is heavily qualified and provides no watertight guarantee of the immunities of innocent civilians. Thus one writer states bluntly of the Spanish school that they are agreed 'once war has been declared any injuries may be inflicted on the enemy which seem necessary to obtain satisfaction or achieve victory ...' (Hamilton 1963, p. 150). Johnson (1975, p. 200) renders an equally harsh judgment on Vitoria and Suarez specifically: 'the arguments of Suarez and Vitoria tend to erode the rights of the innocent whenever necessity – whether military necessity or that of vindicative justice – requires treating them as one with the guilty'.

It is perfectly clear how such judgments are arrived at, as is evidenced by a brief outline of Suarez' and Vitoria's arguments. Suarez (1944, p. 843) permits infliction of damages upon innocent parties: 'if such a course of action is essential to complete satisfaction', he asserts, 'it is permissible to deprive the innocent of their goods, even of their liberty'. The reason he advances for this permissiveness is, in itself, most revealing for he claims that 'the innocent form a portion of one whole and unjust state; and on account of the crime of the whole, this part may be punished even though it does not of itself share in the fault'. Such reasoning, as can be seen, strikes at the very heart of any principle of discrimination in warfare. Moreover, even when Suarez prohibits the actual killing of the innocent, he qualifies this prohibition by appeal to the doctrine of double effect when he concedes that 'incidentally they may be slain, when such an act is necessary in order to secure victory' (p. 845).

Vitoria likewise makes appeal to double effect but goes some way towards restricting what can be done in its name. He allows that 'sometimes it is right, in virtue of collateral circumstances, to slay the innocent even knowingly, as when a fortress or a city is stormed in a just war, although it is known that there are a number of innocent people in it . . .' This resort to indirect collateral damage is, however, subject to Vitoria's general constraint that such an operation be conducted only if it can be expected to have a major effect on the outcome of the war and provided only greater evils do not arise out of the war than would otherwise be the case. If not, it is Vitoria's considered opinion that 'it would not be right, for the purpose of assailing a few guilty, to slay the many innocent' (quoted in Fernández-Santamaria 1977, pp. 136–7). The problem with such a formulation is that the precise contribution of any one operation to the ultimate outcome cannot be known in advance with any certainty, nor can the balance of evils created as against evils averted be calculated with any precision. Vitoria's restrictions are inadequate because they are tantamount to allowing that the proof of the moral pudding is to be discovered in the military eating.

POLITICAL THEORISTS AND CONVENTION A

There have been various times when political theorists, both ancient and modern, have discussed limits to war in such a way that they can be seen to be concerned with issues raised under convention A. The most obvious examples of this will be presented in the following section.

There is one issue that must be dispensed with at the outset. It should by now be clear that all of the traditional restraints of the *ius in bello* can be embraced within convention B as it has been herein described, even though convention B is a wider category and would include substantive restrictions not found in classical *ius in bello* theory or, at any rate, might include motivations for adoption of such limits which did not appear in the *ius in bello* tradition.

At first sight, it is more difficult to provide a satisfactory account of the relationship between *ius ad bellum* and convention A. On closer inspection, however, we discover that, while the two are not co-extensive, they do perform a similar function, with convention A being the broader of the two categories. In its origins, the *ius ad bellum* was simply an attempt to equate a just form of war with a specific set of causes or ends of war – retribution or restitution for a wrong received, or some such, was the general formula. Later, and in the hands of Aquinas, the definition of a just war was expanded to include, not simply a just cause but, in addition, the waging of the war by proper authority and with a right intention. Each of these conditions of a just war in its own way contributed to a definition of the process of just war: each described the essential nature of war, if it was to be a just and not a corrupt one. Convention A, regarded from this perspective, is simply a fuller statement of the nature of the process of war, stripped of the specific moral, religious or philosophical overtones which the *ius ad bellum* had brought to it. In other words, whereas *ius ad bellum* sought to distinguish between just war and unjust war, convention A would have us distinguish between various forms of war or, at the extremes, between what is war and what is non-war.

Such a framework of understanding advances this study because, just as there is an ambivalent relationship between *ius ad bellum* and *ius in bello,* so likewise is there between convention A and convention B.

In order to clarify this point, it is first necessary to describe the elements of ambivalence in the two components of traditional just war doctrine. To some analysts, there is an inevitable tension between *ius ad bellum* and *ius in bello,* to such an extent that whenever the former has been emphasized, it has always been at the expense of the latter: conversely, serious discussion of *ius in bello* became possible, historically, only with the gradual disenchantment with efforts to stipulate the just causes of war. One of the most learned jurists in the field of the laws of war highlights this basic antagonism between the two when he suggests that 'the importance attributed to the idea of the just war throughout the Middle Ages and well into the seventeenth century undoubtedly delayed the appearance of any body of rules restraining the more barbarous practices of warfare' (Draper 1958, p. 222). Invariably, the notion that the cause was just fostered a permissive attitude towards war's conduct. Even those international lawyers who were a universe away from sympathy with doctrines of 'holy war' could nonetheless give expression to principles which were no less inimical to restraint in war, such as in Suarez' rendition of the medieval canonists' precept that 'if the end is permissible, the necessary means to that end are also permissible' (1944, p. 840). This, in concise form, expresses the basic tension between the *ius ad bellum* and the *ius in bello.*

By way of contrast, not all theorists see the relationship in these antagonistic terms. Some writers emphasize the areas of compatability between the two and regard the *ius in bello* as the inevitable offspring of the *ius ad bellum* of which, they argue, it had always been an essential component, even if only tacitly so. From this alternative perspective, the *ius ad bellum,* far from stifling thought on the conduct of war, had always contained, within its definition of just cause, gross limitations upon the means to be adopted in its attainment. The words of one commentary upon the Roman *ius fetiale* would be appropriate in the present context: 'the reason for which the war was begun in the first place was regarded as indicating the object for which it was pursued, and therefore as setting limits to its prosecution' (Russell 1936, p. 78). Certainly, it is possible to discern such a relationship in much of the medieval just war theorizing, even if conclusions about the means of war were seldom explicitly drawn. Miller (1964, p. 258) is, therefore, correct to insist upon *ius ad bellum's* spillover into the realm of the *ius in bello:*

> The rules — the *jus in bello,* or the laws of war — had not been considered as independent of the principles of the *bellum justum* so long as that doctrine was regarded as potentially viable. Throughout the Middle Ages ... the assumption ... was that the war legitimately declared must be waged in accordance with legitimate means. Not only was it required that the amount of force used be proportional to the extent of the injury suffered — Augustine's chief stipulation for limiting war — but the *bellum*

justum doctrine also carried with it requirements as to the rights
of combatants and the proper treatment of prisoners.

Indeed, many writers have pointed to the symbiotic relationship between the two elements of the just war doctrine.
Far from the elements of just cause eclipsing concern for just
means, the just cause itself was not to be regarded as a static
condition, but as something which could subsequently be
changed in the course of the war if the means employed were
such as to corrupt the war as a whole. As has been claimed:
'it may not be argued that ... once the war has started, its
substantial justice has been settled beyond invalidation in
terms of criminality *in bello*' (Midgley 1975, p. 68; *see also*
Melzer 1975, p. 93).

If we accept this analysis, that *ius in bello* can be supported rather than negated by *ius ad bellum,* then there is reason
for accepting also that the relationship between convention B
and convention A might be a similarly positive one. Just as
the proper means of war are deemed to be implicit in its
proper ends, so it could be said that the substantive limitations of war find their origins in those conventions which
stipulate the ground rules of war as a meaningful political
process.

It follows from the similarities between *ius ad bellum* and
convention A that we can interpret the many statements
about the ends and objectives of war, in as much as they
define what war is all about, as instances of philosophical discussion of the convention A of this study. From this perspective, we can see that many political theorists have been
concerned to limit war by stipulating what, precisely, is the
point of such a social activity.

This tradition of argument reaches far back into antiquity
and has been passed down from generation to generation
with little apparent modification of its cardinal principles. Its
recurrent theme is that peace is the object of war and, as far
as the conduct of war is concerned, it follows that war should
not be waged in such a manner as to militate against future
peace. To many political philosophers, limitations on war
could be derived from convention A, from the essential
characteristics and purposes of the activity itself.

We find this view expressed in Plato's injunction that 'he

will never be a true statesman, nor will any man be a finished legislator, unless he legislates for war as a means to peace, rather than for peace as a means to war' (1934, p. 5). This is echoed in Cicero's precept that war 'should be undertaken in such a way as to make it evident that it has no other object than to secure peace' (1913, p. 80). That cry reverberates down the history of intellectual speculation on the subject. It is taken up by Augustine (1972, p. 866) and repeated verbatim by Aquinas, in whom it is further developed as an aspect of the 'right intention' which is a necessary condition of a just war (D'Entreves (ed.) 1948, p. 159). As Johnson (1975, p. 41) correctly insists: 'the concept of right intention can properly be conceived as an important source for the *ius in bello* in Christian theological thought'. Spinoza likewise falls in the mainstream of this tradition when he asserts that 'the sole object of warfare should be to secure peace, so that the sword may be sheathed when the war is over' (Wernham (ed.) 1958, p. 331).

In similar fashion, we can see that another of the classical components of the *ius ad bellum,* the requirement of proper authority, could also serve a limiting function through convention A, as part of our contemporary understanding of what war is, or is meant to be. The war without proper authority which, to the just war analyst was therefore an unjust war, becomes, to the secular political scientist or positivist international lawyer a species of private war or, more commonly, not a war at all but some form of civil disruption, rebellion, sedition or what have you. The semantics of what war is deemed to be, and the conventions of type A which flow from such definitions, are still very much live issues. We need only recall the legal debates of the 1970s as to the applicability of the laws of war to 'guerrilla' or 'national liberation' operations to be impressed by the crucial importance of this issue. It is the provenance of convention A to limit the activities of war by causing us to recognize what war's form is and what its point must be: those conflicts, the processes for the resolution of which are not regarded as war, cannot by definition share in war's limitations.

It remains only to summarize those insights which political philosophers have provided into such other characteristics of convention A as war's processes of initiation, self-regulation and termination, and how, in turn, war is limited by its own necessary features.

That war is a procedure requiring formal initiation is a proposition that has not much interested political theorists, except in an overly-narrow legalistic sense. The notion of formal initiation, what it tells us about war and how it contributes to limitation through regulation, are sadly neglected areas in political thought. Indeed, we probably have to go back to antiquity to find the topic seriously considered at all. It is not in the least surprising that it is a Roman lawyer, Cicero, who suggests, in accordance with the fetial code, that 'no war is just, unless it is entered upon after an official demand for satisfaction has been submitted or warning has been given and a formal declaration made' (1913, p. 36).

Self-regulation in war, or the honouring of agreements entered into in war, is a topic which has received much more extensive scrutiny. As discussed in a previous chapter, the notion of *pacta sunt servanda* is an essential feature of war's limitation and lies at the heart of convention A: without the observance of that principle, war's character would change. We have previously noted the attention devoted by the early international lawyers to the issue of 'keeping faith with the enemy' and to the distinction often drawn between breach of faith, which was not permissible, and stratagems, which were in no way prohibited.

Once again, Hobbes (p. 83) stands out as a lonely, if not solitary, figure on this intellectual landscape: 'to this war of every man, against every man, this also is consequent; that nothing can be unjust . . . Where there is no common power, there is no law: where no law, no injustice. Force and fraud, are in war the two cardinal virtues.'

We would have expected Machiavelli to join company with Hobbes on this question, but Machiavelli virtually recognizes the distinction between fraud and stratagem of which the international lawyers were to make so much, and while he raises no moral objection to the former, he does have some reservations about recourse to it:

> Although in all other affairs it be hateful to use fraud, in the operations of war it is praiseworthy and glorious . . . This, how-

ever, I desire to say, that I would not have it understood that any fraud is glorious which leads you to break your plighted word, or to depart from convenants to which you have agreed; for though to do so may sometimes gain you territory and power, it can never . . . gain you glory (Machiavelli 1883, p. 471).

Machiavelli, therefore, comes close to the predominant strand of political thought which urges that faith, once pledged to the enemy, should be kept. That precept is as commonplace with Cicero as it is with Kant. Not only was this principle accepted as a precondition of limits within war; it was also recognized to be a precondition of the limits embodied in the final termination of war which, as Adam Ferguson correctly pointed out, are no less dependent on keeping faith with the enemy:

> . . . the faith plighted, though even to an enemy . . . is held . . . to be sacred in the highest degree. The obligation . . . certainly rests on a principle of humanity, absolutely necessary to the welfare of mankind, as without it, the calamities of war, once begun, could scarcely ever be brought to an end. Peace itself rests upon the faith of a treaty concluded, while nations were yet at war (Wolfers and Martin (eds) 1956a, pp. 103–4).

This leads us to the final aspect of the process of war, namely the conventions which govern its termination, and the thoughts which political theorists have expressed on the nature of victory and the rights which it confers upon the victor. Almost without exception, those philosophers who have reflected on this issue, have been aware of the important ways in which conventions of termination can serve to limit the spoliation of war.

In an attempt to render manageable the array of theoretical meditation upon victory and its after-effects, it will be argued that political theorists have subscribed to at least three general approaches to the question as to why the termination of war should contribute to limited reprisals in its aftermath.

The first, and probably the most common, is an argument for moderation derived from the purposes of the war itself: since war is a procedure with a point, it follows that when objectives have been realized, the rationale for further violence collapses even if the emotional impulse to indulge in bloodshed long endures. Montesquieu (1949, p. 135) is in this mould when he insists that 'when the conquest is completed, the conqueror has no longer a right to kill, because he has no longer the plea of natural defence and self-preservation'. Rousseau, as is his wont, expresses the same point much more incisively: 'one kills in order to vanquish', he commented, perhaps wistfully, 'but there is no man so bestial that he seeks victory in order to kill' (Forsyth *et al.* (eds) 1970, p. 178).

The second approach is to base the proper moderation of victory upon the residual natural rights of the vanquished. In Locke's theory, for instance, the rights of the victor are curtailed by the persisting rights of the vanquished, or more specifically, by the persisting rights of the vanquished's wife and children. The victor does not, therefore, take title to the vanquished's possessions, as the children have a right to sustenance from that property. Similarly the fields must not be permanently despoiled because this would be akin to visiting the sins of the fathers upon succeeding generations (Locke 1963, pp. 404–9).

Thirdly, and arguably as a specific manifestation of the preceding approach, there are those who would press for the immunity of all members of the defeated state as an extension of the principle of noncombatant immunity. In this situation, we see yet another application of a 'who?' convention in the centre of a process that, we have maintained, is governed by conventions of type A. Once again, therefore, we must concede the arbitrariness and frailty of this continuing distinction. Nonetheless, it does seem valid to point to the identities between the conventions of surrender and the conventions surrounding the immunity of noncombatants. As Johnson (1975, p. 252) has shrewdly observed: 'the limitation on cruel treatment of noncombatants and destruction of their livelihoods during a war implies limitation on any cruelty whose effects persist after the war when all are noncombatants'. It requires little imagination to see how this argument could be extended to support a principle of moderate treatment in victory's aftermath when, in the most fundamental of senses, war's business is already done.

Is it possible, in the light of this brief survey, to make any worthwhile generalizations about the content and main pre-

occupations of traditional political theory and its consideration of limits to war? Is there a traditional theory as such
that can be discerned from the varied and disparate writings
of the past two millennia? At one level, the answer to these
questions must be in the negative: political theorists have
focused upon a bewildering variety of just or necessary causes
of war and a similar array of just or necessary means by
which it should be pursued. Nonetheless, amidst this kaleido-
scopic discussion, two general patterns tend to recur, if not
ubiquitously, then at least amongst a representative sample of
those theorists who have turned their minds to the contemplation of war's means and ends. The first, as suggested in the
review of convention B, is the requirement that the conduct
of war be a discriminating activity in terms of the human
targets towards which it is directed. The second, as suggested
in the review of convention A, is the requirement that war be
pursued with a particular end in view, and that the means
adopted be such as to secure, and not contradict, this end.
The great majority of writings about limits to war has traditionally revolved around one or other of these two principles.
However vague the content of these principles might be, their
elaboration by theorists was predicated on the crucial assumption that war was a bounded form of violence: when these
bounds were crossed, the element of violence negated the
very essence of war.

4

Models of War-Limitation:
Champions, Charity and
City-Swapping

THE CHAMPION

Combat by champions

The settlement of a conflict by means of a combat between champions representing the opposing sides is an extension of some of the principles we have already encountered. For instance, it formalizes observance of the rule of equal advantage, the combat being between equal numbers with identical equipment or, at least, with weaponry of the contestants' own choosing. It epitomizes also the invitation to battle, whereby the time and place of the combat are specified. It delineates who, from amongst the enemy, is a legitimate target and, to be effective, it requires an agreed procedure for determining who is the victor. It should already be apparent that combat by champions is an extremely complex social institution. But is it warfare? Is combat by champions a highly sophisticated and elaborate set of conventions for setting limits to war? Or does it turn war into something else?

To some analysts, combat by champions is a microcosm of warfare, but warfare nonetheless: it is nothing but a manifestation of war in miniature. This is the line taken by Ayala (1912, p. 29) when he describes the combat between the two sets of triplets, the Horatii and the Curiatii, representing Tullus Hostilius, King of the Romans and Mettius Suffetius, King of the Albans, as simply 'an abridged form of the war' that they were already fighting and which was proving too costly. It is a view to which Schelling also appears to subscribe when he is discussing restraints in war and the collaboration between enemies which is necessary for such restraints to be observed. He provides as an example of this 'the duel, *as a method of war*' (Schelling 1966, p. 144). Clearly Schelling recognizes the championship duel as a legitimate and genuine mode of warfare.

Other analysts would demur from such an interpretation and have variously described combat by champions as a form of game, sport or recreation, but certainly not as a form of warfare. The instances of championship contests in medieval Europe have, accordingly, been dismissed as examples of chivalric display with no serious purpose to them, other than as a means of demonstrating the courage, prowess and honour of the knight. The problem here is that precisely the same comment has been made about the battles of that period, which were ironically little more than champion duels on a larger scale. This is how some of these battles have been described:

> Many of the battles of this period were no more than shock skir-mishes between small bodies of armoured knights, in which individual combats were sought, to prove rather the worth of the fighter than his destructive capabilities. The object was to un-horse one's opponent rather than to slay him. In short, battles were frequently little more than sharp-weapon tourneys (Fuller 1946, p. 63).

Presumably, on this reasoning, such battles would also have to be dismissed as instances of some other form of activity and not of warfare itself.

A concise statement of the view that combat by individual champions is not genuine warfare, can be found in one description of the champion practice in the ancient Greek epics. According to this account, the champion combat is a form of theatre:

> . . . a certain artistic ideal was applied in the institution of single combats between chiefs and distinguished warriors, who thus played the part, as it was, of the protagonists of a tragedy, whilst their respective nations filled that of the spectators and judges of fair play. Thus was fought the duel between Paris and Menelaus (Phillipson 1911, p. 209).

More strikingly than any other form of war-limitation, then, the champion confronts us with the question, how far can war be limited while remaining war?

This is not the place to provide a comprehensive history of the contest between champions as a form of combat and as a means of settling disputes. Our purpose is merely to establish the historical manifestations of this combat form as a background to a critical assessment of it in terms of the ongoing discussion of war-limitation.

The precise historical origins of the champion combat are not known to the present author. However, it can be stated with confidence that, as a military practice, it is at the very least four thousand years old. Archaeologists inform us of documents and wall paintings depicting the duel that date from the twentieth century BC. The duel was a contest 'between two warrior-heroes, as representatives of two contending forces. Its outcome, under prearranged agreement between both sides, determined the issue between the two forces' (Yadin 1963, p. 72).

Nor is it possible to be certain about the reasons which led to the adoption of this practice, even if certain conditions which facilitated its adoption can be discerned. For instance, it does seem likely that combat by champions was common practice at periods when the style of battle itself tended to resemble a series of individual duels. We have already mentioned this relationship in connection with the knightly battles of medieval Europe. Clearly, in such circumstances, it becomes easier to conceptualize warfare as an expanded duel and to regard the single combat and the battle as identical in principle, even if differing in scale.

This would appear to be true of other historical epochs. Combat between champions amongst the ancient Greeks was certainly an accepted custom before the development of the phalanx and its peculiar style of warfare. Consequently, as Sealey (1976, p. 29) has commented of the form of battle in Greece prior to the seventh century BC: 'these warriors were not organized in a phalanx; each fought largely on his own, and a Homeric battle tended to become a series of duels'.

Another recurrent theme in the history of the champion combat is the notion that war is a dispute between princes and that it is only fitting that the dispute should be resolved between the princes themselves or between the princes' chosen representatives. Huizinga (1954, p. 96) has developed this point of view:

> The idea of having political differences decided by a single com-
> bat between the two princes concerned, was a logical conse-
> quence of the conception still prevailing, as if political disputes
> were nothing but a 'quarrel' in the juristic sense of the word. A
> Burgundian partisan, for instance, serves the 'quarrel' of his lord.
> What more natural means to settle such a case can be imagined
> than the duel of two princes, the two parties to the 'quarrel'?

Whatever its historical or theoretical origins, the practice
of resolving disputes by single combat has been a trans-
cultural phenomenon. Turney-High (1949, p. 72) regards it as
a war pattern of the Aryans, found across Eurasia from India
to the Vikings. We will quickly review the prevalence of the
practice as well as some of its celebrated highlights.

Combat by single champions is certainly referred to in the
Hindu epics although, as some commentators have insisted,
there is a need for caution in deducing historical facts from a
literary *genre* famous for its tales of courage and chivalry.
Nonetheless, it is unlikely that the championship duel was
wholly a literary invention. Chakravarti (p. 187) provides a
colourful example of the champion combat in conjunction
with the rule of equal advantage, even if the latter is honoured
in the breach on this occasion:

> The Chachnāma relates the story of a war between Rai Chach and
> Mahrat, the chief of Jaipur. When the two armies met, Mahrat
> came forward and proposed, as the matter was a purely personal
> one, to settle the dispute by single combat. 'Chach represented
> that he was a Brāhman, and unaccustomed to fight on horse-back.
> His magnanimous foe then alighted to meet him on equal terms,
> when Chach treacherously sprung upon his horse and slew his
> adversary . . .

Some of the better known champion episodes are to be
found in the Greek epics and histories. Champions were
apparently employed in the wars against the Persians as well
as between the city states themselves. Herodotos mentions
the instance where 'Hyllus made proclamation, that it would
be better not to run the hazard of engaging army with army;
but that from the Peloponnesian camp, the man amongst
them who they judge to be the best, should fight singly with
him . . .' (Phillipson 1911, pp. 209–10).

The most frequently cited instance, again narrated by

Herodotos, dates from the mid-sixth century BC and refers to a perennial dispute between Argos and Sparta over the territory of Thyreae. It is an interesting case because, although an example of combat by champions, it was not a contest between single champions:

> The Argives . . . agreed in conference with the Spartans that three hundred picked men a side should fight it out, and that Thyreae should belong to the victors; the rest of the two armies were to go home without staying to watch the fight, lest either side, seeing its champions getting the worst of it, might be tempted to intervene. On these terms they parted, leaving behind the men chosen to represent them, and the battle began . . . (Garlan 1975, p. 27).

The practice survived into Roman times and is found, as already mentioned, in the contest between the Horatii and the Curiatii. However, of the ancient episodes of champion combat, none can surpass in fame the contest between David and Goliath. Yadin (1963, p. 265) provides the following interpretation of that biblical episode:

> The Philistine and Israeli armies are ranged against each other in battle array on opposite hills. A champion comes forth from the Philistine camp, shouts contemptuously to the Israeli army, and demands that they send a warrior to do battle with him. A close examination of the narrative shows that Goliath is not being simply boastful and provocative. There is a specific intent behind his words. He is offering the army of Israel a method of war which was common enough in his own army but which was still strange to the Israeli forces.

How precisely the champion tradition came to survive in medieval Europe is again unclear. It may simply have reflected a throw-back to Graeco-Roman antiquity, in so far as much of the military tradition of chivalry was derived from classical experience. On the other hand, it is not impossible that the championship duel enjoyed a revival as a result of practical encounters with Islam, in the crusades and in Islamic Spain. Certainly, resort to single combat was accepted practice amongst Islamic countries, either as a preliminary to the main battle or indeed as a substitute for it (Khadduri 1955, p. 92). It is, therefore, not surprising that it is in Moorish Spain that we come across that most celebrated of champions, el Cid, otherwise known as the Campeador.

According to the (legendary) accounts, the Cid served as champion for the King of Castille against a champion of Aragon to settle ownership of the disputed city of Calahorra. The Latin Chronicle called the *Gesta Roderici* testifies that the Cid 'fought with Ximeno Garces one of the best Knights of Pamplona' and that he 'fought also with like success against a certain Saracen at Medini Celi' (Clarke 1902, p. 110).

In any case, the proclivity to settle disputes by single combat was apparent in medieval Europe. Numerous challenges were issued and, as Huizinga points out, the challenges were usually not accepted. The custom reappears as late as the Renaissance with Charles V himself proposing single combat to the King of France (Huizinga 1954, p. 97). Amongst Froissart's many episodes, we find in October 1355 that the King of France proposes to the invading King of England that they meet in single combat (1839, pp. 206–7).

War-limitation and the champion

How are we to understand the champion convention as an instance of war-limitation? According to Walzer, combat by single champions is simply an extension of 'who?' rules in the sense that it extends immunity to members of the army: 'once such a contest has been agreed upon, soldiers themselves are protected from the hell of war' (1977, p. 43).

And yet any analysis of the champion convention reveals that it is much more than this. Indeed, it has to be emphasized that there is a fundamental duality in the champion as a form of war-limitation: not only is it concerned with the saving of lives; equally, if not more importantly, it is concerned with the political question of producing a decisive result to the matter in dispute. As such, the champion is a perfect example of a form of war-limitation which straddles both convention A and convention B. Yadin (1963, p. 267) refers to this fundamental duality when he observes that 'apparently the stimulus of the duel was not primarily boastfulness or conceit on the part of the individual warriors, but the desire of commanders to secure a military decision without the heavy bloodshed of a full-scale battle'.

When two armies confront each other but agree that the

battle will be fought in microcosm between appointed champions, we have a perfectly stylized example of a convention of war-limitation. But what is being limited in this instance? Is the use of champions a meta-rule about the manner in which the dispute will be resolved, or is it a subsidiary rule prescribing limits to the resultant damage? Or is it a convention which necessarily does both of these things?

We can approach this problem from several different angles. Firstly, we may question whether it is possible to make any meaningful comment on the use of combat by champions in terms of a distinction between moral and political conventions of war-limitation. The moral argument would presumably be that there is value in saving lives, and that anything which contributes to this goal in war is morally desirable. In other words, the moral tradition, while accepting that war may be a legitimate device for resolving conflict, does tend to emphasize the limitation of the impact of the conflict and to tell us more about how the effects of conflict should be limited, than about how the conflict itself should be resolved. As a matter of emphasis, therefore, the resort to champions can be regarded as a moral instrumentality in warfare. This is the view put forward by Walzer. Writing of the war convention, he points to one set of rules in the following terms:

> Their tendency is to set certain classes of people outside the permissible range of warfare, so that killing any of their members is not a legitimate act of war but a crime. Though their details vary from place to place, these rules point towards the general conception of war as a *combat between combatants,* a conception that turns up again and again in anthropological and historical accounts. It is most dramatically exemplified when war is actually a combat between military champions (1977, p. 42).

Walzer implies that the significance of the champion convention lies in the moral fact that it saves lives. Put differently, the primary intention of the convention is to extend the category of noncombatants to include everyone except the rival champions. In this respect, Walzer takes over the position, said to be pervasive in the Homeric poems, which regards war as calamitous and which seeks to minimize its suffering: 'the Greeks and the Trojans alike rejoice in the settlement of their dispute by the less destructive single combat of Paris and Menelaus . . .' (Phillipson 1911, p. 172). Huizinga (1959, p. 201), writing of the theoretical attraction to the single combat in the late Middle Ages, explains the rationale of the champion in the following terms:

> The motive, as always, was expressly formulated in the terms: 'to prevent Christian bloodshed and destruction of the people, on whom my heart has compassion, [I wish] that this quarrel may be settled by my own body, without proceeding by means of war, which would entail that many noblemen and others, both of your army and of mine, would end their days pitifully'.

There is, however, an alternative perspective which tends to emphasize the political dimension of the champion convention and its primary contribution to the method of resolving conflict, rather than its secondary effect of saving lives. This perspective is referred to by Huizinga (1949, p. 92) in another commentary on the single combat: 'we must not regard this as having provided an omen or as being an humanitarian measure designed to avoid the spilling of blood, but simply as an appropriate substitute for war, a concise proof, in agonistic form, of the superiority of one of the parties . . .' The author then goes on to reintroduce the former conception and to demonstrate its differing motivation when he notes that 'this archaic conception of war is soon vitiated by specifically Christian arguments advocating single combat as a means of avoiding unnecessary bloodshed'.

What are we to make of these opposed interpretations? Is a convention of war-limitation in the form of single combat by champions co-extensive with the moral and political realms, as in our previous case concerning the prohibition of the use of bows and arrows between our competing cavemen? Tentatively, our reasoning might proceed as follows. In the case of our cavemen, we argued that a complete description of the act of killing would stand as an authentic account of the act of winning, that in analysing the death of one contestant, we are confronted with a full and convincing explanation as to why one caveman should occupy the cave. This is so because the conventional right of the victor to possess the cave is grounded upon the physical realities of the situation, in as much as this right cannot conceivably be negated. When the convention of limitation is introduced, proscribing the use of the decisive and fatal bow and arrow, the convention does more than prevent a death: it also seriously modifies our notion of what is meant by winning. Under the limitation, there can either be no victor at all or, at very best, one contestant's possession of the cave is provisional and contingent, not a reflection of absolute and unchanging physical realities. In other words, winning may mean either eliminating your opponent or getting him to agree (permanently or temporarily) to your exclusive enjoyment of certain utilities, by a continuous process of threatening to beat your opponent in a sequence of contests. Consequently, the introduction of a war-limitation preventing the death of one of the parties has direct effects on the nature of the resolution which is achieved between their competing claims, and on the nature of the possession which the winning party enjoys.

How does this compare with our model of combat by champions? Once again, we can contrast the situation under the application of this convention with the situation in which no limitation is applied. In a total war, the winner is the side which stands in unchallengeable physical possession of the disputed object: winning equals killing. What, then, is the effect of applying the single-combat mode of competition as opposed to all-out war? Clearly, on the one hand, it reduces the number of lives lost. Evidently, on the other, the point of the convention is that it seeks to give the winner an enjoyment of his victory that is tantamount to the physical elimination of the enemy. Trial by champion is a once-for-all resolution of the conflict, just as is the death of one of the cavemen. The victor's possession of the spoils is not assumed to be provisional or open to review. The retention of the spoils is not a sequential situation, dependent on physical resources, where the winner retains the spoils by convincing his opponent that, were they to fight again, he (the former) would win again.

Analytically speaking, the idea of combat by champion is a curious combination of two apparently contradictory ends. It seeks to endow the winner with the total enjoyment of victory that normally comes only from elimination of the opponent; and it seeks to do so while converting absolute war into minimum war. In a word, the champion convention destroys the equation between the act of winning and the quantum of damage wrought: victory no longer equals the body-count, but it is just as decisive. Indeed, paradoxically, it is the absolute decisiveness of the resolution of the conflict that permits the saving of lives.

We have already established how the use of champions relates to the process of conflict resolution. It endows the victor with a quasi-legal entitlement to enjoyment of rights, in a manner normally achieved only by physical extermination of the enemy: victory as a continuing sequence of bodily struggle, or the threat of such struggle, is replaced by victory as a terminal condition. However, the convention also has substantive implications. Even if the saving of life is a subsidiary effect of the convention, it is nonetheless a necessary effect of it: allowing that the use of champions demonstrates a convention about a procedure, we are yet forced to consider why such a procedure is thought desirable or what the point of it might be? It is in this area that the moral ambivalence of the champion convention lies because, even if the convention is not primarily about the saving of life, it makes no sense without reference to the saving of lives.

Finally, we can also penetrate the finality of the decision rendered by the champion method, by comparing the outcome of a single combat with the quite literal trial by champions or 'judicial duel' or, distinctly but relatedly, by viewing it as an instance of divine judgment. Historically, wars have been viewed in this light and various duels or combats have served these functions. For instance, Johnson (1975, p. 62) points out that at the start of the Hundred Years' War 'both sides could still reasonably believe in war as a corporate trial by battle, in which God would grant victory to the side with justice behind its claims'.

In this sense, a champion contest corresponds to a 'judgment'. Huizinga (1949, p. 91) makes the point in elaborating upon the connection between war and divination:

> One wages war in order to obtain a decision of holy validity. The test of the will of the gods is victory or defeat. So that instead of trying out your strength in a contest, or throwing dice, or consulting the oracle, or disputing by fierce words — all of which

may equally well serve to elicit the divine decision — you can resort to war.

We can extend Huizinga's point beyond divination. What is common to the single combat and all the above devices, is that a decision is produced, the finality of which bears no correspondence to the resources expended in obtaining it.

The champion: saliencies, chance and victory

Champions and saliencies

It is one of Schelling's main contentions that for limitations in warfare to be effective, they have to be salient: both parties must be able to recognize that a limitation has been breached or, otherwise, it can scarcely be an effective restraint on conduct. Moreover, even if a party decides to go beyond one particular limitation, that need not entail the overthrow of all limitations whatsoever, as long as there is a subsequent salient limitation at which it can stop and convince its opponent that this new limit will be observed. These saliencies become acute in tacit bargaining between adversaries but they presumably also have relevance to explicit bargaining situations. Thus Schelling underlines the virtues of qualitative limitations. He cites the example of conventions against the use of gas in warfare:

> 'Some gas' raises complicated questions of how much, where, under what circumstances, 'no gas' is simple and unambiguous . . . there is a simplicity to 'no gas' that makes it almost uniquely a focus for agreement when each side can only conjecture at what alternative rules the other side would propose and when failure at co-ordination on the first try may spoil the chances for acquiescence in any limits at all (Schelling 1966, p. 131).

It would be difficult to deny that consideration for such saliencies is embodied in the combat by champions: here we have further symbolic evidence that the champion is to be regarded as a genuinely limited form of war. To fight a champion combat with only one person less than the total strength of the army would not make sense. The fact that champions are to be regarded as a meaningful limitation is avowed by their symbolic quality which marks them off as being saliently different from the army as a whole. The simplest, and logically most attractive, format of this convention is for a single combat involving one from each side. But even when multiple champions have been employed historically, care has been taken to lend a symbolic quality to the champions to maintain their saliency. This can be done by choosing a multiple which is a neat, round number (the Combat of the Thirty in 1351, the 300 that fought for Argos and Sparta) or by a peculiar characteristic of the champions themselves (the Horatii and Curiatii, although a combat of three, was between triplets).

Champions and chance

The champion convention institutionalizes the element of chance in warfare. The characteristics that war shares with 'contracts subject to chance' and with combat between champions were amply described by Pufendorf (1934, p. 767):

> Such pacts are used no less in war . . . when the decision of a whole war is made to depend on the result of a contest between entire armies, or two or more champions from each side . . . Nay more, practically all formal wars . . . appear to suppose an agreement that he upon whose side the fortune of war has rested can impose his entire will upon the conquered . . . whoever resolved to take up war against another . . . is understood to have left the decision of the issue to the dice of Mars.

The champion convention merely institutionalizes this element of chance that is present in all warfare. It is based, if you like, upon a trade-off: the champion trades away a better chance of victory against the higher cost of such a gamble. Thus, other things being equal, the chance of victory remains constant for both parties whilst the costs for both are significantly reduced.

It was precisely this element of chance in the champion convention that evoked the condemnation of the early international legal theorists. Ayala (1912, p. 30), for instance, was not convinced that it was a sensible practice: 'I cannot think that this manner of settling disputes is altogether safe, seeing that it is foolhardy to stake the sum of one's fortunes upon the hazard of the one or the other individual'. He does not explain why full-scale warfare is any safer. Grotius, similarly, denounces the practice of settling wars by drawing lots, which is akin to war by single combat, except that he regards it as a sensible course of action if one party is certain of being defeated in a full-scale war. He allows that: '. . . if on a careful estimate the party attacked in an unjust war is so far inferior that there is no hope of resistance, it is apparent that a decision by lot can be offered, in order that a certain peril may be avoided by recourse to an uncertain one' (1925, p. 820). The comment is, however, naive: it takes two to agree to a convention and Grotius seems not to realize that, in the situation he describes, there would be no possibility of the stronger party consenting to the arrangement. Why should it trade off a certain victory against an uncertain one? In other words, as a game of chance, trial by champion makes most sense the more doubtful the outcome of the intended full-scale battle and the more even the contending forces. In such a situation, there is no diminution in the chances of victory for both sides, but there is a diminution in the costs.

As Grotius continues, his objection to the champion duel becomes even more fundamental in that he regards such a token effort, employing champions alone, as inconsistent with the very purpose of warfare. Accordingly, he sets forth the following position:

> If the issue at stake, such as the safety of many innocent persons, is worthy of war, we must strive with all our strength to win. To use a set combat as an evidence of a good cause, or as an instrument of divine judgement, is unmeaning and inconsistent with the true sense of duty (p. 821).

This takes us back to the idea that the only way of showing proper intention in war is to fight it without any limitation whatsoever, which is certainly not Grotius' overall position. If we do not literally have to strive with all our strength, how far short of this can we fall while still insisting that we are engaged in a serious purpose? Is an army that is conscripted by lottery as a token force any more representative of a warlike intent than a combat between champions? As with all conventions of war-limitation, we are again faced with the vexing question of where to draw a logical line, beyond which we fight a war and short of which we are engaged in some other social activity.

Champions and the problems of victory

As previously argued, victory in war can be at least partly conventional. However, in the case of a completely structured encounter, such as that between champions, the need for specific rules of victory and unambiguous evidence of victory become even more pressing: as a formal system of conflict resolution, it requires a formal procedure for termination. This is revealed in a fictional recreation of the combat between el Cid, as the champion of Castille, and Gonzales, the champion of Aragon. When the Cid had unhorsed his opponent he 'dismounted and slew him and asked if anything more remained to be done for the right of Calahorra. The umpires answered, No' (Clarke 1902, p. 41). The formalities having been observed, the decision could then be awarded.

The problems surrounding victory in a championship duel can be found at two distinct levels. The first group concerns the problem of recognizing who has actually won the contest; the second concerns the vulnerability of a victory that is conventional and rests, therefore, upon mutual observance. These two situations may be treated separately.

The first problem is likely to arise when ground rules specifying the constituents of victory have not been elaborated in advance. The previously mentioned contest between Sparta and Argos is the most memorable case in point:

> So closely was it contested that of the six hundred men only three were left alive — two Argives, Alcenor and Chromios, and one Spartan, Othryadas — and even these would have been killed had not darkness put an end to the fighting. The two Argives claimed the victory and hurried back to Argos; but the Spartan, Othryadas remained under arms and, having stripped the bodies of the Argive dead, carried their equipment to his own camp . . .
> The two armies met again on the following day, to learn the result of the battle. For a while both Argives and Spartans maintained that they had won, the former because they had the greater number of survivors, the latter because the two Argives had run away, whereas their own man had remained on the battlefield and stripped the bodies of the dead. The argument ended in blows, and a fresh battle began . . . (Garlan 1975, p. 27).

The case is apparently not unique. In an analysis of a biblical passage describing a combat between twelve men representing the House of David and twelve representing the

House of Saul, Yadin (1963, p. 267) concludes that the outcome was indeterminate:

> For reasons we can only guess at in the absence of firm details, the result is indecisive for the contestants 'fell down together'. And this explains the next phase of the story − 'And there was a very sore battle that day'. The duels had been fought, neither contestant had won, and so there was no alternative but to gain a military decision by the committal to battle of the whole of both armed forces.

It is this problem that is tackled by Grotius (1925, pp. 822–3) in a passage entitled 'In such combats who is to be judged the victor?' The best solution that he could come up with was that of territorial possession as evidence of victory but he conceded that when 'there are no sure proofs of victory, the issue remains in the same condition as before the battle, and must be referred either to battle or to new agreements'.

The other problem is a more fundamental one, not one of recognizing victory but of preserving it: the task is to ensure compliance with the outcome of the combat on the part of an army that has been 'defeated' symbolically, but which still exists as a physical reality. Why should the vanquished party abide by the decision when, having already 'lost', it has no more to 'lose'. The problem was recognized by Ayala. He recalled that the victory of the Horatii for the Romans was short-lived because the Albans subsequently tried to betray the Roman armies. Ayala concludes, therefore, that champion duels cannot, in themselves, furnish victory and that there is no alternative to an all-out competition between the forces available to both sides: conventional 'victory' is an insecure victory. As Ayala (1912, p. 30) states, 'wherefore, when the safety and liberty of us all, or the whole of our possessions, is in the balance we ought to fight with all our available strength: for otherwise not only will the conquered blame his rashness, but the victor will also not gain complete safety'.

CHARITY

The principle of charity

The champion convention shares certain similarities with our two other models of war-limitation but is also distinct from both. Before examining such comparisons and contrasts, however, we must establish the outline of the other two types of war-limitation. Firstly, we can consider the manifold moral theories of limitation under the generic heading of traditions of charity.

It should be emphasized that there are many moral theories relating to war, some of which are permissive, others of which impose absolute prohibitions. There is some intellectual violence, therefore, in speaking of *a* tradition of charity. Nonetheless, as we are concerned with ideal-types and with the tendency of war-limitations to have this or that intention and this or that effect, there is some justification in grouping moral theories together, in order to demonstrate what they collectively have in common with each other, in contrast to the champion convention and the city-swapping convention.

Charity, as a model of war-limitation, is mostly associated with varieties of just war theories. Although such theories have differed both in content and in motivation, we might accept the general formulation that 'the just war stops short of countenancing the utter destruction of the adversaries and tends to limit the incidence of violence by codes of right conduct, of noncombatant immunity and by other humanitarian restraints . . .' (Russell 1975, p. 2). Regardless of the specific moral content of the doctrine, there is a general insistence that charity constitutes a limitation beyond which it is not possible to go even in the prosecution of a war with just ends. Vattel (1916, pp. 289—90) was to make the point succinctly and his observation can stand as a general depiction of charity as a form of limitation: 'let us never forget that our enemies are men. Although we may be under the unfortunate necessity of prosecuting our right by force of arms, let us never put aside the ties of charity which bind us to the whole human race'.

Seen in this context, the tradition of charity stands in juxtaposition to, and usually in antagonism with, principles of military necessity and *raison d'état*. In the words of Osgood and Tucker (1967, p. 303): 'whereas reason of state must reject the claim that there are any inherent limits on the means that may be threatened or employed to preserve the state, *bellum justum* must insist that there are such limits and that they may never be transgressed, whatever the circumstances'. This is the assertion of the principle of charity in its absolute form. It may, of course, be diluted to incorporate *raison d'état* rather than to contradict it. It is thus common to find the principle of charity expressed in qualified form where it may, in dire circumstances, be overridden by the pressing necessity of state security. It is this form which is adopted by Wolff (1934, p. 410) when he contends that 'charity so moderates the use of the right to punish an enemy, that nothing may be done which seems hostile to it, except in case of conflict between love for one's self and for one's enemy'.

The principle of charity urges us to refrain from doing certain things to the enemy during war. We must be clear about the reasons why we should so refrain and this can best be done by contrasting charity with alternative motivations.

Firstly, we could refrain from certain military actions out of prudential or utilitarian considerations. In this case, the principal consideration, inducing restraint on our part, is the prospect that it might induce reciprocal restraint by the enemy: the restraint becomes an attribute of our relationship with the enemy rather than an attribute of the action that we are refraining from doing.

Secondly, we may refrain from doing something to the enemy in order that we might be able to threaten to do it in the future. Here again we have a form of war-limitation which is, in principle, different from that derived from charity. This second motivation for restraint is most clearly expressed in Schelling (1966, p. 24) when he argues that 'each might feel the sheer destruction of enemy people and cities would serve no decisive military purpose but that a continued *threat* to destroy them might serve a purpose. The continued threat would depend on their not being destroyed yet.' What induces restraint in this case is neither the intrinsic moral repugnance of the act, nor the prospect of reciprocity, but simply the utility of not doing now what we may wish to do, or threaten to do, in the future. As Schelling (p. 193) again says: 'the reason for not destroying the cities is to keep them at our mercy'. Objectively, the restraint is

similar in both cases but the motivation which leads to the
restraint is fundamentally different. The principle of charity
accordingly asserts itself by limiting war neither for reasons
of reciprocity nor for reasons of mounting a future threat.

As previously indicated, charity may find its source in a
multitude of philosophical and metaphysical considerations
— moral, humanitarian, religious and natural law amongst
them. In general, whatever its source, we may refer to
charity, with Johnson (1975) as an 'ideological' limitation
upon war. It manifested itself in ancient times:

> Even in the heat of battle or the intoxication of victory, men at
> war had to conform to a number of customs aimed, in a general
> way, at limiting the blind use of force. Though never codified,
> these customs were widely and correctly enough observed, even
> in relations with barbarians, for anyone contravening them to be
> blamed and to have sanctions imposed. The reasons were, in the
> first instance, religious, but increasingly, as philosophical thought
> developed, truly humanitarian as well (Garlan 1975, p. 57).

During the Middle Ages, the two dominant ideological
underpinnings of the just war doctrine were the overtly
religious concept of charity and the more secular concept of
natural law. The distinction, according to Johnson, begins to
disappear from the time of Grotius in the mid-seventeenth
century:

> Such a reversal in the conception of the relation of charity to
> nature is of the greatest importance for the development of just
> war doctrines in international law after Grotius. Though Grotius,
> as a bridge figure, continues to write of the dictates of nature and
> those of charity as differing, he has removed the fundamental
> divider that separates nature and supernatural morality in the
> followers of Thomas Aquinas (1975, pp. 229–30).

The confluence of moral, religious, humanitarian and
natural law elements in Grotius is evident, and he makes little
effort to stipulate precisely the grounds upon which he seeks
for the limitation of violence in war. In his famous Prologo-
mena to *De Jure Belli ac Pacis,* Grotius was to denounce the
contemporary practice of war for the reason that 'when arms
were once taken up, all reverence for divine and human law
was thrown away, just as if men were thence forth authorized
to commit all crimes without restraint'. In a similar passage,

Grotius again indicates the catholicity of his ideological position:

> An enemy therefore who wishes to observe, not what the laws of men permit, but what his duty requires, what is right from the point of view of religion and morals, will spare the blood of his foes ... Furthermore, from humanitarian instincts, or on other worthy grounds, he will either completely pardon, or free from the penalty of death, those who have deserved such punishment (p. 733).

In however tentative a form, what Grotius is articulating here is the principle of charity as a model of war-limitation. It is a position which has taken on multifarious forms. Indeed, as in the case of Walzer (1977), it is an ideological theory of human rights which may constitute the moral basis of rules in warfare. In this wider sense, Walzer's human rights' position locates itself within the tradition of charity. It is Walzer's argument that the war convention, the body of rules stipulating what may, or may not, be justly done in warfare derives from a theory of human rights. This theory is, however, left hanging by Walzer and is as insecure in its philosophical basis as that of Grotius mentioned above. Note, for instance, Walzer's discussion of the origins of the claim to rights:

> Individual rights ... underlie the most important judgments that we make about war. How these rights are themselves founded I cannot try to explain here. It is enough to say that they are somehow entailed by our sense of what it means to be a human being. If they are not natural, then we have invented them, but natural or invented, they are a palpable feature of our moral world (1977, p. 54).

Although arriving there by an alternative philosophical route, Rawls apparently acknowledges a similar naturalist or humanitarian restraint on warfare when he would prohibit means of war that 'encourage a contempt for human life' (quoted in Amdur 1977, p. 453).

Whatever the source of the doctrine of charity, it is usually thought to express itself in the twin principles of proportionality and discrimination. It is to these two aspects of charity that we must now turn.

The rudimentary notion of proportionality is straightforward but beyond that there are hidden complexities. Clearly, the principle implies that, as regards the application of military force, there is such a thing as sufficiency beyond which the military returns do not justify the humanitarian costs. Vattel (1916, p. 279) expressed the principle succinctly when he said 'a lawful end confers a right only to those means which are necessary to attain that end. Whatever is done in excess of such measures is contrary to the natural law'. Of course, there is an indication of some of the problems of proportionality even in this formulation, in as much as we are left to wonder whether the proportionality is to be between the means and the end (in which case we have a right to any means necessary to the attainment of a justified end) or between the costs and benefits of the means themselves (in which case some means would be unjustified, even for justified ends, if they were intrinsically too costly).

The principle of proportionality has served as a limitation on war in various capacities. It has been appealed to in order to limit the number of lives lost on both the attacking and the attacked side, where the overall military returns would not appear to warrant the expenditure of lives required. It has been appealed to in order to mitigate the execution of reprisals, by requiring that they be similar both in kind and in severity. Although perhaps not so apparent, the principle of proportionality has also been of importance in the limitation of the weaponry employed in warfare. Tucker (1975, p. 162) explains the application of the principle to types of weaponry:

> ... the principle of humanity is used to determine the lawfulness of weapons of war in terms of their military necessity. The principle of humanity thus forbids the employment of any weapon that is unnecessary for the purposes of war or that needlessly or unnecessarily causes human suffering or physical destruction. It should be apparent that the principle of humanity is dependent for its application upon the principle of proportionality. It is not human suffering or physical destruction that the principle of humanity forbids, but such suffering and destruction as are disproportionate to the military utility thereby obtained.

The second aspect of charity is usually taken to be a principle of discrimination, a principle which once again has variously manifested itself. Many attempts have been made to distinguish between gradations in enemy character, whether in terms of guilt versus innocence or combatancy versus non-combatancy or some variation on these central themes. This is to say that charity has underwritten limitations to war in the form of 'who?' rules which argue that what may legitimately be done in warfare is frequently dependent upon whom one is doing it to.

At the heart of the principle of discrimination lies a recognition that the enemy is not an amorphous collective but that it is possible to make moral judgments as between various categories within the enemy. As Grotius (1925, p. 741) was to point out 'nature does not sanction retaliation except against those who have done wrong. It is not sufficient that by a sort of fiction the enemy may be conceived as forming a single body.'

The attempt to determine which categories are morally meaningful has preoccupied much of the discussion of the *ius in bello*. As has been shown, the issue has hinged, at times, on a notion of political guilt: those alone who are responsible for the initiation and political direction of the war are to be considered the true enemy. The guilt—innocence dichotomy has also been interpreted as denoting a moral rather than a political condition. Certainly this was the meaning placed upon it in many of the classical just war doctrines and this is still the meaning placed on it by one contemporary just warrior. Ramsey (1968, p. 152) is representative of this viewpoint when he demonstrates the interaction between the *ius ad bellum* and the *ius in bello* in Christian thought:

> Since it was for the sake of the innocent and helpless ones that the Christian first thought himself obliged to make war ... how could he ever conclude from this that it was permitted him to destroy some 'innocents' for the sake of other 'innocents' closer to him in natural or social affinity? Thus was twin-born the justification of war and its limitation ...

The other traditional expression of a morally significant distinction in enemy character is that between combatants and noncombatants, in some theories equated with the guilt—innocence categorization, in others not. There can, however, be no doubt that the tradition of charity, expressed as a principle of right conduct in war, has dwelt at length on the combatancy—noncombatancy distinction and its implication for the conduct of warfare, both in theory and in practice. Thus, it has been contended that the distinction has, more than any other, served to civilize European warfare:

> Despite its imperfections and lapses in practice, the principle according immunity from direct attack to the civilian populations of belligerents formed the core of the restraints traditionally imposed on the conduct of war. On its observance the not inconsiderable achievement of 'civilized warfare' essentially rested (Osgood and Tucker 1967, p. 216).

Given its prominence in discussions of *ius in bello,* it is not surprising that the combatant–noncombatant distinction should find itself at the centre of a variety of philosophical debates. Of these, three only will be mentioned: the status of the distinction as a moral norm; the relationship between the distinction and military necessity; lastly, the problem of developing substitute distinctions if this one is obliterated.

The precise moral status of noncombatant immunity has been the subject of some contention. The assumption that the legal norms and conventions surrounding noncombatancy derive from fundamental moral principles has, indeed, been a dominant one. Accordingly, Osgood and Tucker (1967, p. 306) suggest that 'in the doctrine of *bellum justum* . . . the norm forbidding the direct and intentional attack on noncombatants represents an absolute injunction . . . For it is only where the prohibition against the deliberate killing of noncombatants is considered absolute that a clear conflict may arise between the necessities of the state and the requirements of an ethic that presumably sets limits to these necessities.'

However, this notion that noncombatancy derives from universal and absolute moral principles has been challenged in recent years. Hartigan (1965, p. 214) argues that noncombatant immunity developed out of historical accident, the actual practice of a certain type of warfare and 'an ill-defined and unconscious belief on the part of the mass of the affected population that war ought to be the reserved business of the warrior' and concludes that 'there is certainly room for legitimate doubt as to whether the norm of civilian immunity enjoys the status of an absolute moral imperative' (p. 218). Accordingly, the immunity granted to noncombatants was merely a phase in the history of warfare and it has wrongly been perceived as a universal and absolute moral prescription. It is in the context of contemporary debates about the justice of nuclear deterrence, and about forms of nuclear war, that this issue has significance.

Closely related to this point is a second which concerns the relationship between noncombatant immunity and military necessity. The fundamental question in this respect is the extent to which noncombatant immunity can be eroded or breached, while still leaving the principle intact as a meaningful limitation upon warfare. Thus even those who would maintain that noncombatant immunity is a fundamental moral precept in war, have also argued that the principle can accommodate military necessity while persisting as a moral force. The previous point examined the black and white contrast between noncombatant immunity as mere military practice and that immunity as moral imperative. In this second debate, we must countenance the grey area where morality and necessity overlap, and ask how flexible can the immunity be in the face of demands of necessity without becoming morally redundant? Tucker (1960, pp. 92–3) has provided a useful summary of the problem when he states that 'with a sufficiently elastic definition of what constitutes a legitimate military objective, and a sufficiently broad interpretation of what constitutes permissible "incidental" injury to the civilian population, there is no need ever to deny the continued validity of the principle distinguishing between combatants and noncombatants'.

The third issue that has been debated follows on from the previous two. If it is conceded that there are problems in either defining a noncombatant category or in restricting military activity to take cognizance of it, the alternatives would be to define a new category of immunity or to have none at all. Thus when Hartigan (1965, p. 217) asserts the non-universality of noncombatant immunity as a moral principle of warfare, he suggests that other restrictions could be developed to take its place:

It would seem that too much of the concern exhibited by jurists and moralists over limiting nuclear warfare has focused on the question of the seeming impossibility of protecting noncombatants from attack. With this extremely constrained view of the alternatives open to belligerents, noncombatant immunity has perhaps received more than its due share of attention while other equally or more essential norms that might serve as limiting principles in a nuclear war have been ignored.

What might these other norms be? Hartigan's own response is to adopt a principle of flexibility in defining the innocent, as those deserving immunity may vary from situation to situation: 'the task becomes one of drawing new and flexible lines of distinction between participants and non-participants' (p. 220). But this solution seems inadequate on at least two counts. Firstly, Hartigan's flexible categories are extremely vague and have little or no substantive content. How can we operationalize rules for the protection of the innocent if not on the basis of a combatancy distinction? There does seem to be some force to Walzer's contention, although made in the different context of terrorism, that permitting attacks on un-armed civilians 'breaks across moral limits beyond which no further limitation seems possible, for within the categories of civilian and citizen, there isn't any smaller group for which immunity might be claimed' (1977, p. 203). The second criticism would be that the very flexibility which Hartigan urges upon us, would serve to undermine the effectiveness of his rules of limitation. We are back to Schelling's insistence that limits be salient ones and the pervasive question 'if not here, where?' Hartigan's chameleon-like conventions, adapting themselves to individual circumstances, infringe the saliency principle that Schelling has demonstrated to be essential to any effective limitation.

Charity and nuclear weapons

The development of nuclear weapons and the adoption of strategies of nuclear deterrence posed new challenges for a charity-based *ius in bello* and sparked off a voluminous debate about the just war in the nuclear age. It is not the present intention either to contribute to this debate or to review it comprehensively, merely to indicate how the principle of charity has been related to discussions of nuclear war-limitation.

The reasons why nuclear weaponry stimulated a new round of just war literature are many and mostly obvious. It might not be too superficial to say that the twin manifestations of charity in warfare, in the shape of the principles of proportionality and discrimination, were those which seemed most obviously challenged by the new means of warfare. Accordingly, it has been around these issues that most of the debate has revolved.

The very nature of the weaponry calls into question the application of traditional principles of proportionality. As Walzer (1977, pp. 276–7) has suggested: 'the collateral damage likely to be caused even by a "legitimate" use of nuclear weapons is so great that it would violate both of the proportionality limits fixed by the theory of war: the number of people killed in the war as a whole would not be warranted by the goals of the war ... and the number of people killed in individual actions would be disproportionate ... to the value of the military targets directly attacked'.

Similarly, there is the even more widespread argument that nuclear weapons render obsolete any attempt to apply a principle of discrimination in warfare, either that between combatants and noncombatants or between any other 'flexible' categories that could be devised. Thus at the heart of the moral dilemma presented by nuclear weapons is the consideration, as O'Brien (1967, p. 31) states, that 'in all present forms of warfare ... literal application of the rule against intentional, direct attack on non-combatants ... would make moral engagement in warfare virtually impossible'. The choices offered in these terms are stark ones: either we do not fight morally necessary wars or, if we do, we cannot help but fight them immorally.

In accordance with the classic just war doctrine, the issues most closely investigated have been the related ones of just intention and double effect, as means of making nuclear instrumentalities of warfare conform to the demands of charity: if nuclear warfare is to be saved as a just form of warfare, then, according to most commentators, the questions of intention and double effect become paramount.

The issue of intention has been of primary significance in analyses of nuclear deterrence. Assuming that the threat of nuclear devastation is an immoral one, and one that exceeds the normal limitations of the just war, can we make such a threat without intending to execute it? Opinions, naturally, have been ranged on both sides. Walzer (1977, p. 270) is reluctant to see the threat divorced from its execution: 'the reason for our acceptance of deterrent strategy, most people would say, is that preparing to kill, even threatening to kill, is not at all the same thing as killing. Indeed it is not, but it is frighteningly close — else deterrence wouldn't "work" — and it is in the nature of that closeness that the moral problem lies.' Amongst the many who have maintained that there is a morally-relevant distinction between doing something, and threatening to do it, we find Paul Ramsey. Ramsey's case seems to rest on the assumption that preparing to do an act, and even preparing in such a way as to convince the enemy of its execution, is not at all the same thing as intending to do it. We can, therefore, prepare for counter-city war even if it is only our intention to execute a counterforce war. Ramsey (1963, pp. 53—4) summarizes his argument by way of analogy:

> Then it may be possible to put, not nuclear weapons as such, but the inter-city use of nuclear weapons into a category by itself, so that, while the capability still exists, the intention to attack cities will recede into the background so far as not to have actuality. Things as strange have happened before in the history of warfare. Tribes living close to death in the desert have fought cruel wars. They even used poisoned arrows, and certainly to a limited extent they fought one another by means of direct attack upon women and children. But they knew *not to poison wells*! That would have been a policy for mutual homicide, and a form of society-contra-society warfare ... In refraining from massive well-poisoning, or in keeping that ambiguous, did these tribes, in any valid or censorable sense of the word, still 'intend' to poison wells?

It is but a small jump from a discussion of intentions to a discussion of effects, intended or otherwise. The problem then becomes one of determining whether effects which are not directly intended, are to be assessed by the same moral standards as effects which are so intended. By extension, this leads again to the doctrine of double effect.

The distinction between direct and indirect killing may, or may not, be crucial. Ramsey (1968, p. 316) thinks it is and sees in it the evident workings of the principle of charity: '. . . the heart and soul of it was charity seeking to save human life when not all killing could responsibly be avoided . . . the rule of double effect was the immediate result of charity forming the consciences of men . . .' But the very same distinction between intentional and unintentional killing has also been employed to limit the provenance of charity and to constrain the very conventions of warfare which flow from it. This occurs in the corrupt form of 'double-think about double effect' (Anscombe 1970, p. 50), by means of which any secondary or collateral damage is justified by the principal or direct intent. The problem seems to lie in the definition of an unintended effect, when it is an effect that follows inescapably from the projected action. The doubt is expressed by O'Brien (1967, p. 27) in his conjecture 'whether the double effect concept is sufficient to justify the use of modern means of war whose lethal effects on noncombatants are better described as "inevitable" than "incidental" . . .', and in Walzer's critique of Ramsey:

> If counter-force warfare had no collateral effects, or had minor and controllable effects, then it could play no part in Ramsey's strategy. Given the effects it does have and the central part it is assigned, the word 'collateral' seems to have lost much of its meaning. Surely anyone designing such a strategy must accept moral responsibility for the effects on which he is so radically dependent (1977, p. 280).

The function of the principle of charity is to serve as a constraint on military necessity. And yet there is reason for thinking that the doctrine of double effect, having thrown military necessity out the front door, permits it to re-enter by the back. One is left to wonder which is the more harmful to the principle of charity, an explicit statement of its limitations, or an attempt to preserve it by accommodating elements of military necessity within it? Vitoria was at least candid when he asserted that 'it is never right to slay the guiltless, even as an indirect and unintended result, except when there is no other means of carrying on the operations of a just war' (Scott 1934, p. 231). Arguably, it is less destructive of the principle of charity to have its limits firmly demarcated than to render them infinitely flexible: at least in the former case, we know when the principle has been transgressed.

One last comment can be made upon the relationship between nuclear weapons and *ius in bello*. It was one of the perennial problems for the medieval just war theorists that they could not be precise about what was permissible in war for the reason that there was uncertainty about the precise purpose of war. Although they were agreed that part of the just cause of war was that covered by the formula *ulciscuntur iniurias,* that very term concealed moral ambiguities. As Russell (1975, pp. 66–7) has demonstrated, the root of the verb means variously repulsion, vengeance and punishment and, consequently 'the phrase *ulciscuntur iniurias* perpetuated the ambiguities inherent in Augustine's treatment, for it could entail merciless and unrestrained revenge for a trivial injury, restrained defense against hostile attack, recovery of stolen goods, or even the punishment of evil-doers'. In this context, it has to be said that nuclear weapons have functioned as a moral solvent. Like the medieval theorists, we can allow these moral distinctions to remain hidden, not because they are unimportant, but because our military technology does not allow us to respect them in practice. To the extent that charity, with its proportionality and discrimination, is challenged by nuclear weaponry, it matters little what are the finer moral purposes of our warfare, because our instrumentalities are too blunt to attain them except in an indiscriminate, all-or-nothing, package.

Charity and war-limitation

If there was difficulty in drawing some distinctions in our discussion of the champion, because of the ambivalence of that convention, there is less confusion with conventions deriving from charity. We can, for instance, start by saying that a charity model assumes a clear distinction between limitations based on political reasoning, and limitations based on moral reasoning as the charity model belongs in this second category. Ramsey (1963, p. 42) provides the skeleton of the charity model when he insists that 'the traditional limits upon the "just" conduct of war were a product not so much of man's sense of justice as of "social charity" determining, in crucial situations in which the use of force cannot be avoided, how force can be directed to the saving of human life'.

The primary and overwhelming consideration in charity-based war conventions is the saving of lives or, in less dire straits, the mitigation of suffering. This certainly appears to be the position which Potter (1973, p. 14) urges upon us when he maintains that 'we are allowed to use force only to restrain. In this mission we cannot ignore the obligation to respect human life even in the person of our enemy.'

How, then, does the tradition of charity, as a source of war-limitation, relate to the previous discussion concerning conventions A and B? Can we, as a matter of emphasis, distinguish whether charity primarily embodies one or other of the conventions? Given these alternatives, we would argue that the tradition of charity tends toward a convention of type B, that is one about how the impact of conflict may be limited while the conflict is resolved. This can be seen in the fact that if the convention were pushed to the extreme, it would save lives to the point where no forceful resolution of the conflict were possible: while the tradition of charity certainly cannot be equated with moral pacifism, the latter is the extreme tendency of the principle of charity. Once again we are dealing with matters of degree rather than with clear-cut distinctions; but it is possible that these matters of degree have great moral significance and important practical implications. The difference might be highlighted in the following formulation. Convention A tends to argue 'let us resolve the conflict and see how we can save as many lives as possible' whereas convention B tends to argue 'let us save as many lives as we can and see how we can resolve the conflict'. In the nuclear age, the arithmetic difference between these two formulations may amount to millions of lives. In these terms, the tendency of the tradition of charity is to provide a convention of the latter kind.

Similarly, we would regard the tradition of charity as tending to underwrite a substantive convention rather than a procedural one. This can again best be understood by stating the principle in its extreme form, which is admittedly an overstatement, but which serves to demonstrate the logical tendency of the principle: its extreme formulation might be 'save all lives and then settle the matter how you can'. In other words the principle tells us much more about the permissible substantive impact of the conflict, than it does about the permissible procedures for resolving it.

The tradition of charity may also be approached in the context of a discussion of immunity and withholding, to see whether this tells us more about the nature of the limits deriving from this convention of limitation. Here, it would have to be said that the overwhelming emphasis of the tradition is upon immunity and only secondarily, although relatedly, upon withholding. It is the right to immunity which demands the withholding, and not the need for withholding which permits the immunity. What the tradition of charity asserts is that there is an absolute right to immunity, except in so far as legitimate grounds can be provided for *not withholding* in certain specific cases. Withholding requires no moral explanation whatsoever: it is the exceptional cases, in which force is not withheld, that demand moral argumentation and sanction.

Such a charity-based conception of immunity finds perfect expression in the recent argument of Paskins and Dockrill (1979). Their case for noncombatant immunity in warfare can be seen to be similar to the argument from immunity and in contrast with the argument from withholding:

> Many see the just war ideas as a worthy effort at limiting war: war is something given and the task is to do what one can to mitigate its disasters. But for Jim this is to begin at the wrong end. His problem is not how far war can be limited, but how far it can in conscience be extended. He has ... great difficulty in accepting war at all. But his difficulties with the killing of noncombatants are still more formidable (p. 229).

The logic of the charity model takes the following form and, as will be seen, contrasts starkly with the city-swapping model: it is a strategy of immunity, because it makes no moral sense not to withhold (as there are no morally significant grounds for revoking the right to immunity) and it saves lives because there are good reasons to save them in the absence of better reasons not to. In the charity model, immunities persist even when additional bloodshed might yield a politically-favourable resolution of the issue.

CITY-SWAPPING

The model of city-swapping

In this section, a third distinctive conception of war-limitation will be outlined. Firstly, we will describe its general characteristics and then, as with the previous two models, we can move on to examine it in greater detail in terms of the analytic categories already established. What we are concerned with in this section is a generalized notion of what constitutes limited war, as it emerges from the analyses of the nuclear strategists. The strategists have, of course, developed a mind-boggling array of escalatory stages, each of which is limited in relation to the next rung on the escalation ladder, and there are therefore as many accounts of what constitutes limited war as there are gradations in the threat and exercise of military force. The nomenclature 'city-swapping' should not be taken literally to mean only a countervalue strategy in which cities are taken out alternately but rather as a generic term referring to a type of relationship between limitation and bargaining before and during warfare.

What, then, are the general characteristics of this third model? What we are dealing with here is a form of limited war in which the limits are as much an outcome of the bargaining between belligerents as they are conventions about how the bargaining shall be conducted: chronologically, the limits cannot actually be known until the conflict is resolved. In a very important sense, therefore, we are confronted here with a model of limited war which has no intrinsic limits.

In its essentials, this model of limitation is equivalent to Halperin's strategy of 'limited retaliation' of which he states that 'this strategy involves severe quantitative restraint. Both sides fire few missiles, perhaps one at a time, increasing to larger numbers if one side does not back down after the initial exchanges' (1963, p. 96). As such, this form of warfare shares the characteristics of two of Schelling's models being both a war of 'risk' and a war of 'pain and destruction' (1966, pp. 166–7). As will be seen shortly, this warfare is a competition in risk-tasking and the risk is of increasingly greater quantities of pain and destruction. Despite all this, city-swapping has to be regarded as a principal model for the limitation of contemporary warfare.

There is debate in the literature as to the novelty of this form of limitation, with its proponents seeing it as a model elaborated systematically only during the nuclear age. The argument seems to be that this model of limitation is predicated upon collaboration, which is conscious, even if tacit, between enemies in wartime itself; such collaboration is deemed to be a development of the theory of limited war in the nuclear era. It is a theme which Schelling had done so much to elucidate and to popularize:

> It is in the wars that we have come to call 'limited wars' that the bargaining appears most vividly and is conducted most consciously. The critical targets in such a war are in the mind of the enemy as much as on the battlefield; the state of the enemy's expectations is as important as the state of his troops; the threat of violence in reserve is more important than the commitment of force in the field ... And, like any bargaining situation, a restrained war involves some degree of collaboration between adversaries (1966, pp. 142–3).

Why should enemies collaborate in warfare, especially after a nuclear war has broken out? We might complacently assume that they would collaborate because they have no reason not to—that once nuclear war has commenced, the two sides no longer have any interest in prosecuting it. Halperin (1963, p. 100) makes this kind of naive suggestion when he maintains that 'once deterrence fails, neither side has any interest *per se* in destroying the other's homeland'. Of course, once nuclear war breaks out, both sides may not simply have an interest in attacking the other, they may have several such interests. Amongst the possibilities are that they might wish to raise the stakes in the ensuing competition with the enemy or that they might want revenge for damage already suffered. Additional reasons have been suggested by Knorr (Knorr and Read (eds) 1962, p. 17):

One purpose is to demonstrate one's resolve, one's determination not to accept defeat but, if necessary, to broaden and deepen the conflict that has broken out. Another is to inflict on the opponent damage and pain, to punish him and to weaken his resolve by the prospect of further punishment. A third is to reduce the enemy's military capabilities . . .

These might all be good reasons for non-collaboration with the enemy with the intention of securing unilateral victory.

What, then, might induce enemies to enter into tacit co-operation with each other? Why, if they are both trying to win, should either of them withhold forces that it has available to it. What is the incentive that will induce 'a deliberate hobbling of a tremendous power that is already mobilized' (Brodie 1959, p. 311)? The recurrent answer to this question is that the belligerents will agree to restrain their available forces only if they perceive it to be in their respective self-interests to do so. As Brodie (1954, p. 19) was to point out in an early contribution to the theory of limited war in the nuclear age: 'the reciprocity of restraint, whether openly or tacitly recognized, will have to be on the basis of mutual self-interest'.

We must now briefly consider the sense in which city-swapping constitutes a limited form of warfare, as well as some of the restrictions upon such a usage. If two belligerents are engaged in war, and if their convention is to destroy targets on either side slowly, selectively and alternately, in what sense does this represent a limited form of warfare?

Ramsey (1963, p. 20), in the very act of disparaging such a model of limitation, implicitly concedes that it may nonetheless limit the destruction of warfare:

This is the secret meaning of the statement that countervalue warfare can, as a test of wills, have only *quantitative* limitations. This really means that there are no limits, except that quantity of destruction which will cause one side to give up first. If there had been more resolution to continue fighting . . . the quantity would have been higher.

Evidently, however, despite Ramsey's protestations, if the punishment inflicted in the initial stages of war is sufficient to diminish the resolution of one of the parties, the war will be limited, in the sense that the quantity of damage wrought will be less: two cities destroyed on either side is a limitation in comparison with ten cities destroyed on either side. City-swapping may, therefore, be described as a model of warfare which is quantitatively limited.

Or, at least, it *may* be so limited. The problem with this form of limitation is that it is impossible to know beforehand at what point the war will, in fact, be limited. What appear as limitations, as terminations to the war, may be no more than breathing spaces or breaks in the sequence of action. We do not know in advance where the limits, if any, will be found. It is for this reason that Ramsey (1963, p. 23) denounced the 'abyss of infinitude and illimitability into which strategic city exchange has already plunged'. His specific argument is that 'to this there are no real boundaries: and to speak of "quanti-tative" limitations is misleading and dangerous language. Even the understandings reached during the fighting will be arbitrary ones, maintained only by encounters of resolve.' On this issue, Ramsey's reasoning is supported by that of Schelling, even if otherwise the two have little in common. The problem with all limitations which are purely quantita-tive is, as Schelling would argue, that they are not salient: there is no logical reason for stopping at one quantity rather than another. As Schelling (1966, p. 164) noted: 'to argue that one can as readily stop after the third city, or the thir-teenth, or the thirtieth, detracts from the more promising boundary at zero'.

It might, therefore, be suggested that city-swapping, as a form of warfare, is an all-out fight (potentially) with the significant qualification that it is in slow motion and that its sequential nature allows the action to be broken into. This permits the action to be broken off but does not in itself guarantee that it will be.

There is an additional reason why the limits of city-swap-ping are not predetermined. The very consideration which can induce the belligerents to stop − namely the prospect of an extension of the conflict and the intensification of pain − is opened up as a possibility, not by accident but by delib-erate design: war is to be limited, not simply by fear of worse to come, but because the limits themselves are means to the very extension of the conflict that is to be avoided. Schelling

(1966, p. 106) exposes the logic of this form of limited war when he remarks that 'the risk has to be recognized, because limited war probably does raise the risk of a larger war whether it is intended to or not. It is a consequence of limited war that that risk goes up; since it is a consequence, it can also be a purpose.' Martin (1979b, p. 115) makes precisely the same point when he discusses the limitation on the use of nuclear weaponry to a tactical level and comments on the 'paradoxical nature of the search for a doctrine of limited nuclear war. For the tactical or theatre-nuclear element, which is by definition a limited concept, depends for its limitations upon a link to the limitless possibilities of the strategic balance.' We induce limits by holding out the prospect of war without limits and by making that prospect even more real.

City-swapping and war-limitation

The structure of this model is most vividly captured in Schelling's account of San Franciscan duels: 'in early days, wealthy San Franciscans, it is said, conducted their "duels" by throwing gold coins one by one into the Bay until one or the other called it quits' (in Knorr and Read (eds) 1962, pp. 243–4). We might call such a conflict limited in two distinct senses. Firstly, the two contestants are not trying to throw each other into the Bay, which is to say that neither is seeking to eliminate his opponent physically. Secondly, the two contestants do not simultaneously throw into the Bay their entire holdings of gold coins. In some sense, therefore, we are confronted with a limited contest and yet, equally, we have no way of knowing beforehand at which limit the contest will stop: the coin-swapping may conceivably continue until all coins have been expended on both sides (assuming they have equal amounts); conceivably, also, when this has happened, one party might, in exasperation, throw the other into the Bay. The likelihood of the latter outcome is dependent upon the strength of the conventions of the contest but clearly the former outcome is not equally proscribed.

Accordingly, we can accept Knorr's analysis of limited strategic war as serving as a general description of the city-swapping model of limitation currently under discussion:

> ... limited strategic war ... is primarily a contest of resolve. The
> military actions are part of a bargaining process. They are designed
> to precipitate bargaining in order to bring about an agreed ter-
> mination of hostilities before these escalate to a less controlled,
> or perhaps uncontrolled, cataclysm of destruction (Knorr and
> Read (eds) 1962, p. 4).

But how does this bargaining come about, and what is the
likelihood that there will be agreed limitations to it? If the
interests of the two parties are completely opposed, there can
be no possible basis of accommodation and no reason to stop
before the cataclysm eventuates. We, therefore, need a clearer
perception of the basis of any agreed limitation and that
basis can be provided only by a common interest in avoiding
suffering. As our two San Franciscans throw their coins
away, in ritual fashion, the only thing which can call a halt is
the pain caused by the loss of each coin and the cumulative
impact of this pain. Read provides a full description of the
logic of this relationship and is worth quoting at length in
this context:

> The territorial contest is an example of pure conflict — or, in
> technical terms, a zero-sum game, which means that what one
> side gains the other loses. By contrast, punishment in itself is not
> necessarily a gain for the side inflicting it, or at least not a gain
> commensurate with the loss to the side suffering it. An army can
> cancel out the enemy's territorial gains by retaking the same
> ground in a counterattack, and the final result is as though the
> ground had never been lost. But casualties and pain are an abso-
> lute loss for which there is no compensation in reprisal, however
> necessary reprisal may be. Other things being equal, both sides
> prefer a battle in which punishment is low to one in which it is
> high. Thus, although the contestants have incompatible interests
> in the territorial aspect of war, they have some degree of common
> interest in the punitive aspect. This common interest makes bar-
> gaining possible and provides a motive both for limiting the
> violence of combat and for terminating the war in a negotiated
> settlement reflecting limited political aims (Knorr and Read (eds)
> 1962, pp. 81–2).

There is, then, as we have said, a sense in which we must
regard city-swapping as a model of limited war. However, it is
worth noting at this stage that critics have attacked such a
notion of limitation, and have done so from two distinct
positions. The one would be the essentially political objec-

tion that the limitations may not hold, and any expectation that they will is an act of faith rather than of policy. The other might be regarded as the moral objection that even if the limitations should 'bite', they would bite too high. Schelling and Ramsey may be taken as representative of these two positions respectively. Schelling specifically warns that 'there is no logical reason why two adversaries will not bleed each other to death, drop by drop, each continually feeling that if he can only hold out a little longer, the other is bound to give in' (in Knorr and Read (eds) 1962, p. 255). Ramsey's objection to the notion of limits through bargaining is close to Schelling's but goes further. While Schelling contends that there is no assurance that the parties will not go beyond the destruction of one city apiece, Ramsey urges that if they stop at one city they have *already* gone too far. He agrees with Schelling that when war is viewed as a test of resolve 'there is no end here, no limits' (Ramsey 1963, p. 17). He then proceeds to the additional critique of counter-city retaliation as a bargaining tactic:

> The question is not primarily whether cities can be deliberately exchanged with coolness and control enough to prevent this from at once becoming a spasm of countercity devastation. To this there is a prior question: whether exchanging cities for bargaining purposes and to play on the will of the adversary and break his resolve has not already transgressed the limits that are clearly present when war is understood as a trial of the actual military strength of nations. War as a test of the limitlessly variable 'strength' of resolve may go as high as strategic city exchanges. War as a test of real strength to defend or effect objectives can and will go no higher than counterforces warfare (1963, p. 19).

We must now move on to consider this third model of war-limitation in terms of our various analytical categories. Firstly, can we distinguish the city-swapping limitation as pertaining more to convention A or to convention B? The contention of the study is that the city-swapping convention as a means to limiting war shares the characteristics of convention A to the extent that it is primarily a convention about how conflict may be resolved while limiting the impact of the conflict.

What is the reasoning underlying this conclusion? A case might be developed along the following lines. The point of the bargaining between two parties, in the form of exchange of cities or throwing of coins into the bay, is to make the opponent back down. The only limitation to which this is subject is the injunction that it is better to win cheaply than to win dearly; however this, in turn, may be overridden by the consideration that if one tries too hard to win cheaply, one may in fact lose and it may be preferable to win dearly than to lose; but if one knows that one will lose in any case, it might be better to lose cheaply than to lose dearly. What emerges from this tangled situation is the message that there is no logical way of knowing what the price of victory or the price of defeat will be before the bargaining commences. It is the bargaining which sets limits to the suffering, and only secondarily the suffering which sets limits to the bargaining. The convention tells you how you may win (and best done cheaply) and how you may lose (and best done cheaply) but it tells you also that you may win or lose *at any price*: to that extent, it is the outcome which is more important than the price at which it is achieved, even if both sides have an interest in keeping the price low. Arguably, then, city-swapping is a convention concerned with the resolution of conflict which *may* also limit its impact; but it tells you much more about the former than about the latter. In that sense, the city-swapping model stands in stark contrast to the charity model: in the former, winning is more important than saving lives, though it makes sense to save lives; in the latter, saving lives is more important than winning, though it makes sense to win. The champion straddles the two: according to it, it makes sense to win and it makes sense to save lives and the only manner in which this can be done is by wrenching the notion of winning away from either the lives saved or the lives lost.

It follows from this conclusion that we would view city-swapping as tending towards the definition of a specific process for resolving conflict, rather than as requiring particular substantive limitations in war. It is a convention about how to resolve conflict, not about the price of a settlement: even if it favours a low price, it cannot guarantee such an outcome.

It remains, therefore, only to consider the city-swapping model in the light of our two modes of limitation, by immunity or by withholding. As a matter of emphasis, do the conventions of city-swapping derive from a concern with immunity or from a strategy of withholding? The answer to this question has already been suggested. We have noted that city-swapping is concerned with winning (cheaply if one can) or losing (cheaply if one must) but that winning dearly may be deemed preferable to losing at any price. On this basis, it is difficult to argue that the limitations of city-swapping, such as they are, stem from the recognition of inviolable rights to immunity. Force is withheld out of consideration of the costs to oneself, in future suffering, not out of recognition of the opponent's immunities. Moreover, as winning can outweight even these costs, such withholding as occurs is contingent and provisional: the area of immunity is dictated by the degree of withholding, but the degree of withholding is not determined by a fixed area of immunity.

There may be some overlap here between our immunity/withholding distinction and Schelling's analogy of the shooting gallery: 'if we were at a shooting gallery, had paid our fee and picked up the rifle and could shoot either the clay pipes or the sitting ducks, "shoot the pipes" would mean the same as "don't shoot the ducks"' (1966, p. 193). In accordance with the charity convention, we might shoot the pipes but not the ducks because the ducks enjoyed immunity. In the city-swapping convention, we might not shoot the ducks because we had specific reasons for wanting to shoot the pipes. If shooting the pipes did not achieve our objectives, we might then shoot the ducks. In the former case, there is a fixed area of immunity; in the latter there is not. The city-swapping model is a strategy of withholding all your forces in the shortest run, in case they might all be utilized in the longest run.

5

Forms of Nuclear War-Limitation

POST-1945 THEORIES OF LIMITS TO WAR

In this chapter, writings on the possible forms of war-limitation, in a nuclear context, will be reviewed. This body of ideas and argumentation is diverse in character and mixed in its origins. For instance, it combines statements about limited nuclear war that have been made by US government officers, and which thus have official standing, with a wide spectrum of semi-official and academic speculation on the same topic. We are, therefore, concerned in this section with ideas which have been variously related, or unrelated, to governmental thinking and policies.

The literature is also diverse in the sense that it is an inter-mix of hypothetical argumentation with insights derived from concrete experience. Many of the scenarios described in these analyses of limited war are no more than theoretical constructs − predictions, more or less plausible, about the conceivable forms of future wars. Others, and especially those of a policy-prescriptive nature, recall the actual limited-war experience of the post-1945 period and draw their lessons for statesmen from that experience. From this perspective, Kolkowicz (1980, p. 1) has contended that the reality of limited-war thinking can be contrasted with the purely theoretical dimensions of nuclear deterrence: '. . . the empirical validation of strategic deterrence doctrine is ambiguous at best, while what is referred to as limited war theory and doctrine is as real and pervasive as the last war in Asia or the next one in the Middle East'. We are, in consequence, dealing not with idle theory: the ideas produced by the theorists of limited war have helped shape the strategic

142

doctrines and postures of at least one of the world's superpowers; in addition, limited 'local' wars have actually been
fought.

It should also be pointed out by way of initial clarification
that, for the moment, we are concerned only with Western
notions of limitation. This is to say that while the focus of
this book is upon bilateral conventions of war-limitation, we
must for the moment adopt a unilateral perspective upon
these conventions. The fullest and most explicit official discussions of limits to nuclear war are, understandably, to be
found on the Western side and the whole question of reciprocity — whether the Soviets too might be prepared to play
the limiting game — is one that will be taken up in due
course. To the extent that American notions of limited war
are unilateral, and presented in isolation from Soviet reac-
tions, they fall less clearly within the ambit of our discussion
of reciprocal war conventions. If it were true, therefore, as
one analyst of the limited nuclear options strategy of the
United States has argued, that the doctrine was not predicated on mutuality, then it would not so obviously be a part of
our general theme. As Davis (1975–6, pp. 7–8) was to observe of the Schlesinger doctrine: '. . . the desirability of the
new doctrine was not linked with any specific Soviet response. Because Soviet forces had an inherent degree of
flexibility, many hoped that the Soviet Union would eventually introduce limited-use concepts into her own strategy, but
the American doctrine was not predicated upon this'. Whether
such a claim can be accepted at face value, or whether the
Schlesinger doctrine was but a unilateral statement about an
anticipated bilateral convention, will be reserved for later
comment.

The first substantive issue to be referred to is whether, in
speaking of limits to war in a nuclear context, we are considering a novel phenomenon or merely the re-appearance of
an age-old practice. There is a general, if not absolute, consensus amongst commentators that war-limitation in the
nuclear age is qualitatively different from previous historical
manifestations of limited war. In fact, it is only with trepidation that we can use the term 'limited war', as a self-conscious
theory for restricting the mode of war's conduct, with refer-

ence to the pre-1945 period, because many leading analysts hold the position that such a theory has only been elaborated in response to the development of nuclear weaponry. This is certainly the position adhered to by Osgood (1970, p. 94):

> The detailed elaboration of a strategic doctrine of limited war, the formulation of specific plans for carrying out this doctrine, and the combined efforts of government, the military establishment, and private analysts and publicists to translate the doctrine into particular weapons and forces are developments peculiar to the nuclear age.

However, in many cases, such a conclusion is merely asserted, or the grounds advanced in support of it are themselves questionable. It is surely difficult to maintain, as Åkerman (1972, p. 47) has done, that 'limitation in the form of collaboration with the enemy was something that could not be conceived in the pre-nuclear world'. In varying degrees, all of the historical conventions of war-limitation, previously presented, depend upon some collaboration between belligerents, even if only tacit.

A more convincing case for the novelty of war-limitation can be made on the basis of the weapons themselves, rather than on the degree of collaboration between the fighting parties. Thus Aron (1956, p. 104) placed limited war in the nuclear age in the context of a longer military tradition but at the same time recognized revolutionary changes within the tradition of limited war: '. . . the appearance of A- and H-weapons will result, in the next historical period, in bringing back, in an unprecedented form, the classical distinction between limited and total wars . . . The new aspect of it is that the limitation is this time imposed by the character of available weapons.' Brodie went even further in specifying which of the weapon characteristics lent the novelty to the practice of contemporary limited war: it was their military efficiency. Thus Brodie (1957, p. 114) argued that:

> In using the term 'limited war' today, we are not talking about a return to something. We are talking about something quite new . . . The problem of modern limited war is the problem of sanctions for keeping out of action, even though in being, precisely those instruments which from a strictly military point of view are the most efficient.

But even in saying this, Brodie seems to shift attention away from the weapons, and their characteristics, to the problem of ensuring compliance with a convention of non-use. The problems of observance, and the motivations for respecting mutual restraints, are by no means peculiar to nuclear conditions, even if nuclear technology adds a special edge to the discussion. It is not uncommon, therefore, for analysts to arrive at ambivalent conclusions, in which they refer to the persistence of traditional problems of limited war, but then proceed to highlight their intensified nature, given the penalties for non-compliance in the form of nuclear reprisals. Even Osgood, who so unequivocally pronounced the novelty of nuclear theories of limited war, had earlier advanced a more circumspect position in claiming that '. . . limited war would be equally desirable if nuclear weapons had never been invented. However, the existence of these and other weapons of mass destruction clearly adds great urgency to limitation' (1957, p. 26).

The argument that there is something new to war-limitation in the nuclear age is sometimes made from another angle. It is difficult to imagine a previous age in which the enunciation of a limited military strategy could, in any sense, be regarded by the other side as a threatening posture. While, historically, various belligerents have had interests in various forms of limitation, and these interests have not always been mutual and equal, it is probably true that, at no previous time, would one country's adoption of a limited strategy have constituted an act of aggression, or been seen as being more provocative than a threat of total war. Whatever other arguments might be levelled against limited-war strategies, they have seldom been charged with being more hostile than their total war counterparts.

In the nuclear age, this situation may well have eventuated: the attempt to create the infrastructure of a future convention of limited nuclear warfare could easily be interpreted by the opponent as threatening and provocative, and as being more aggressive than the simple espousal of total war threats. How has such a paradoxical situation come about?

The explanation is to be found in the similarity between the technological and weapon system prerequisites of a selective targeting capability and the requirements for a successful pre-emptive first-strike capacity. Not surprisingly, therefore, one of the principal arguments employed by the opponents of Schlesinger's counterforce targeting proposal was that it would provoke fears in the Soviet Union that the United States was developing a first-strike capability: the attempt to limit war, whatever its motivation, could not but be seen as an aggressive action. It was this argument that was used by Ian Smart in a letter to *The Times*:

> Choosing to exploit current missile technology in order to achieve such accuracy . . . may reflect an intention no more sinister than the desire for greater flexibility in retaliation. The choice itself, however, entails building forces whose capability, in terms of accuracy, is not essential to a deterrent second-strike threat but is essential to an effective first-strike . . .
> The intention behind the choice is immaterial; it is the capability it entails which will be interpreted, or mis-interpreted, by the other super-power (*The Times,* 17 January 1974, p. 5).

The argument which proceeded during the middle 1970s was, therefore, about the wisdom of the United States acquiring a flexible counterforce capacity and the likely effect of this on Soviet policy. It was in this vein that Martin (1974, p. 158) was to note that 'so long as the targets for selective strikes include hard sites . . . it is clear that the technology necessary for selectivity will be closely related in kind, if not quantity, to that demanded by a full competition in counterforce capability'. The unfortunate side-effect of this was that the attempt to limit nuclear war might lead to its over-hasty initiation because of the incentives for pre-emption. The critics thus fastened onto the theme of greater instability associated with limited options, especially in a crisis situation. Rathjens (1974, p. 683) contended that the policy might lead to 'reciprocally reinforcing incentives to initiate a disarming first strike against adversary missiles', and Carter (1974, p. 27) took the position that 'a substantial US counterforce capability against Russian ICBMs is more likely to create an incentive for the USSR to adopt a hair-trigger, launch-on-warning posture . . .'

We need not take sides on the merits of these arguments. It is sufficient for the present purpose to point out that the issue demonstrates a rather novel complication in the discussion of limited war in the nuclear age, when weapons' technology itself can make the effort to control and mitigate warfare appear as a provocative and aggressive posture.

The experience of two World Wars of the twentieth century implanted the conviction that wars would tend henceforth towards their total form. The invention of a weapon, total in its effects, enhanced this assessment of the military situation. What is surprising, given this technological and intellectual context, is not the large number of statements proclaiming the totality of war in the nuclear age, but the rapidity with which ideas of limited warfare re-emerged from their recent eclipse and the robustness which they displayed, despite the inhospitability of the climate in which they made their appearance. It is a striking event in the history of ideas, that the supreme fruition of the notion of the totality of nuclear warfare, and the resurgence of a theory of limits to war, should have been virtually simultaneous occurrences: the thesis of total nuclear war immediately evoked a variety of antitheses in the form of theories of nuclear war-limitation.

The limitation envisaged in these theories was to take a variety of forms, the details of which will be presented later in this chapter. By way of introduction, it may be useful to present a brief review of the major landmarks in the discussion of post-1945 limited warfare.

We tend to think of the theory of limited war as emerging in the 1950s, but the chronological gap between total weapons and the first theoretical explorations of limited forms of warfare did not endure as long as this. One survey in fact maintains that 'the notion of developing tactical nuclear weapons ... developed quite early. The first theoretical studies in the area of "limited nuclear war" began in 1948 ... at the Californian Institute of Technology' (SIPRI 1978a, p. 10). Moreover, no sooner had the Second World War ended than a prominent military publicist gave expression, in however general and undetailed a form, to a vague optimism that limited war might once again re-emerge to take the place of the recent European orgies of destruction. Liddell-Hart (1946, p. 203) foresaw the possibility of the revival of 'a code of limiting rules for warfare' and based his guarded optimism on a sense of history and the recovery of sanity after the Thirty Years' War. 'It is not impossible,' he argued on the basis of this precedent 'that a reaction from the disorders of the past thirty years might see a twentieth-century revival of reason sufficient to produce self-control in war.' Meanwhile, on the other side of the Atlantic, theoreticians like Bernard Brodie were soon to provide some kind of detailed rationale for the adoption of limited war strategies.

This antithesis between total war and limited war expressed itself also at the level of bureaucratic or personality politics within the United States at this time. It was reproduced, for instance, in the late 1940s in the competing claims amongst scientific advisers for research, on the one hand, into smaller tactical nuclear weapons and, on the other, into the development of the 'super' or hydrogen bomb. The clash of views came, of course, to be personalized in the giant figures of Robert Oppenheimer and Edward Teller. It is clear that Oppenheimer had early advocated further development of tactical weapons, at least partially as a counter to Teller's importunings on the super bomb. Oppenheimer, for example, was to state in his security hearings that during the late 1940s: 'the prevailing view was that what we had was too good – too big – for the best military use, rather than too small' (Wharton 1955, p. 100). A former Department of Defense official recalled that 'always Dr Oppenheimer was trying to point out the wide variety of military uses for the bomb, the small bomb as well as the large bomb' (Gilpin 1962, p. 117). Accordingly, the General Advisory Committee, of which Oppenheimer was chairman, included in its controversial report of 30 October 1949, along with the recommendation against crash development of the hydrogen bomb: 'an intensification of efforts to make atomic weapons available for tactical purposes . . .' (York 1976, p. 152). It is interesting to note also that in the course of the 1950s Teller himself was to become a vocal champion of tactical nuclear weaponry, expressing the view that limited use of nuclear weapons 'would do no more damage to the face of a nation than conventional weapons' (Teller and Brown 1962, p. 281), and promoting for that reason the development of 'small, "clean" nuclear arms that would be needed for limited nuclear conflicts' (p. 287).

These early pioneering efforts were to be given a major stimulus by two discrete developments at the end of the decade. The first was the Soviet acquisition of its own atomic weapon and the concomitant realization that the destruction of future large-scale war could be mutual. This, in turn, directed intellectual energy into the exploration of forms of military contest which might make some political sense for nuclear-armed antagonists. A note of desperation was to creep into some of the analyses, the limitation of nuclear warfare being presented as humanity's only hope. During the 1950s, a chorus of voices was to sing the refrain that attempts to prevent war were not sufficient; measures must be taken to restrain war in the event that it should occur. Typically, Aron (1958, p. 69) was to declaim that 'it does not seem to me either intellectually right or politically opportune to assert that nothing could stop a total war the moment the atomic taboo was violated'.

The other development was the experience of the Korean war. As Brodie (1957, p. 112) was to recall: 'the Korean war demolished the basis for the glib axiom that all modern wars must be total, and demonstrated conspicuously some of the major constraints necessary to keeping a war limited'. The experience of a war that had actually been kept limited, even if that limitation was not itself universally popular, served to promote further consideration of the military and political problems associated with limited wars, and of the reasons for which such wars should be undertaken. Above all, the experience focused attention on limited war as a war which was geographically confined, and which did not directly impinge upon the homeland of the major powers. For many writers during the 1950s, such geographically-delimited wars were to provide the main model of limitation in the nuclear age.

From the middle 1950s onwards, the focus of debate shifted. As the American defence community became increasingly concerned with the theoretical weaknesses of massive retaliation, the debate came to concentrate upon the precise strategy that the West should adopt and the question turned, specifically, on the relative virtues of conventional and tactical nuclear capabilities. In short, the issue at stake was twofold: which form of defence would provide the greater security to Western interests; secondly, which form of warfare would offer the greater possibility of keeping a war limited, in the sense of avoiding an all-out nuclear exchange? The answers to these two questions were possibly not the same but, amongst some of the more partisan advocates, there was a natural tendency to conflate the two.

Initially, the purveyors of tactical nuclear war-fighting strategies were the more vocal and appeared to have the better of the argument. Their cause was popularized in Kissinger's *Nuclear Weapons and Foreign Policy* in which the virtues of limited defence options, *vis-à-vis* sole reliance upon massive ones, were celebrated, and use of tactical nuclear weapons was advocated. Kissinger's starting point was that 'strategy can assist policy only by developing a maximum number of stages between total peace . . . and total war' (1957, p. 136). In other words, a politically-meaningful military strategy must allow for choices between the two extremes and limited war described the totality of that inner spectrum. Seldom have the niceties and formalities of limited warfare been so fully elaborated as in the writings of this period. Kissinger, for instance, set out the following ground rules of limited war and deserves quotation at length to convey the full grandeur of this code of nuclear chivalry:

> We should leave no doubt that any aggression by the Communist bloc may be resisted with nuclear weapons, but we should make every effort to limit their effect and to spare the civilian population as much as possible. Without damage to our interest, we could announce that Soviet aggression would be resisted with nuclear weapons if necessary; that in resisting we would not use more than 500 kilotons explosive power unless the enemy used them first; that we would use 'clean' bombs with minimal fallout effects for any larger explosive equivalent unless the enemy violated the understanding; that we would not attack the enemy retaliatory force or enemy cities located more than a certain distance behind the battle zone or the initial line of demarcation (say five hundred miles); that within this zone we would not use nuclear weapons against cities declared open and so verified by inspection, the inspectors to remain in the battle zone even during the course of military operations (1957, pp. 231–2).

Similar arguments had been advanced in the United Kingdom. Buzzard had coined the term 'graduated deterrence' as his preferred substitute for massive retaliation and had urged

NATO to acquire the military capabilities necessary for fighting limited wars and the doctrines necessary for their successful prosecution. He was optimistic that meaningful limitations could be found, even in the midst of nuclear war, and that the prospects for observance of such limits were sufficiently good to warrant preparations on that basis. In his own words: 'the problems of making useful distinctions between hydrogen and atomic weapons, and of defining centers of population and their geographic limits, are certainly difficult ones. But provided they are thoroughly studied beforehand, there is no reason to suppose that they are insuperable' (Buzzard 1956a, p. 234). The same general position was advanced by a Royal Institute of International Affairs study group of which Buzzard was a member. Its report urged that Western deterrence would be augmented by increasing the certainty of a response, even if its severity was reduced, and it foresaw the possibility that future wars, even nuclear ones, could be limited as regards extent of theatre, weapons used and targets attacked (Buzzard *et al.*, 1956b).

As the decade wore on, there was growing disenchantment with some of the arguments deployed by the champions of tactical nuclear weaponry and eventually even Kissinger, the best-known of the nuclear advocates, defected and urged that greater emphasis be placed on conventional defence capabilities to supplement the existing nuclear ones. The possibility of limited conventional wars gained greater credence, although limited nuclear wars were not completely discounted. What must be stressed, however, is that even with this change of emphasis from nuclear to conventional warfare, there was no radical questioning of the very principle of limitation in warfare: on the contrary, as the Soviet Union developed its own nuclear arsenal and the days of American ability to inflict massive retaliation with impunity became a distant memory, the arguments in favour of *some* form of limited strategy became all the more compelling. As one writer was to phrase it: 'it was the appearance of the H-bomb, the supposed implications of "massive retaliation", and, above all, the unexpectedly rapid Soviet acquisition of nuclear weapons, that stimulated the search for alternatives to all-out war' (Martin 1977, p. 64).

At the more theoretical level, Schelling (1960) was developing his study of the role of bargaining in limited warfare and of the nature and possibilities of tacit agreements. Some of these studies were pursued using techniques of simulation and models derived from game theory. Meanwhile, with less scholarship but possibly greater public impact, Kahn (1960) was trying to sell to the American people the idea that nuclear war need not mean apocalypse and that there are recognizable degrees of nuclear destruction: such notions are essential for the contemplation of limited war-fighting strategies in the nuclear age.

The next important phase in the evolution of post-war thinking on limits to war was the debate, albeit short-lived, which was engendered by the brief espousal by the Kennedy administration of a 'limited counterforce', or 'no-cities' strategic doctrine. The posture was outlined by Secretary McNamara during 1961–2, but was to disappear from official statements shortly after this period. However, as will be argued shortly, the seeds of that abortive policy were to bring forth a richer harvest in the course of the 1970s.

The McNamara 'no-cities' posture was a perfect example of an attempt to create conventions of nuclear war-limitation. In fact, in reaching backwards to the traditional usages of military power and to the targets against which such power should be directed, and by suggesting that nuclear power might be tailored to recognize such traditional constraints, McNamara was implicitly arguing that the nuclear revolution was less than total, and that nuclear wars could be limited in a manner not entirely remote from traditional practice. In his famous Ann Arbor speech of June 1962, McNamara outlined the basis of the new policy in the following terms:

> The US has come to the conclusion that, to the extent feasible, basic military strategy in a possible general nuclear war should be approached in much the same way that more conventional military operations have been regarded in the past. That is to say, principal military objectives ... should be the destruction of the enemy's military forces, not of his civilian population (quoted in Kissinger 1965, p. 99).

What McNamara was doing was to take the 1950s theorizing about limited war to its logical conclusion and to suggest that reciprocal restraints might be observed even in a nuclear war in which the superpowers themselves were struck. Even in these dire circumstances, there was no need for everything to be lost. Schelling (1966, p. 162) described the McNamara strategy in the following words:

> Even a major attack on military installations need not, according to McNamara's declaration, have to be considered the final, ultimate step in warfare, bursting the floodgates to an indiscriminate contest in pure destruction. He was talking about a much larger and more violent 'limited war' than had theretofore received official discussion, but the principle was the same. What he challenged was the notion that restraint could pertain only to small wars, with a gap or discontinuous jump to the largest of all possible wars, one fought without restraint. His proposal was that restraint could make sense in any war, of any size . . .

In terms of this study, the McNamara 'no-cities' posture is a clear example of an effort to develop conventions of nuclear warfare. Indeed, another theorist of limited war has described the McNamara proposal as 'the most far-reaching application of the idea of contrived reciprocal limitation of warfare' (Osgood 1970, p. 103). McNamara was not claiming that the United States had any assurance of Soviet reciprocity: but that he thought the securing of Soviet compliance a worthwhile objective, there can be little doubt:

> It would certainly be in their interests as well as ours to try to limit the terrible consequences of a nuclear exchange. By building into our forces a flexible capability, we at least eliminate the prospect that we could strike back in only one way, namely, against the entire Soviet target system including their cities. Such a prospect would give the Soviet Union no incentive to withhold attack against our cities in a first strike. We want to give them a better alternative . . . (Kaufmann 1964, pp. 92–3).

In subsequent years, McNamara's statements suggested the abandonment of a counterforce posture in favour of the stability of mutual assured destruction. It would, however, be misleading to conclude that counterforce capabilities were no longer a consideration in the framing of United States' strategic doctrine. Indeed, there are important continuities, in the direction of strategic selectivity, throughout the 1960s and 1970s, and only by bearing these continuities in mind can the significance of Secretary James Schlesinger's later adoption of selective targeting and counterforce capabilities be properly understood: the continuities in the American strategic posture throughout this period belie the appearance, created by the various proclamations of the Schlesinger doctrine, of revolutionary changes in that posture.

The public pronouncement of a switch in US strategic targeting policy, with the intention of targeting a larger array of non-civilian sites and of permitting greater flexibility and selectivity, was prompted by the felt inadequacies of sole reliance on the deterrent threat of assured destruction. President Nixon had repeatedly asserted his dissatisfaction at the possibility of being presented with all-or-nothing choices − the option of doing nothing or launching all-out nuclear attack on Soviet cities. Wohlstetter (1974, p. 1133) had articulated the unease with mutual assured destruction when he had written that 'a policy of unrestrained, indiscriminate attack on Russian civilians, executed without reserve, with no attempt to induce restraint in the Soviet leadership, can serve no purpose of state under any circumstances. If "Mutual Assured Destruction" means a policy of using strategic force only as a reflex to kill populations, it calls for a course of action under every circumstance of attack that makes sense in none.' Even more trenchantly, and with a sense of outrage, Wohlstetter (p. 1127) has commented that 'not even Genghis Khan tried to avoid military targets and to concentrate *only* on killing civilians'.

Schlesinger himself advocated limited nuclear options on two principal grounds: firstly, that such a posture would serve as a more credible deterrent and, secondly, that in the event of deterrence failing, it would provide a better guarantee against the rapid escalation of fighting to an orgy of destruction. Schlesinger's official statement claimed that 'what we need is a series of measured responses to aggression which bear some relation to the provocation, have prospects of terminating hostilities before general nuclear war breaks out, and leave some possibility for restoring deterrence' (Department of Defense 1974). In other words, a limited nuclear war capacity would have a better prospect of deterring war but, should war nonetheless occur, it could be fought with greater control and restraint.

The policy of limited nuclear options was not the radical innovation in American strategic practice which its advocates claimed it to be. The administration's constant reiteration of the novelty of the programme, the better to highlight its superiority over postures past, served only to draw the attention of analysts to constant trends of development. Schlesinger himself conceded that the United States had had options in the past but argued that they had all been relatively massive. The critics of the Schlesinger doctrine were thus able to maintain that the United States had already gone far enough in the direction of a counterforce capability and that to go farther would be acutely destabilizing. Carter (1974, p. 22) accordingly asserted that 'the simple fact, which cannot be stressed too strongly, is that the US strategic forces are now capable of carrying out a large array of alternative missions, far in excess of assured destruction'.

The retargeting that occurred at the beginning of the Kennedy administration, and that was embodied in the Single Integrated Operational Plan, had evidently become a permanent feature of the US posture. As one commentator has remarked: 'even in the brief period of least ambiguous emphasis on MAD – the time surrounding the SALT 1 negotiations – the counterforce mission was never removed from the SIOP. Emphasis on nuclear warfighting and deterrence based on counter-military options, as opposed to countervalue deterrence, has fluctuated . . . but it has never been abandoned' (Betts 1979, pp. 91–2).

That there should have been these strategic continuities is in no way surprising and that Schlesinger should have been articulating in public what was already well-established strategic practice, can be partially explained by Schlesinger's own intellectual background. Schlesinger had spent several years at the RAND Corporation, the think-tank which had carried out various of the seminal studies of limited war; its personnel had been closely associated with the earlier McNamara 'no-cities' initiative (*see* Ball 1975).

Another way of making the same point is to suggest that the central issue of the strategic debate surrounding the selective targeting announcements of 1974 was not, despite the polarized manner in which many of the arguments were presented, whether the United States should have limited options, as against an assured destruction capability alone, but rather what degree of options should be acquired. As two authors were to state: 'the issues are not either—or, as frequently suggested, but more or less: more or less enhanced flexibility; more or less selectivity; more or fewer options; more or less emphasis in planning on limited strikes, on restraint, on precision, on military targets' (van Cleave and Barnett 1974, p. 659).

Even if the Schlesinger statements did not reflect radical changes in the United States' force posture, they did serve to promote a debate on the desirability, or otherwise, of counterforce options and served to focus attention in the latter 1970s on the subject of limited nuclear warfare. From that perspective we can agree with the observation that 'the combination of new technology and evolving doctrine for both strategic and theatre nuclear operations has made the late seventies an unusually active phase in the evolution of the idea of limited nuclear war' (Martin 1979b, p. 118). The issuance by President Carter in 1980 of Presidential Directive No. 59, which affirmed selective and limited nuclear options as American strategic policy, was, in proper perspective, merely the culmination of two decades of strategic restructuring, rather than a new point of departure.

It may be appropriate at this stage to consider briefly the place of these various proposals for limited nuclear war in the longer tradition of restriction on the means of warfare, namely the *ius in bello*. Did the various writers and policy makers who made statements about limits to war in the nuclear age see themselves as self-consciously contributing to that older tradition, or was their intention quite different?

The question may be approached indirectly. One of the principal issues, associated with the counterforce debates of the 1960s, and even more so of the mid-1970s, was whether the purpose of a strategic policy was war-avoidance or, alternatively, the creation of a capacity for war-fighting. Even more fundamentally, the point at issue was whether the pursuit of the latter goal might not undermine the attainment of the former in as much as a capacity for fighting nuclear war in a controlled and restrained fashion might undercut the very deterrence that keeps nuclear war at bay. Garnett draws attention to this dualism in the discussion of limited war when he notes that 'limited war strategies were advanced as a response to two quite different pressures. First, they developed because if deterrence failed men wanted an alternative to annihilation, and second, they developed because many believed that the ability to wage limited war enhanced deterrence. Most limited war theorizing has therefore to be considered from two distinct perspectives; that of those who are interested in waging wars in a controlled fashion, and that of those who wish to avoid war altogether (in Baylis *et al.* 1975, pp. 116–17).

The issue was debated in more strident terms during the 1970s and there is, perhaps, a contrast here with the more traditional search for restraints in war, if we can accept the contention of Geoffrey Best's study *Humanity in Warfare.* Best maintains that the pursuit of restraint in war is supportive of restraint in recourse to war and, as such, the two goals are complementary rather than antagonistic. As Best has argued:

> One cannot contemplate restraint in the conduct of war without being driven to consider restraint in the recourse to war. The law of war on its *jus in bello* side . . . says nothing, dares not say anything about *jus ad bellum*. But thought about the one is barely separable from thought about the other . . . Only a mentally-dulled militarist could study . . . [the laws of war] . . . and be made more warlike; they must make mentally and morally active people less accepting of war (1980, p. 9).

The paradox is that the present purveyors of restraint in the conduct of nuclear war are accused by their critics of trying to make people, like mentally-dulled militarists, more accepting of war and it is in these terms that the most vitriolic parts of the debate have been conducted.

The opponents of the selective and limited options policy accordingly criticized it on the grounds that thinking about limited conduct of war might well hasten its initiation. Carter (1974, p. 30) denounced the counterforce option because 'the Administration's promotion of the option and its general public advocacy of a counterforce strategy might have a pervasive, if subtle, tendency to reduce the inhibitions against the use of nuclear weapons'. Wolfgang Panofsky and Herbert Scoville were similarly fearful that the administration might be leading the American public into a world of dangerous delusions. Panofsky suggested that 'any successful attempt to project an image — however ill-founded — of a "clean" nuclear war generating minimum civilian casualties could make the use of nuclear weapons in limited conflicts more acceptable' (Pranger and Labrie 1977, p. 77). Scoville (1974, p. 175) developed the same line of argument:

> The initiation of nuclear war at any level is a disaster that is more likely to occur if national leaders can fool themselves into believing that it might be kept small and that they might come out the victors. This is less likely to occur in any specific crisis if the military have not prepared plans long in advance and acquired specially designed weapons to fight a limited war.

In other words, if we accept these arguments at face value, we have a situation unique in the history of the *ius in bello* in which the promotion of restraints in the conduct of war exposes the advocate to charges of militarism and incitement. The only just warriors in the past who might have had such charges levelled against them were the 'holy warriors' — those who deemed a just cause of war to override the necessity of observing rules of just conduct. In the present case, however, we have the wholly paradoxical situation in which a policy of restraining the conduct of war is itself deemed execrable.

These critics did not have it all their own way: assertions that limited options would promote war were met by counter-assertions that this was not so. Wolfers (1956b) had two decades earlier emphasized the dangers of *not* thinking about limited war. To conclude that wars must inevitably be unlimited, and to base strategy on this assumption, could lead to dangerous self-fulfilling prophecies. Wolfers had also noted with optimism that 'no government in its senses will conclude that, simply because war could be limited, it necessarily would be' (p. 214).

Other writers in the 1970s refused to see the validity of any relationship between force structuring and the frequency of war. In a balanced review of the various arguments surrounding the Schlesinger programme, Greenwood and Nacht (1974, pp. 771—2) reached the following conclusion:

The history of warfare suggests that decisions to initiate hostilities more frequently than not derive from perceptions and misperceptions of political will. They are rarely triggered by an increase in the real or perceived flexibility of available weaponry. Particularly in the nuclear age, details of military hardware and intricate war plans are unlikely to be crucial in decisions about war and peace between major powers.

If the arguments that the new stragegies would bring on nuclear war were discounted, the case that the limited nuclear warriors belonged to a venerable tradition of moderation in warfare was strengthened. Moreover, the fundamental philosophic premise from which their arguments sprang was identical to that employed by past proponents of limits to war, namely, that wars will occur in any case and the only sensible, the only moral, course of action is to plan to conduct them with as much moderation as is humanly possible. Writing in the 1950s, Osgood (1957, p. 16) had given a full description of the philosophic premise from which limited war strategies derive:

> Because of the imperfection of man, force is a moral necessity . . . Therefore, men are confronted with the fact that their own imperfection makes both force and restraint of force equally imperative from a moral standpoint. There is no way to escape this dilemma. Men can only mitigate its effects. The aim should be, not to abolish force in society, but to moderate it and control it . . .

Kissinger, too, had deprecated the tendency to think in terms of extremes of all-out war or of all-out peace and had urged upon his readers the preferable course of developing principles of war-limitation 'which may not prevent war, but which could keep any conflict that does break out from assuming the most catastrophic form' (1957, p. 206). This was precisely the case that was to be deployed most frequently by the supporters of the new limited war strategy, that deterrence might fail in any case and then what?

> . . . deterrence may fail in any case, and the weapons may have to be used. The ability to conduct selective and limited nuclear strikes for express and restricted purposes . . . promotes the possibility of escalation control, and increases opportunities for war termination without major urban damage (van Cleave and Barnett 1974, p. 661).

There is then a genuine dilemma in locating the current generation of limited warriors within the tradition of *ius in bello*. So much depends upon individual assessments of the intentions underlying their preferred strategies and of the effects of these strategies, intended or otherwise: war-fighting may be less acceptable than war-avoidance, but it is not as clear that limited-war fighting is less acceptable than unrestrained war-fighting. When one also recalls the complex interplay between the preparation for the fighting and the avoidance this may induce, the choices of appropriate action in the nuclear age are seen in their many-sided subtlety.

There are two general issues that remain to be discussed in this overview of proposals for limits to war in the post-1945 period. They concern the role of command and control systems, and the advance planning of such systems, in the effective implementation of conventions of limited warfare. Secondly, and relatedly, the broad theme of technological advance, and its impact upon limited-war thinking, requires some brief exposition.

Analysts were quick to realize that while the central problem of limited war was one of policy — the effective relating of means and ends — there was also a problem of implementation: wars would not remain limited simply by administrative *fiat*. They would have to be effectively controlled so that they might be kept within preordained limits.

Arguably, the notion that one can control war might tell us more about the national traditions of the people holding such a view than about the prospects of controlling war in practice. To the extent that this is so, it may come as no surprise that it is in recent American strategic thought that both the need for, and the possibility of, controlled military action have loomed so large. Kolkowicz (1980, p. 23) locates this tendency in the mainsprings of American intellectual traditions when he expresses the view that 'the roots of modern American strategic theory and doctrine lie in the scientific spirit of the Enlightenment and in the optimistic tradition of the more recent period which envisaged man's ability to control, manage and order conflict by rational scientific and technological means'. The problem of limits to war becomes, then, administrative and technological, rather than political or military in character.

That command and control lay at the heart of limited-war practice was emphasized in the early McNamara proclamations of a counterforce strategy. McNamara told the House Armed Services Committee that America needed a force 'of a character which will permit its use, in the event of attack, in a cool and deliberate fashion and always under the complete control of the constituted authority' (Kaufmann 1964, p. 53). A task force had already been established to investigate problems of command and control and this Partridge Report included details of a command structure which would survive a nuclear attack (Ball 1975, p. 166). This was in line with McNamara's call for the 'machinery for the command and control of our forces which is itself able to survive an attack and to apply the surviving forces in consonance with national security objectives' (Kaufmann 1964, p. 74).

Not only was there a requirement for command and control facilities in the event of war, but detailed operational plans would have to be established in advance. Without such advance preparation, the heat of battle might take the course of war in a direction not sought by either of the belligerents. As Kahn (1960, p. 163) was to express it: 'one of the reasons why modern war is likely to be excessively destructive is that, with events moving so fast, unless pre-attack preparations for evaluation, negotiation, and operational flexibility have been made there is no way for knowledge of the actual military course of events to improve the conduct of operations'.

The European theatre, given the number of tactical nuclear weapons assembled within it, was to present acute problems of command and control for those who favoured limited nuclear operations on that continent. It was difficult to see how effective use could be made of tactical weapons by field commanders while preserving the central direction of a campaign necessary to maintain it within its intended limits. Kissinger (1965, p. 178) had admitted as much: 'controlling a few hundred strategic weapons during military operations is difficult but soluble. Controlling thousands of weapons of many different ranges and characteristics in the confusion of combat is another matter.' Without such control, how are limits to be observed or the intended limits to be communicated to the other side? One author, in fact, fastens on this

problem of communication, between national and field commanders, as the Achilles heel of limited nuclear operations:

> The core of the problem is the conflict between the need for a
> control capability at a national level and the dynamic aspect of
> limited warfare which seems to require some delegation of con-
> trol to field commanders. Establishing a 'balance' between local
> and national command levels is of particular significance under
> conditions of limited nuclear war, especially following the initial
> introduction of nuclear weapons and at the onset of subsequent
> escalatory stages. To the extent that this centralization-decentra-
> lization dilemma remains unresolved, the unmanageability of
> limited nuclear war is vividly apparent (Nash 1975, p. 91).

The other factor to be mentioned is that of technological
advance. Broadly speaking, the extent of options in warfare,
limited or otherwise, is partially dependent on the state of
the technological art. It was to be expected, therefore, that
there would be some interrelationship between limited-war
theory and technological innovation, both feeding on each
other: as weapon design improves, more options are opened
up; simultaneously, the demand for options provides a
stimulus to the design of more flexible weaponry. In any
case, there can be no arguing with one author's general assessment to the effect that 'a wider range of options are tech-
nically possible now than in the 1950s and 1960s when the
first wave of strategic studies emerged' (Wilborn 1977, p. 366).

Indeed, the initial technological impact on early nuclear
strategy was experienced in two forms, one direct, the other
indirect. The direct impact was in the shape of the technical
limitations of the first generation of nuclear weapons which
stamped on post-war strategy its massive, counter-city characteristics. As Iklé has remarked: 'a nuclear weapon small
enough to avoid vast civilian damage, yet accurate enough to
hit most military targets, was not within the technology of
the first nuclear decade' (in Pranger and Labrie 1977, p. 68).
Early nuclear weapons were little more than city-busters and
did little to contribute to theories of limited warfare.

Indirectly, initial thinking about nuclear war was dominated by the technological limitations of a previous generation
of weaponry. The area bombings and counter-city bombings
of the Second World War were shaped, to a large measure, by

the shortcomings of precision bombing and had fostered a strong belief, not to be shaken in some quarters for many years, that the principal function of air power in modern warfare lay in attacking civilian morale by the bombing of cities. From that perspective, as Howard (1970, p. 145) has commented: 'Hiroshima and Nagasaki seemed only a continuation, or at most a culmination, of all that had gone before'. Technology dictated the dominant mode of Second World War bombing: subsequently, Strategic Air Command, which would deliver the atomic bombs, relied upon its wartime experience in thinking about the task with which it was now confronted. In this way, the limitations of the weaponry of the Second World War had a formative influence on attitudes towards the likely nature and conduct of military operations in a world of nuclear weapons. To the Air Chiefs of the period, the conclusion was apparent: 'the strategy that had not fully succeeded against Hitler because of technological limitations', in the words of Iklé, 'now seemed feasible thanks to the atomic bomb. Our new weapons could administer the "knock-out blow" against Russia's cities' (Pranger and Labrie 1977, p. 66).

Then, as subsequently, a more selective and flexible strategy was dependent upon better weapon design (*see* Cane 1978). During the course of the 1970s, the future of selective targeting was regarded as being closely allied with one particular weapon characteristic, namely accuracy. Hitting what you wanted to hit, while not hitting what you did not want to hit, required accurate missiles. One analysis of Schlesinger's limited options programme makes amply clear the importance of accuracy to the strategic directions which Schlesinger wished to follow:

> The Secretary stated candidly that we want to improve our counterforce capability somewhat, particularly through better accuracies. Although he requested research and development funding for a follow-on Minuteman warhead with larger yield, as well as improved accuracy, it is clear that the fundamental vehicle will be the removal of past restrictions on accuracy and other improvements to make selective targeting and retargeting possible (van Cleave and Barnett 1974, p. 670).

So integral was the relationship between the new limited nuclear options and weapons improvement seen to be that the critics of the programme rested a major part of their case on the stimulus which pursuit of counterforce would give to a new round of the technological arms race.

NUCLEAR WAR-LIMITATION AND CONVENTION B

One of the problems in coming to terms with the idea of limited war in the nuclear age is the many possible manifestations of the limits themselves. In response to the initial question of this study – what is limited when war is limited? – theorists in the post-1945 period have produced a variety of answers. One writer tells us that amongst the variants of limited war are to be found such things as local war, theatre war, theatre nuclear war, conventional war, limited nuclear war and wars of national liberations (Kolkowicz 1980, p. 1). These all embody forms of limitation and some of them have actually been experienced in the post-1945 period.

Apart from listing distinct *genres* of limited war, there are other ways of categorizing limitations in the nuclear age. Halperin (1963, p. 28) makes the distinction between limitations of a quantitative and limitations of a qualitative nature:

> One side, for example, may use none of its planes or it may use some of them; one side may bomb none of a particular class of targets or it may bomb some targets in that class, but not others. In the local wars which have taken place in the postwar period both qualitative and quantitative limitations of geography, kinds of targets and kinds of weapons have been observed by the major powers and their allies.

As in Chapter 2, we can begin a survey of forms of nuclear war-limitation by considering instances of convention B, those predominantly concerned with limiting the impact of war, with substantive principles of limitation, with the conduct of warfare rather than the processes of settlement and with humanitarian considerations as opposed to fundamental political procedures.

'What?' conventions

Little need be said in this section that cannot more appropriately be discussed elsewhere. In the context of nuclear weapons, given their tendency towards indiscriminate effects, the issue of what may be done to the enemy has virtually been collapsed into the issue of how it may be done. Nearly all attempts to maintain traditional distinctions between stopping and killing the enemy, or militarily incapacitating as opposed to maiming him, become pointless in themselves: in an age of nuclear weaponry, the purpose of such a distinction can only be served by instituting 'how?' conventions which restrict the nature of the weaponry itself.

Two brief comments may, however, be in order. Firstly, as already stated, the residual elements of a distinction between what is appropriate, and what inappropriate, to do to the enemy have survived in efforts to have nuclear weapons outlawed on the grounds that they are immoral weapons, or illegal weapons, or both. It need scarcely be said that this approach has not inspired much interest on the part of the nuclear powers themselves, and there is no indication whatsoever of the emergence of any conventions of limitation on this particular basis.

Secondly, a possible exception to these broad claims is to be found in some of the literature discussing theatre warfare, mainly in its European variant. In some of these analyses, the use of tactical nuclear weapons, in certain restricted ways, has been recommended on the grounds that it would convey to the enemy an intention to defeat him militarily rather than to inflict punitive damage or to seek his annihilation. Conceivably, a limitation could be devised, and observed, on this basis. But this is to beg the question whether nuclear weapons can be employed only with such selective effects: even the most ardent champion of tactical nuclear war-fighting capabilities would probably concede that, as far as the immediate target is concerned, the effects of such use would tend to be total, since the targets struck would be militarily incapacitated, stopped, maimed and made to suffer.

'Who?' conventions

Stipulation of the legitimate targets of warfare has been one of the most common conventions of limitation in warfare. In consequence, it is scarcely to be wondered at that the issue should have re-emerged as an important one in the analysis of limits to war in the nuclear age, even though the problems of implementing and respecting any such distinctions are greatly magnified by the indiscriminateness of modern-day weapons. Despite this unfavourable weapon environment, the attempt to predicate war-limitation upon 'who?' conventions has been one of the more conspicuous endeavours of limited-war theorizing since 1945.

In this sense, as will become apparent, the primary thrust of the Schlesinger doctrine of 1974 was in the direction of laying the basis of a 'who?' convention. Nor, perhaps, were theories necessarily fanciful that wars might be kept limited as regards the nature of the targets selected for attack. The proponents of such theories could point to numerous positive examples of target restriction in the wars of the post-1945 period, even if these were not central nuclear wars between the major powers. Halperin (1968, p. 96) for instance, appeared to be impressed by the record of such limitations that had been observed, either unilaterally or bilaterally:

> Even within the area of combat both countries have observed limitations on targets attacked, particularly by air power. The United States observed a whole series of different limitations during the Korean War. In the initial stages, it attacked only military targets in North Korea; later it extended the area under attack to industrial targets, but not those close to the Soviet and Chinese borders. Then restrictions on attacks close to the Chinese border were removed. The Chinese, on the other hand, engaged in no bombing at all in South Korea except for some minor heckling raids. In Vietnam, again, the United States observed a varying series of limitations on the targets which it would attack in North and South Vietnam.

Had Halperin written several years later, he might have found the record much less impressive. The point, nonetheless, stands that restrictions on the nature of the targets to be attacked have been observed in post-1945 wars. In the 1967 and 1973 Middle East wars, both sides eschewed the option of large scale strikes against each other's major population centres.

While it has already been argued that early attitudes towards war in the nuclear age were formed by bombing experience during the Second World War, it could also be said that there was an earlier, and intermittent, tradition of attempting to restrict the targets of aerial bombardment which pre-dated that wartime experience: arguably, while total-war theories derived from wartime experience, early limited-war thinking was attracted to those pre-war efforts, however abortive, to establish conventions about the legitimate targets of air attack.

These inter-war efforts had taken various forms and both the British and the Germans, for their own respective ends, had taken the initiative at one time or another. Both had made proposals for conventions of air warfare during the 1930s. The international legal community had also attempted to develop a code of aerial combat which would protect vulnerable civilian populations. Bialer (1980, p. 109) outlines these efforts in the following terms:

> ... three main groups of proposals had been advanced in an attempt to protect the civilian population by a restriction of air bombardment. The first consisted of a corpus of rules governing air warfare (an example of which was provided by those drafted at the Hague in 1923 in an effort to define the legitimate objects of air attack). The second consisted of proposals for the restriction of bombing to such specified areas as 'the battle zone' ... Third, there were proposals made at the Hague for the delimitation of geographical areas which did not contain legitimate military targets and were therefore to be immune from air bombardment.

Even if these efforts were unsuccessful, they created precedents and provided a stock of ideas to which a later generation of limitationists was able to return and to shape to the needs of the nuclear age.

It also has to be recognized that even if no legal code of warfare had been agreed by the outbreak of hostilities, the mode of air warfare from 1939 through to mid-1940 has given encouragement to subsequent theorists that tacit conventions, not to strike population centres, might emerge spontaneously. That fact impressed Bruce Russett and seemed to be important in his own proposal, to be outlined below, for a countercombatant deterrent. In Russett's words; 'the point is not that most of World War II was fought with little restraint on bombing civilian areas – that is obvious. Rather, it is equally important that for quite some time each side did limit its actions and was aware that the other side was doing the same' (1972, p. 208). Even such a seasoned student of military affairs as Liddell-Hart was impressed by this fact and placed responsibility for the infringement of this convention squarely upon allied shoulders:

> Though the bombing of Warsaw and Rotterdam horrified a world not yet acclimated to such air-massacres, these did not take place till the German troops were fighting their way into those cities, and thus conformed to the old rules of siege bombardment ... The Germans' departure from this code during the war can hardly be dated before September 1940 when the night bombing of London was launched, following upon six successive attacks on Berlin by the RAF during the previous fortnight. The Germans were thus strictly justified in describing this as a reprisal (1946, p. 199).

Accordingly, when post-war theorists began to think of the possibilities of limiting war in the nuclear age, it was natural that they should be led to contemplate restrictions on targets as a mode of limitation because there were positive historical precedents which, although by no means completely reassuring, at least seemed worthy of emulation and development.

Within the general strategy of placing restrictions on targets, there seem to have been two dominant avenues of approach. They were outlined in an early study of the possibilities of limiting atomic war:

> In trying to establish distinctions between one type of target and another, there are two lines of thought to follow. One is to consider drawing a line between civilian and military objectives. The other line of thought broadly relates to the conception of distance from a front line, the idea being, of course, to limit atomic attacks to something like a battle area, in its widest sense, but to allow all kinds of attack within that area (Buzzard *et al.* 1957, p. 220).

In seeking limitations upon the nature of targets, post-war theory and policy has explored both of these avenues, although it would probably be true that the former has had greater appeal than the latter. Most of the following discussion will be devoted to the military—civilian dichotomy, but the theories of restriction based on the notion of a battle-zone will also be mentioned.

The theme of restricting warfare to military, rather than civilian targets has manifested itself most clearly in various counterforce targeting proposals of the past three decades. Early discussions of limited nuclear war considered target restriction to be the most likely form of limitation. Thus Wolfers (1956b, p. 228) thought that 'attacks pin-pointed on enemy long-range air bases and even on his nuclear production facilities . . . may also prove compatible with limited warfare'. Similarly, Buzzard, in advancing his case for graduated deterrence, thought that even in a nuclear war, intentional attacks on cities might be avoided: indeed, he was sufficiently sanguine to believe that, in the interests of preserving conventions of target limitation, both sides might be prepared to overlook even the occasional atomic bomb that went astray:

> With some distinctions established well in advance, the problem of limitations seems far from hopeless. For the difference between a bombing policy intentionally designed to strike the middle of cities with hydrogen bombs, and one designed to strike other targets with atomic bombs, but occasionally near-missing a city by mistake, would be obvious. Moreover, the Communists, like us, would be desperately anxious for cities to be spared from mass destruction. Thus both sides would be eager — not reluctant — to overlook an occasional accidental breach of the rules . . . (Buzzard 1956a, pp. 234–5).

Counterforce, as we have seen, soon became an important aspect of the United States' strategic posture and was to remain so from the Kennedy years onwards, periodically receiving reaffirmation and refinement. Even in the late Eisenhower years, US strategic forces were targeted against non-civilian objectives. A study, commissioned in 1959, and finally produced as NESC 2009, developed a targeting policy for the United States in which a mix of counterforce and countervalue targets was created (Ball 1975, p. 163). The emphasis on targeting of military objectives was increased in the first two years of the Kennedy administration, culminating in the promulgation of the McNamara 'no-cities' doctrine. There could be no more patent instance of a 'who?' convention than this design for the conduct of strategic nuclear exchanges in which cities might be spared.

The theme resurfaces once again in the counterforce debates of the 1970s, in the wake of the announcement of the Schlesinger targeting proposals. Once more, the focus of attention was clearly upon choice of targets, and upon the possibility of limited nuclear wars in which initial salvoes would be directed against enemy military installations rather than against centres of population as such. Schlesinger himself, in his previous work with the RAND Corporation, had shown that his own personal preferences lay in the direction of a strategic posture that held out some prospect of sparing cities. He was to write, back in 1967, that, in comparison with city-busting, 'far more rational under almost any imaginable circumstances is to reserve one's own forces ... and thereby create every incentive for the enemy to refrain from striking at one's own cities' (quoted in Martin 1974, p. 161). This was precisely the rationale that was to accompany the targeting proposals announced in 1974.

All along, Schlesinger's case was that a nuclear war fought on selective and limited lines had some chance of confining the number of those at risk in war. In response to the criticism that limited exchanges might not remain limited, Schlesinger restated the wisdom of at least attempting to implement target discrimination as a form of limitation:

> We simply are stating that because there is a possibility of a small exchange escalating to the top, there is no reason why we must make it a certainty by going all the way to the top ourselves. Just because you reach that pessimistic conclusion at the outset does not mean that you must go and bash up the urban industrial base of your opponent ... (Pranger and Labrie 1977, p. 140).

By not doing so, and by trying to preserve 'who?' conventions in a nuclear exchange, Schlesinger argued, both sides could save many millions of lives. In his own scenario of a limited Soviet counterforce attack upon the United States, Schlesinger estimated casualties of one and a half millions. While he conceded that these were 'highly undesirable circumstances', he nonetheless maintained that 'the number of fatalities here is a relatively small fraction, less than one per cent, of the fatalities associated with a massive attack against the United States which includes direct attacks on our cities' (Pranger and Labrie 1977, p. 129).

The fact that limited nuclear war could be spoken about in these terms in the mid-1970s demonstrated, perhaps, how far the centre of intellectual gravity had moved on this issue since the 1950s. While it was commonplace for the debates of the 1970s to be framed in terms of limited attacks on military sites in the United States and in the Soviet Union – that was, after all, the contingency to which Schlesinger's statements were addressed – in the 1950s Bernard Brodie, who was not otherwise known for his 'softness', had been confident that limited wars could be ones only in which the homelands of the superpowers were left completely inviolate:

> Limited war might conceivably include strategic bombing carried on in a selective or otherwise limited manner, for example bombing with nuclear weapons on selected targets such as airfields while being as careful as possible not to hit cities . . . But usage has already crystallized enough to indicate that such strategies are not generally included in the meaning of the term 'limited war' (Brodie 1959, p. 310).

By the 1970s, it was precisely such a situation that was the most widely discussed variant of limited war: Brodie's limits on targets had, by that date, seemingly come to be considered by policy makers as overly-restrictive for proper strategic management.

A major qualification needs now to be introduced into this review of counterforce postures and their relationship to target restrictions in war. What has to be emphasized is that in no case mentioned so far was it the intention that counterforce targeting be adopted to the complete exclusion of countervalue objectives: rather what was being proposed was that the United States should target other sites *in addition* to cities, *not instead* of them. As the basis of a convention about discrimination in war targets, the various counterforce doctrines enumerated so far must therefore be appreciated as extremely tenuous conventions. This becomes apparent in the official descriptions of both the McNamara and Schlesinger programmes. A summary of McNamara's rationale for his 'no cities' posture, provided by a close associate of the Secretary, makes this point unequivocally when it says that 'it would be foolish . . . automatically to destroy cities at the outset of the war when they could always be taken under attack by reserve forces at some later stage . . .' (Kaufmann 1964, p. 52). Likewise, various elaborations of the subsequent Schlesinger position demonstrated that counterforce was an addition to countervalue targeting, rather than an alternative to it. Schlesinger commented revealingly upon an assured destruction capacity against Soviet cities that 'our intention is that this should not be the only option and possibly not the primary option' (Ball 1975, p. 152). On any intelligent reading of this statement, attacks against cities were still accorded a high priority: Schlesinger's demotion of city-busting was nothing if not circumspect.

In as much as the principal intent of the counterforce warriors is to discriminate between various targets of war, this would seem to place them within the mainstream of the classical *ius in bello* tradition. At any rate, in some of the counterforce literature the argument is presented in moral terms and explicitly hearkens back to that earlier notion of just conduct of war. Thus one writer concedes that Schlesinger's counterforce doctrine 'does recognize the combatant—noncombatant dichotomy, and focuses its primary threat against combatants and military facilities. It accepts the notion of proportionality and at least implies the use of minimum necessary force' (Wilborn 1977, p. 355). Likewise, Gray and Payne (1980, p. 17) employ a crude just war standard to conclude, on the grounds of its assured destruction component, that 'US nuclear strategy is immoral'. At the time of the McNamara proposals, Roszak (1963, p. 102) had denounced assured destruction as a basis of strategic policy for the reason that 'minimum deterrence fails wholly to qualify as a form of justified warfare. The threat it makes is made directly against civilian populations'. The same author, however, was less than convinced that McNamara's counterforce programme came any nearer to satisfying just war criteria.

In most discussions of this issue, the just war reasons for discrimination in targeting are accorded a much less prominent place: even when moral reasons are acknowledged, they are presented as supporting arguments, and not necessarily the most important. Herman Kahn provides a succinct demonstration of this. Having asserted that 'bonus' damage in the form of civilian deaths is 'basically an immoral idea', Kahn (1960, p. 171) proceeds to outline the basis of this judgment:

> It became reputable and could be justified in World War I and World War II, only because of military necessity. In those wars civilian morale played an essential role in furnishing men and materials to the fighting fronts. This is no longer true, and therefore civilians and their property are no longer military targets. The idea of bonus nonmilitary damage is now not only immoral, it is senseless.

One gets the impression that it is the senselessness of civilian slaughter, in military and political terms, rather than its immorality, that evokes Kahn's condemnation.

If this eschewing of the moral case for target discrimination in warfare is evident amongst the theorists of limited war, it is even more so in the case of the policy makers. Thus one commentator pronounces without qualification that 'the issue of the morality of a policy which deliberately holds civilians hostage was not a part of the official justification of Schlesinger's doctrine' (Wilborn 1977, p. 347). When allusion was made by the administration to the moral dimensions of strategic policy, it was done in a perfunctory manner. President Nixon had, in his May 1973 foreign policy report, intimated rather vaguely that deterrence based on a capacity for massive civilian carnage was 'inconsistent with American values' (quoted in Ball 1975, p. 192). Meanwhile, Schlesinger was to make token reference to the moral issue while revealing the more profound reasons for his disquiet with the policy of assured destruction: 'not only must those in power consider the morality of threatening such terrible retribution on the Soviet people for some ill-defined transgression by their leaders; in the most practical terms, they must also question the prudence and plausibility of such a response . . .' (quoted in van Cleave and Barnett 1974, p. 669).

The recent targeting literature most closely approximates traditional just war doctrine, and its emphasis upon noncombatant immunity, at the hands of a specific group of 'moral counterforce' theorists. This approach to the morality of establishing 'who?' conventions in nuclear warfare is best exemplified in the writings of Paul Ramsey, Arthur Burns,

Bruce Russett and Fred Iklé and it may be useful to provide brief summaries of the arguments for counterforce postures advanced by these various writers. Let it be noted, however, that while these are being presented as moral theories in support of counterforce warfare, such views have been dismissed by other writers as immoral, and their authors as mere apologists of nuclear war. Had Kant been alive today, he might well have regarded them as the new breed of 'miserable comforters'.

The case that those authors deserve the appellation of just warriors, is most conspicuously based upon the centrality of targeting discrimination to their various proposals. In particular, all seek that the strategic posture of the West be directed principally against the combatant capabilities of the Soviet Union. For Paul Ramsey, nuclear war should still be governed by a code of just conduct and he believes that a counterforce policy is the only one consistent with such a code. Moreover, he believes that the unintended collateral damage flowing from even a counterforce strike would be sufficient to deter aggression, without the need to take the additional step of threatening to inflict massive civilian casualties intentionally. As Ramsey (1963, p. 48) expressed his case:

> The collateral civilian damage that would result from counterforce warfare in its maximum form may itself be quite sufficient to deter either side from going too high and to preserve the rules and tacit agreements limiting conflict in the nuclear age. In that case, deterrence during war and collateral civilian damage are both 'indirect effects' of a plan and action of war which would be licit or permitted by the traditional rules of civilized conduct in war.

It is on precisely these grounds – that Ramsey's deterrence depends crucially upon collateral effects which are 'unintended', although foreseen – that he has been most severely criticized.

Arthur Burns may also fairly be offered as an example of a contemporary just warrior whose theory is predicated upon observance of 'who?' distinctions. Burns (1970, p. 15) contends that deterrence, based upon holding cities hostage, and threatening to obliterate them, cannot be reconciled with traditional principles of the just employment of armed force, and suggests as an alternative strategy 'nuclear retaliation against combatant forces and against instruments of war only'. The moral tone of Burns' argument is pervasive, as in his statement: 'I cannot escape the ethical conclusion that a strategy of nuclear deterrence and nuclear combat which sought deliberately to spare noncombatants is less evil than counter-city or mixed-target strategies of deterrence' (p. 26).

Writing at approximately the same time, Bruce Russett arrived at a position similar to that of Burns. He, too, advocated a countercombatant strategy and did so on primarily moral grounds. What does he mean by a countercombatant strategy? He intends that nuclear weapons be used against the enemy's military, and military-related, facilities:

> By countercombatant I mean to include first all of the basic nuclear striking forces of the enemy and their immediate support facilities: missile silos, military air bases, nuclear submarines and submarine bases, air defense and ABM systems, and weapons-oriented atomic energy plants. More than that, it would include internal security forces, all military bases of any kind, and those transport facilities devoted primarily to the movement of troops and military supplies (Russett 1972, p. 218).

It is immediately clear that Russett's list of targets, albeit limited, is nonetheless extensive. Despite this, he remained confident, in sentiments to be expressed virtually verbatim by Secretary Schlesinger some few years later, that 'a countercombatant strategy *could* be implemented, indeed even to the extent of striking at a wide range of military facilities without much regard to their location, without inflicting nearly such a high level of civilian casualties as would be implied by a deliberate countercity strategy' (pp. 220–1).

Fred Iklé might be considered to be on the fringes of this 'moral counterforce' school of thought. His design was for the targeting of military, industrial and transportation facilities in the Soviet Union — what he was to term 'the sinews and muscles' of the country. He saw this as an infinitely preferable strategy to the barbarities of assured destruction of populations:

> The jargon of American strategic analysis works like a narcotic. It dulls our sense of moral outrage about the tragic confrontation of nuclear arsenals, primed and constantly perfected to unleash

> widespread genocide. It fosters the current smug complacence
> regarding the soundness and stability of mutual deterrence. It
> blinds us to the fact that our method for preventing nuclear war
> rests on a form of warfare universally condemned since the Dark
> Ages – the mass killing of hostages (Iklé 1977, p. 70).

However, Iklé's deprecation of city-busting, like Schlesinger's
subsequent attempt at target discrimination, was subject to
the significant qualification that 'the risk of the destruction
of cities would still loom in the background' (p. 73).

One last proposal should be mentioned in the present context, although it is substantially different from those so far
presented. It is to be found in the argument of Gray and
Payne (1980) that even the counterforce proposals of
Schlesinger fall short of providing the United States with a
genuine nuclear war-fighting capacity and, what is more, fall
short of providing the United States with a war-winning
capacity. Regardless of the ultimate objectives of the Gray
and Payne strategy, its operational mode is predicated upon
discrimination in targets and the avoidance of all-out nuclear
attacks on population centres. As already mentioned, the
authors criticize assured destruction on the grounds that it
fails to measure up to just war criteria for the conduct of
warfare. In its stead, they recommend a variant of counterforce with an important embellishment: 'the first priority of
such a targeting scheme would be Soviet military power of all
kinds, and the second would be the political, military, and
economic control structure of the USSR' (p. 24). In amplification of the second aspect, they suggest that 'striking the
USSR should entail targeting the relocation bunkers of the
top political and bureaucratic leadership, including those of
the KGB; key communication centers of the Communist
party, the military, and the government; and many of the
economic, political and military records' (p. 24).

In the context of a study of conventions of limits to war,
such a proposal raises fundamental problems. Is not such an
approach to limited warfare self-negating? To their credit,
Gray and Payne intimate as much when they ask: 'is it
sensible to destroy the government of the enemy, thus
eliminating the option of negotiating an end to the war?'
(p. 24), but unfortunately the authors offer no answer to this

question. Surely a strategy of limited nuclear warfare directed against the command and control system of the other side hopelessly undermines any prospect of continued limitation and is bound, sooner rather than later, to destroy itself? After all, theorists of limited war had long ago insisted that 'unless both sides are determined to fight out the war until all strategic forces have been employed, they will be as interested in having the enemy maintain control over his strategic forces as they are in maintaining control over theirs' (Halperin 1963, p. 101).

So far we have considered those 'who?' conventions that are based upon an explicit distinction between combatants and noncombatants, or between counterforce targets and countervalue targets. As previously suggested, another, although less common, line of thought has been to propose a distinction between so-called tactical targets and so-called strategic targets (*see* Osgood 1957, pp. 254–5, Buzzard *et al.* 1957, p. 220). As a form of war-limitation, such proposals would tend to have the effect that civilians outside the battle-zone, however defined, are accorded protection, whereas those within the battle-zone become legitimate targets. Such a convention would still be essentially of a 'who?' type but the immunity would be accorded to persons as much on the basis of their location as of their function.

However, there are major difficulties with this approach and Arnold Wolfers was quick to seize upon them in the mid-1950s. What concerned Wolfers was the imprecision, or inappropriateness, of the idea of a battle-zone in the context of nuclear war. Wolfers (1956b, pp. 217–18) feared that, rather than target discrimination deriving from the confines of the battle-zone, it would be the battle-zone which would be defined by the actual choice of targets:

> Tactical targets are understood to be those that lie inside the battle and communication zone. However ... the notion of such a geographically limited battle and communication zone has lost most of its earlier meaning ... [T]here is no way of deciding on the targets of nuclear warfare by reference to an ill-defined tactical zone. Instead one has to reverse the process, calling 'battle and communications zone' of the land armies that area to which one intends to limit nuclear bombardment ...

In these various ways have theorists and policy makers alike proposed to reintroduce into contemporary warfare a form of limitation that has been historically prevalent. Given the steady obliteration of the combatant–noncombatant distinction in the course of twentieth century warfare, and given the indiscriminate effects of most nuclear weapons, these proposals could not have been made in less auspicious circumstances. That they should nonetheless have been made, despite the multiplicity of their precise forms, seems once again to lend weight to Walzer's suggestion that, of all the limits to war, the 'who?' conventions are the most important.

'How?' conventions

The very indiscriminateness of weapons impresses upon us the intimate relationship between 'who?' conventions and 'how?' conventions: given weapons that are not themselves discerning, which targets are struck is in large measure dependent upon how targets are struck. It must be conceded, therefore, that there is some artificiality in treating the instruments of war in isolation from the targets at which they are directed. However, it is to those limits to war that are based upon discrimination in its weapons that we must now turn.

In this nuclear age, there seems to be no consensus as to whether limits to war are dependent upon discrimination in types of weapons used. To some people, it is evident that non-use of nuclear weapons is the *sine qua non* of war-limitation at the present time. Alternatively, at least as many writers have denied that there is an essential link between nuclear self-denial and limitation *per se*: the limits to war might be discovered at higher levels, but this is not to say that limits cannot be found, or will not be observed, even if nuclear weapons are introduced. For instance, it was Osgood's considered opinion that 'nothing inherent in a wide range of atomic weapons renders them incompatible with limited war, apart from the targets towards which they are directed and the political context in which they are employed' (1957, p. 248). It is apparent from this formulation that Osgood considers conventions about the political objectives of war, and about legitimate targets, to be more important to the limitation of war than conventions about use or non-use of specific weapon systems.

Part of the explanation as to why Osgood should have reached this conclusion, lies in the confidence with which early theorists of limited war believed that meaningful distinctions between types of nuclear weapons could be monitored and, in consequence, the observance of agreed limitations enforced. Typical of this early optimism was one study group's conclusion that, as the blast of atomic explosions could be measured, 'once an agreement had been reached, either tacit or explicit, a country over-stepping the limit could be detected by means of the effects left by the explosion of its weapons' (Buzzard *et al.* 1957, p. 219).

Moreover, as in the case of target restrictions, the belief that conventions governing the instruments of war were possible, was strengthened by post-1945 examples of the actual observance of such codes. Admittedly, there was no instance of discrimination as between different types of nuclear weapon, but there were precedents in the non-use of some other weapon categories. Thus Halperin (1968 pp. 96—7) eagerly drew attention to recent experience in this area:

Not using nuclear weapons has been perhaps the most significant limitation which has been adhered to by the superpowers . . .
Other limitations on weapons have been observed . . . No countries have, for example, used biological or chemical weapons; and the Chinese Communists and the Russians have refrained from introducing various kinds of weaponry, including submarines and bombers, into a number of limited-war situations.

An important observation that should be made upon the early post-war history of proposed weapons' limitation is that there was a powerful tendency for the technology of the weapons themselves to dictate the nature and scope of possible limited usage, rather than for a doctrine of limitation to direct and stimulate weapon development: the technology tended to dictate the strategic theory rather than vice-versa. Nowhere was this better exemplified than in the statement in 1952, by Gordon Dean, the Chairman of the US Atomic Energy Commission, in support of an appropriation for research into tactical nuclear weapons. 'The setting in which this request is made,' explained the Chairman, 'stems from recent revolutionary developments in the field of atomic weapons technology. Through these developments, the whole concept of how atomic weapons can be utilized in warfare has been radically revised. No longer are they to be used in a "Hiroshima-type" way against cities and industrial areas' (quoted in van Cleave and Cohen 1978, p. 4). The sequence of development is therein clear: it is the state of the technical art which dictates the strategic practice and the possibility of limited use of weapons depends more upon the weapons themselves than upon conscious theories of limitation. Another writer has discerned this same chronological order:

> In 1953 and 1954, Administration spokesmen did not clearly differentiate between different types of nuclear weapons and the different purposes to which they might be put. However, as the weapon development programmes progressed, tactical nuclear weapons began to be linked more and more with 'limited' war. The appearance of the weapons in sufficient numbers for battlefield use in 1954 and 1955 helped to legitimize limited nuclear war in the thinking of the Administration. Once again one has an example of doctrine, and the years of its subsequent evolutions, following from a particular achievement in weapon development (SIPRI 1978a, pp. 11–12).

To the extent that this suggestion is valid, we would have to recognize that doctrines of limited war have been promoted, not only by political and strategic theorists, but also by physicists, technicians and engineers.

Insofar as limits to war in the nuclear age have been discussed in association with limitations upon the nature of weapons to be used, the issues have centred on the distinctions between strategic nuclear, tactical nuclear and conventional weapons, and upon the possible relationships between these categories. For the most part, the limits upon the means of warfare have, therefore, been conceived in terms of thresholds between these types of weapons. Most of the following discussion of 'how?' conventions in contemporary warfare will, accordingly, be structured around the strategic, tactical and conventional instruments of combat.

As to the employment of strategic nuclear weapons, least need be said. Although various authors believe that strategic nuclear exchanges can be conducted in a limited fashion (*see* Knorr and Read 1962, Halperin 1963), there is no way in which the use of strategic weapons can, of itself, constitute a limitation: as far as the destructiveness of weapons goes, use of a strategic nuclear arsenal cannot be *preferred* to some more hideous option. When, therefore, we speak of limitation in relation to strategic warfare, the limitation cannot be a function of the weapons themselves, but only of the manner of their use. Most obviously, the employment of strategic weapons might be subject to quantitative restraints – the number of ICBMs fired, or subject to chronological restraint – fired in sequence with pauses inbetween, but there is no way in which the weapons themselves can limit war by preventing escalation to a grosser form. The most likely pattern of limitation in strategic exchange is with regard to the targets at which these weapons are directed, but at that point we revert from a 'how?' convention back to a 'who?' convention. In the strict sense of a 'how?' convention, strategic weapons are illimitable because when they are employed, nothing remains to be withheld.

In the light of this, it follows that much of the discussion has concerned itself with the use of weapons short of strategic capabilities, namely tactical nuclear and conventional weapons. During the 1950s, it was the use of tactical nuclear weapons that provided the most popular vision of future limited wars. Some of the reasons for this had little to do with the limitability of these weapons, but were related to NATO's perceived inferiority in conventional forces and to the economic pressures for reduced defence spending. To some commentators, however, the utility of tactical weapons lay not only in the fact that they served these Western ends, but also in their specific characteristics which held out the prospect that wars could be fought with them while remaining at a restrained level. It was on the basis of this conviction that Osgood (1957, p. 251) declared that 'for the foreseeable future the peculiar importance of tactical nuclear weapons lies in the fact that they carry greater promise than any other weapon of enabling us to fight limited wars on an equal basis against numerically superior forces'. What was novel about the doctrine created around tactical nuclear weapons during the mid-1950s, was that their employment was envisaged as a substitute for strategic exchanges, rather than as a supplement to them. It was from this perspective that their contribution to limited-war theory was to be increasingly appreciated.

Kissinger's was the name most closely associated with this new version of tactical limits to war. Like the other exponents of tactical nuclear warfare at this time, Kissinger believed that the collateral damage resulting from battlefield use of these weapons could be kept at acceptably low levels, and this in spite of some early evidence to the contrary: a wargame, conducted in 1955 under the name of Carte Blanche, had suggested much higher levels of civilian death and damage than previously expected. In the first flush of enthusiasm, the pro-tactical lobby made elaborate suggestions as to how nuclear weapons, of restricted sizes only, might be used without further escalation. Kissinger himself produced the magical figure of a 'limit' of 500 kilotons upon the explosive power of weapons to be used, in the hope that the Soviets might reciprocate (1957, p. 228).

Subsequently, of course, Kissinger was to recant. He felt less confident that a tactically-limited war would remain so and saw greater virtue in conventional defences. Kissinger (1960, p. 803) noted the argument of some of the critics that 'if the distinction between the low-yield and high-yield weapons is so difficult, if so much depends on the manner of employing them, any effort to set limits based on explosive equivalent will be meaningless'.

By the early 1960s, this scepticism about the limited impact and non-escalatory properties of tactical nuclear weapons was being voiced in the highest échelons of the Kennedy administration. McNamara made it plain that he was less than convinced of the virtues of tactical weapons:

> Nuclear weapons, even in the lower kiloton ranges, are extremely destructive devices and hardly the preferred weapons to defend such heavily populated areas as Europe. Furthermore, while it does not necessarily follow that the use of tactical nuclear weapons must inevitably escalate into global nuclear war, it does present a very definite threshold, beyond which we enter a vast unknown (Kaufmann 1964, p. 97).

It is arguable that there was some internal inconsistency between McNamara's policy on the limited and selective use of the strategic arsenal and his doubts about the damage-limiting and non-escalatory prospects of a tactical nuclear war. What is noteworthy in this regard is that precisely the same charge was subsequently to be levelled against Schlesinger: it would seem that for some reason those policy makers who have most emphasized the possibilities of limited strategic war have also been those who have been least encouraging about the prospects of restraining a tactical one. At any rate, van Cleave and Cohen (1978) complain of Schlesinger that he suffered from a form of schizophrenia in his attitudes towards limited war. They observe bitterly of the *Department of Defense FY 1975 Report* that it conveys the impression that:

> ... strategic nuclear exchanges with the USSR can be controlled and should be planned for, while tactical use of nuclear weapons ... cannot be; ... that it is possible to be very discriminate and to reduce collateral damage meaningfully, while carefully controlling escalation, in a strategic nuclear exchange, but not in the tactical use of nuclear weapons ... (pp. 18–19).

Underlying almost all of the arguments against employment of tactical nuclear weapons lies the contention that, however limited their use, they adversely affect limitation by their very breach of the nuclear threshold. This argument recurs in many discussions of limits to war in the nuclear age. No one emphasized the point more lucidly than did Schelling. ' "No nuclears" is simple and unambiguous,' he wrote, ' "some nuclears" would be more complicated' (1966, p. 132). It was this reasoning, Schelling concluded, which had prevailed during the Korean war: 'in Korea, weapons were limited by the qualitative distinction between atomic and all other; it would surely have been much more difficult to stabilize a tacit acceptance of any limit on size of atomic weapons or selection of targets' (1960, p. 76).

Kissinger's attitude toward the nuclear threshold appeared more ambivalent. While, by 1960, he was prepared to concede that a nuclear war would be more difficult to limit than a conventional one, he remained suspicious of the argument that when that nuclear barrier was violated, there was no prospect of subsequent restraint. On the contrary, Kissinger (1965, p. 181) was insistent that limitation in the conduct of war could still be a characteristic of the post-nuclear phase of hostilities:

> There may be no *logical* stopping place once nuclear weapons are being used. There is, however, a very crucial *psychological* obstacle to automatic escalation. When mutual invulnerability guarantees catastrophic destruction and offers no prospect of great military advantage, neither side can be very eager to let escalation proceed automatically. Both sides are likely to look for excuses to limit, not expand, military operations.

Perhaps Kissinger was being overly-sanguine on this occasion. He does not explain why a psychological obstacle which has failed once, should succeed second time around – why an obstacle breached once should later prove impregnable, and should moderate that very nuclear war which it had failed to prevent.

If the nuclear threshold were not to be breached, the only remaining option was that war be limited to a conventional contest. Thus at various times from the late 1950s onwards, theorists of limited war have directed their attention to the problems, and to the opportunities, of restricting warfare to the conventional realm. From the point of view of Western strategy, the main incentive for a concentration upon conventional defence was to provide a flexible response capability by means of which any Soviet probe, however small, could be responded to on an appropriate scale: the smaller the deterrent value of a massive nuclear retaliatory strike was perceived to be, the greater was the attention devoted to sub-nuclear forms of warfare. McNamara, amongst others, was to voice this rationale:

> Even in limited war situations, we should not preclude the use of tactical nuclear weapons, for no one can foreshadow how such situations might develop. But the decision to employ tactical nuclear weapons in limited conflicts should not be forced upon us simply because we have no other means to cope with them . . . What is being proposed at this time is . . . an increase in our non-nuclear capabilities to provide a greater degree of versatility to our limited war forces (quoted in Kaufmann 1964, pp. 59–60).

Conventional war was, therefore, to appear both in the theoretical literature and in policy statements as a major possible form of future limited war. To the extent that wars would be fought on a 'conventional weapons only' basis, they would represent perfect embodiments of 'how?' conventions in that they would be predicated upon the withholding of other, more powerful, weapons. Just as Eretria and Chalkis were to eschew the use of long-range missiles, so contemporary warring states might agree not to employ their nuclear arsenals. As Martin (1977, p. 71) was to put it: 'insofar as the theory of conventional defense requires both sides to prefer the verdict of the battlefield without appeal to nuclear weapons, either tactical or strategic, it is something of a limited option, even though it accepts the possibility of a very substantial war . . .'

To conclude this section, it should also be stated that, apart from discussion of limited war in its specific strategic, tactical or conventional variants, theorists have posited the limitation of war in terms of a bewildering array of mutually-reinforcing and mutually-undermining relationships between these various forms of combat. To some analysts, it is the strategic threat that will keep war within its conventional confines; others have reversed the relationship and argued that it is successful conventional limitation that will prevent nuclear escalation; to others again, tactical nuclear weapons provide the linchpin that will relate the various forms of limitation to each other.

These complex arguments may be briefly illustrated as a demonstration of the subtleties of 'how?' conventions in the nuclear age. Kissinger is an example of the first train of thought and maintained that it was the real prospect of nuclear war that would strengthen the conventional limits. 'Conventional war can be kept conventional,' he asserted, 'only if we maintain, together with our retaliatory force, an adequate capability for limited nuclear war' (1960, p. 810). Others insisted that it was conventional limitation which was the essential element if nuclear escalation was to be forestalled. In the words of one writer: 'unlimited, or total, conventional war in the age of nuclear plenty is a contradiction' (King 1957, p. 244). Both are saying much the same thing:

the difference is in perspective, the former looking down from the nuclear heights, the latter looking up from the conventional basement. Tactical nuclear weapons were deemed to occupy an uncertain limbo between the other two: their proponents thought they might strengthen the prospects of conventional limitation by providing a link in the chain which would make credible the ascent to strategic nuclear exchange.

'When?' conventions

These have not occupied a prominent place in post-1945 proposals for setting limits to war. To a large extent, this is so because of the feeling that future wars, especially in the missile age, would be compressed in time and that they would not be amenable to chronological limitation: nuclear war would tend to be spasm war and, whatever other aspects might lend themselves to limitation, the temporal dimension did not. The truce, holy or otherwise, has as a consequence not greatly exercised the minds of the theorists of limited nuclear war.

There are two possible exceptions to this general statement. The time dimensions of limits to war have been raised in the proposals which focus, firstly, upon the notion of slow-motion warfare and, secondly, upon the notion of the pause or 'breathing space'. In some versions, the two propositions are almost indistinguishable, but they can be briefly described in separation.

The first idea refers to the fact that nuclear exchanges could occur in a rapid or virtually instantaneous salvo and, as a result, if there is to be any prospect of limiting the course of the war, this can be done only by breaking into the sequence of action and by conducting operations at an artificially slow pace. Given the speed of modern war, if policy is to be allowed to exercise some controlling influence on its course, its tempo must be slowed down. It was with some such notion in mind that Kissinger (1957, p. 226) recommended that 'strategic doctrine should address itself to the problem of slowing down, if not the pace of military operations, at least the rapidity with which they succeed each other'.

The second possible form of time convention is associated with the doctrine of the pause, which has, at various times and in various guises, been a part of NATO's strategy for the defence of Western Europe. What was implied by the doctrine was that at some crucial stage in the fighting, almost certainly at one or other threshold, the antagonists might desist from their military operations, in order to ponder the consequences of crossing the next threshold. Although such a pause might be of only brief duration, it would be the nearest nuclear analogue to the traditional military truce. This formed a part of McNamara's thinking when he was attracted to counterforce options: apparently he requested the Joint Chiefs to prepare plans which would allow for 'negotiating pauses' in the event of nucleear war (Ball 1975, p. 164).

What should be apparent from these sketchy comments is that neither slow-motion nor pause conventions, in themselves, limit war. What they could do, in an otherwise frenetic atmosphere, is to provide the essential preconditions for other conventions of limitation to come into operation.

'Where?' conventions

The possibility of geographical constraints upon war has played an important role in the elaboration of recent theory on limits to war. This is not to be wondered at: early on, Schelling impressed upon readers that it was vital that limits in war, to be observed successfully, be salient. This was a virtue of spatial limits for, in one author's words, geography 'is the easiest, most practicable limitation to establish, to observe, and to communicate' (Osgood 1957, p. 244).

This salience had led, so limited-war theorists argued, to the actual observance of geographical restriction in post-1945 local wars. Almost all writers pointed to the role of the Yalu River in the Korean war as an instance of this salience in operation. Some writers saw the Cuban crisis and Vietnam (albeit before the Cambodian imbroglio) as providing promising examples of wars, or major crises, which were played out in confined, and mutually recognized, geographic theatres.

Apart from those investigations of geographically-limited

war that examined the role of sanctuaries, the two most obvious manifestations of spatial conventions are to be found in
the notions that major wars might be confined to theatres
outside of Europe, or, in complete contrast, that a war might
be confined to the European continent itself.

The former of these scenarios owes its lineage directly to
the Korean experience. This had fostered the belief that even
major confrontations betwen the blocs might conceivably be
restricted to the region in which the conflict manifested itself. One group of writers, reasoning along these lines, even
expressed the opinion that 'there is no inherent reason, for
instance, why all-out war with full-scale hydrogen bombs
should not develop in the Far East without spreading to
Europe' (Buzzard *et al.* 1957, p. 221).

Just as Asians might have been less than enthusiastic about
such a convention, so Europeans have for many years har-
boured resentful suspicions that the most likely form of
limited war between the two blocs would be one fought on
European soil in which the limits redound to the benefit of
the two superpowers. Myrdal (1980, p. 84) is one of the
many to voice this apprehension:

> The increasingly unthinkable danger to both the contesting super-
> powers of a head-on war explains their interest in planning for a
> 'limited' war. Such wars do not imply the use of available stra-
> tegic nuclear weapons against each other. Rather the homelands
> of the superpowers become 'sanctuaries', while wars . . . are to be
> fought in the territories of lesser powers.

The same anxiety had a venerable heritage in European
thought. It had been expressed two decades earlier by
Raymond Aron. 'This sort of limitation,' Aron (1958, p. 72)
complained, 'the big powers dealing gently with one another
but devastating the territories of their allies – would seem to
the Europeans on both sides of the Iron Curtain the culmination of irony and horror'. Indeed it was this fear, that
McNamara's 'no-cities' doctrine might be the first stage in the
creation of continental sanctuaries for the superpowers, and
that it might decouple intercontinental deterrence from the
European battlefield, which accounts for the rather cold
reception received by McNamara's proposals in Western

Europe. More so than any other of the limitations which have been suggested for war in the nuclear age, these geographic conventions have aroused cynicism and hostility in those not fortunate enough to inhabit either the Soviet Union or the United States.

NUCLEAR WAR-LIMITATION AND CONVENTION A

So far, we have considered those writings and policy statements which have been concerned with conventions which, individually, would result in substantive limitation upon the conduct of nuclear war. Now we must turn to discussion of those conventions of type A which, to a greater or lesser degree, seek to define the process of nuclear war.

The immediate conclusion to which we are drawn, on the basis of a review of theorizing on limited nuclear war, is that the problems of engendering limitation in war *via* a politically-meaningful stipulation of the process itself, have received less frequent and less penetrating analyses than have the details of individual forms of limitation. We are thus faced with a curious paradox. On the one hand, theorists have responded to nuclear weaponry by quickly reasserting traditional forms of limitation in warfare, or by adapting these forms to nuclear conditions: even nuclear wars, they have assumed, can be meaningfully limited. On the other hand, it is apparent that the confident reassertion of limitation in warfare is in no way accompanied by comparable expositions of the fundamental nature of the war that is to be limited. It is not too much to say that theorists of nuclear warfare, in attempting to come to political terms with the new technologies of destruction, have placed the cart of practical limitations before the horse of the theory of war. Instead of deducing the relevance of traditional measures of limitation from a continuing concept of war, they have conversely assumed war's continuing nature from the persistence of its modes of limitation. Not only is this to get the argument the wrong way round, but it is also to create a hopeless divorce between the practical implementation of limits in war and any theoretical underpinning which could lend those limits credence.

In what ways are limited nuclear options intellectually integrated with the process of nuclear war? What is the precise point of such war and how does substantive limitation in its conduct contribute towards that end? These are the major issues associated with limited nuclear warfare but, as yet, there has been only faltering investigation of them.

In no respect is this more so than in the examination of that crucial aspect of war's process, namely, the reasons for, and the manner of, its termination. There can be no realistic appreciation of the nature of warfare in the nuclear age without clear and rigorous thought as to what objectives are to be attained by recourse to it, as to how these objectives are to be attained and as to how the attainment of them is to be recognized. Without any such politically-meaningful termination, warfare loses its point. It has to be said that the problem of termination, which is such an integral element of the very process of war, appears in an especially acute form when nuclear weapons are employed. Coser (1961, p. 348) has written about the general problem of termination in 'non-institutionalized' conflict situations and his remarks have particular relevance to nuclear hostilities:

> In conflicts not fully institutionalized, assessment of relative strength is not an easy matter so that the loser may not in fact concede that he has lost, nor may he even be aware of it. Therefore, it is to the interest of both contenders that the point at which victory is attained, or the point beyond which no more gains can be anticipated, be marked as clearly as possible so as to avoid unnecessary exertions on both sides. Termination of conflict becomes a problem to be solved by both parties.

Regrettably, it is speculation on the political meaning of termination in nuclear war that has been most wanting. We can therefore agree with the judgment expressed elsewhere (Foster and Brewer 1976, p. 1):

> While our understanding of conventional war termination is not well developed, at least some descriptive analyses of that process have been done, there is a rich history on which to base analyses, and historical experience supports the assumption that conventional war can be terminated short of mutual exhaustion or annihilation. The state of the art for analyzing nuclear war termination is quite different. There are no historical precedents, and nowhere in the literature of nuclear warfare is the termina-

tion problem systematically addressed. Scholars, in emphasizing
the differences between conventional and nuclear warfare,
routinely suggest that there is no interesting terminal point to
nuclear war short of mutual annihilation.

The last claim is an overstatement. Clearly, the theorists of
limited nuclear war have worked on the assumption that such
wars could, indeed, be terminated short of mutual annihilation. However, the general thrust of the criticism is accurate
in that, while there has been much discussion of the limits to
be observed in the conduct of nuclear war, there is a singular
lack of any penetrating analysis which relates limitation in
war to an over-arching theory of war itself. Above all, what is
lacking from a viable theoretical treatment of nuclear warfare
is a compelling account of the point of termination – of
what brings it about, at what point it is brought about (and
whether sooner or later), of what is achieved politically by
the war's ending and of how, in fact, the point of termination is to be recognized.

The absence of systematic exploration of these issues cannot be attributed to lack of awareness of their existence.
Brodie (1959, p. 404) had long since remarked that 'the un-
solved problem of modern total war is that of how to stop it,
quickly, once it is decided'. His formulation of the problem
was, however, lacking in precision; he did not draw attention
to the prior problems of how the war is decided and how we
recognize the decision. The same nagging issue, of making
sense of termination in nuclear war, apparently also vexed
Defense Secretary Harold Brown, even as he defended limited
options:

> I do not wish to pretend . . . that anyone has found a way of con-
> ducting a strategic nuclear exchange that remotely resembles a
> traditional campaign fought with conventional weapons . . . Ad-
> mittedly, counterforce and damage-limiting campaigns have been
> put forward as the nuclear equivalents of traditional warfare. But
> their proponents find it difficult to tell us what objectives an
> enemy would seek in launching such campaigns, how these cam-
> paigns would end, or how any resulting asymmetries could be
> made meaningful. We are left instead with large uncertainties
> about the amounts of damage that would result from such ex-
> changes, about escalation and about when and how the exchanges
> would terminate (Department of Defense 1979, pp. 75–6).

Clearly, then, there is more to limited war in the nuclear age than the enumeration of a variety of substantive constraints. For such limitations to make any kind of political sense, they must be integrated with a theory of war in which war's nature and objectives are fully articulated. Without this, we have but half of a theory of limitation. Regrettably, however, it is in this latter respect, of providing a coherent conception of the process of nuclear war, and of where it leads us politically, that the theory of limited nuclear war is most deficient. Without it, an essential source of limitation in warfare is lost.

In Chapter 2, historical examples of convention A were presented in terms of the convention *pacta sunt servanda*, conventions about the formal initiation of war, conventions of equal advantage, and conventions of surrender and victory. We can briefly review what has been said in the theoretical literature and in policy statements about conventions of type A, before returning to a closer examination of the deficiencies in this area and of the crucial implications that follow from them for limitation of nuclear war.

Pacta sunt servanda

As previously argued, this principle is essential to any form of limitation and wars fought in adherence to this principle would be different in kind from wars fought without it. The issue immediately raised by this concerns reciprocity, and the means of knowing whether this principle is to be applied or not. The question of Soviet compliance with conventions of nuclear war-limitation is an exceedingly complex one, and the implications of the answer to this question are enormous. One student of Soviet attitudes towards limited nuclear war has drawn attention to some of the uncertainties:

> The rationality of using selective nuclear strikes to deter the Soviet Union from continuing an aggression depends, above all, on the probable Soviet response to such strikes. Will the Soviets agree to play according to the ill-understood and esoteric rules of intrawar deterrence ...? Or will they see any limited nuclear attack as voiding all rules of restraint, presaging inevitable escalation ...? If the Soviets can be expected to respect American

rules, limited options might provide an effective means of demonstrating resolve, inflicting pain, and coercing the opponent. If not, limited strategic strikes would be a foolhardy provocation (Snyder 1977, p. 2).

This question of the Soviet attitude towards limitation will be reviewed in the following chapter. However, there are two separate issues involved. Not only do we have to ascertain the nature of the projected conventions, and of the Soviet attitude towards them, but also we must consider the means for, and the obstacles to, their observance. In other words, there are two distinctive aspects to *pacta sunt servanda*. The first, inasmuch as most conventions are assumed to be tacit, pertains to the communication of the content of the 'pacta' themselves. The second pertains to the problems of 'servanda': observance of limits is not simply a matter of will but also of effective implementation.

Before the Soviet Union could be expected to comply with conventions of war-conduct, it would need to know what the conventions are and this is, at least in part, a problem of communication and co-ordination. As has been suggested by one group of authors (Brennan 1975, p. 19): '. . . increasing the likelihood that a conflict could be terminated short of escalation to large-scale nuclear exchanges requires that both the American intention to respond initially with a selective and discriminating use of force and the limited scope of American objectives be communicated clearly to Soviet leaders'. When analysts have turned their minds to the principle of *pacta sunt servanda* in nuclear warfare, it is this problem of communicating the nature of the conventions themselves which has absorbed much of their attention (*see* Davis 1975–6, p. 16).

The other aspect of the problem is that pertaining to 'servanda'. An indication that the parties are willing, in principle, to observe constraints in war is of little value if there are practical obstacles in the path of such adherence. The theorist of limited nuclear war has, therefore, been compelled to explore the nature of conventions which would facilitate observance in cases where both parties sincerely wished to comply with restraints, but feared that they might be unable to do so.

What are the practical difficulties that might lead to such an unhappy outcome? They are to be discovered at several levels. There is, for instance, the problem of perception – the basic task of distinguishing whether an enemy action is one which falls within, or without, tacit restrictions. In order to reciprocate a constrained military act by the opponent, it is first of all necessary to recognize that the act was, in fact, constrained. Here, it has been suggested, there are major obstacles to detection and recognition. How, for example, can it be known before the event whether an enemy missile attack has been launched with a view to minimizing collateral civilian damage? By the time the nature of the attack is fully monitored, it may be too late to respond and certainly to respond appropriately. It was this line of argument which was pressed against Secretary Schlesinger during Senate hearings in 1974. Senator Muskie stated the problem in suggesting that 'the decisionmaker responsible for determining the nature of the response, he will not know what the limitations are until the strike is over?', to which Schlesinger responded, without reassurance: 'quite right, Mr Chairman' (United States Senate 1975, p. 26).

Even allowing for accurate monitoring of an attack that has been experienced (in terms of the targets, yield, number of warheads and height of detonation), there is the additional task of interpreting the significance of this information. How clear-cut must the information be to convey the message that the attack has been a limited one? If the information is ambiguous, should the enemy be given the benefit of the doubt?

Finally, assuming accurate perception and interpretation of the enemy's communication of limits, there remains the operational difficulty of maintaining such tight command and control over your own forces as to permit of an appropriate response. The degradation of the package of control systems is recognized to be a major impediment to escalation-avoidance in a limited nuclear war. A 'headless' war would, by any political criteria, degenerate into a 'pointless' war.

Accordingly, a convention closely related to that of *pacta sunt servanda* would be one of mutual agreement to refrain from striking each other's command and control centres. By itself, this could not avoid degradation of control (because of inadvertent damage to these centres) but its intention would be clear. Accordingly, proposals for such mutual self-restraint have abounded both in the theoretical literature and in the pronouncements of policy makers. Their thrust has been to facilitate adherence to other conventions of limitation in cases where the parties desire to do so.

This motif is recurrent in strategic debate and practice over the last decades. According to Ball (1975, p. 165) the search for a convention of this nature bore fruit in 1961 when 'to provide the Soviet Union with the option of fighting a "controlled" nuclear war, Moscow was taken off the initial US target list . . .' More recently, spokesmen for the Carter administration displayed sensitivity to the same issue. Defense Secretary Harold Brown was pessimistic about the prospects of avoiding escalation in a nuclear exchange 'especially if command-control centers were brought under attack' (Ball 1980a, p. 4).

Similar considerations have led to even more elaborate theorizing. One journalistic account of Presidential Directive 59 went so far, citing administration officials, as to suggest that the United States might tacitly spare the top Soviet political control centres, while taking out those lower down the hierarchy. The reasoning, as always, was based on the need to permit survival of the means for abiding by conventions of limitation:

> . . . the President would retain the flexibility, at least theoretically, to kill, in a first strike, only second-échelon military and political leaders. Defense officials say they can wipe out communications systems needed to conduct detailed combat operations and spare those relied upon by top Soviet leaders to start and stop wars.
> 'The President might want to launch a crippling retaliation, and then call Brezhnev on the hot-line to say that, unless he stops the war, some further strike will land on his personal bunker,' the Wall Street Journal of 27 August 1980 quotes one official.

This scenario is somewhat more exotic than most. Nonetheless, there is no denying the persistent attention given by policy makers to the requirements of *pacta sunt servanda,* as a necessary prerequisite for limitation in nuclear war. Charac-

teristically, in his final report as Defense Secretary, Harold
Brown was to revert to this theme:

> We must, and we do, include options to target organs of Soviet
> political and military leadership and control ... A clear US
> ability to destroy them poses a marked challenge to the essence
> of the Soviet system and thus contributes to deterrence. At the
> same time, of course, we recognize the role that a surviving
> supreme command could and would play in the termination of
> hostilities, and can envisage many scenarios in which destruction
> of them would be inadvisable and contrary to our own best
> interests (Department of Defense 1981, pp. 41–2).

Formal initiation and equal advantage

These two aspects can be dealt with in summary form as
neither has held the interest of recent theoreticians. Of the
various ways in which contemporary nuclear war might be
limited, these are amongst the least promising.

It is most unlikely that a nuclear war would be accompanied by formal procedures of initiation, or, even were it to
be so, that this would be of much practical consequence. In
any case, all the technological features of nuclear weaponry
that serve to undercut the value of formal initiation simply
add force to a post-1945 trend which is already firmly established. Even in its conventional forms, recent warfare has
been less concerned with the formality of the procedures for
its commencement. As Seabury (1970, p. 98) has remarked:
'since World War II there has been a decline of symbolic
formalism in the endings of wars. But there has also been an
erosion of formalities in their commencement, too.' There is
no reason to assume that a nuclear war would reverse this
trend and, certainly, theorists have given no indication that
this would be so. Discussion of conventions of initiation of
nuclear war has, in consequence, been conspicuous by its
absence. One minor qualification to this general judgment
might be in respect of agreements between the superpowers
to communicate formally to each other that war has *not* been
initiated, in the event of nuclear accident or attack by a third
party. These conventions were, for instance, formalized in
the 1971 package entitled *Agreement on Measures to Reduce*

the Risk of Outbreak of Nuclear War Between the USA and the USSR.

As to the notion of equal advantage in warfare, it is difficult to assess its impact on theories of limited nuclear war. We might wish to conclude that the SALT agreements and SALT 1's ABM Treaty were examples of conventions which, although negotiated in peacetime and with a view to stabilizing the balance of deterrence, would affect the conduct of a future war and might, accordingly, be viewed as partial embodiments of the idea of equal advantage. The logical conclusion of this line of argument would be that essential equivalence is to the code of nuclear chivalry what equal advantage was to the medieval tournament. The Department of Defense's (1979, p. 76) policy statement could be seen in this light:

> The Soviets have made a great deal of requiring equality with the United States in strategic nuclear forces, and we do not disagree. But since precise equality is impossible to define when the forces of the two sides differ in so many respects, we have adopted the principle of essential equivalence as a surrogate for equality ... We must insist on essential equivalence with the Soviet Union to symbolize the equality that both sides accept in this realm.

However, this line of argument can easily be overstated. While it is surely true that the various nuclear test and arms control agreements of the 1960s and 1970s would have an affect on the conduct of a future war, and while the thrust of SALT 2, if not of SALT 1, was in the direction of reducing major asymmetries between the two parties, it goes too far to claim that the present-day superpowers are operating on the basis of an explicit convention that unilateral advantage in military hardware is to be foresworn. Such an assertion simply does not square with the dynamics of the qualitative arms competition in which the superpowers have been engaged, nor does it take account of the restless search for the doctrinal and technological underpinnings of strategic advantage. Conventions of equal advantage or of essential equivalence may well have inspired the rhetoric of the strategic balance, but it is doubtful that they have had much impact on its practical development.

Conventions of termination

Wars are limited, in the most fundamental of senses, because there is some point to them. Without such a point, an important source of limitation, deriving from the intrinsic nature of the process of war, is lost. It is surprising, not to say alarming, that consideration of the political implications of termination of nuclear war should be relatively rare and, for the most part, deficient. We can, therefore, accept the judgment of Gray (1979, p. 82), if not the conclusions from it, when he claims that 'Western commentators continue to be bemused by the reality-numbing concept of "war-termination". Wars are indeed terminated, but they are also won or lost.' While much lip-service has been paid to the requirements of termination in nuclear war, its precise political significance, attributes and implications have seldom been fully articulated. Conventions of termination lie at the very heart of the discussion of limitation in nuclear war but the means by which they will be operationalized in war remains, so it seems, in the realm of political faith, rather than in the realm of creative political intelligence.

Fashions as to what the precise point of a nuclear war might be, in American eyes, have changed over time and been reflected in the various adjustments to US strategic targeting policy. Reducing these fluctuations to a crude summary, we might say that the point of nuclear war has been variously perceived as being the punishment and destruction of the Soviet population, the interdiction of a Soviet retaliatory capacity, the prevention of Soviet post-war economic resurgence, the blocking of Soviet military victory and, to some, the securing of United States' victory. This list is not intended to reflect the evolution of official policies, nor a correct chronological sequence, but merely to depict the spectrum of thought in recent years as to what the objective of a nuclear war would be if one had to be fought. Each has its own ambiguities and peculiar difficulties of termination, and some objectives are more amenable to limitation than others. Even more difficult to come to terms with are those formulations of nuclear war objectives which posit termination as the only goal of war once it has broken out. While 'the war to end war' has been a recurrent martial appeal for pacific ends, the slogan is given a new twist in the collapsed time-frame of nuclear confrontation, when the war to be ended is the one which is currently being fought. What are we to make of a concept of war the sole goal of which is its own cessation?

Hitherto there has been some difficulty in analysing the declared strategic war aims of the United States for the reason that a policy shaped as a deterrent is not necessarily an accurate guide to action policy: what US officials have said they would do, and why they would do it, before the event may be, at best, a vague approximation to what they would actually do in the event when, necessarily, prevention of war is a goal no longer to be attained. However, if we can accept official protestations at face value, this should no longer present an analytic problem as the distinction between deterrent objectives and war-fighting objectives is now deemed to be a misleading one. This was the message conveyed by the Secretary of Defense in 1978 when he insisted that 'we cannot afford to make a complete distinction between deterrent forces and what are so awkwardly called war-fighting forces' (Department of Defense 1978, p. 54). Inasmuch as US strategic forces are now presented as having a war-fighting function and a deterrence function in war (not to deter war but to deter a worse war), the ground has been cleared for an unequivocal assertion of the political objectives of nuclear war and of their relationship to, and compatability with, a termination of the war short (well short) of mutual destruction. Viewed from this perspective, have the theorists of limited nuclear war provided us with a convincing account of the nature of nuclear war termination and of the rationale which might underlie the adoption of conventions of limitation?

At one level, the problem has been approached simply as one of execution. Providing that the machinery exists, and survives intact, a war can be stopped. At this level, then, discussion of war termination blends into the general pursuit of effective command and control systems and war termination becomes subsidiary to this more important concern. As a defence official in the Kennedy days, J. T. McNaughton, was to suggest: 'command and control flexibility means there will be a way to stop a war before all the destruction of which both sides are capable has been wrought' (quoted in Moulton 1973, p. 82).

The problem, however, is more deep-seated than this. To provide the means to stop a war is not at all the same as providing a convincing rationale for doing so. What cannot be emphasized too strongly, is that adequate provision for termination of nuclear war, and for conventions which might facilitate it, while it depends upon executive machinery, is, in a much more fundamental sense, a problem of political theory rather than a task for administrative mechanics. Command and control is by all means necessary for the termination of war, but it is by no means sufficient.

When we advance from the machinery for execution of war termination to an anlysis of its political premises, we find the subject receding before our eyes. The strength with which the conviction, that war will be limited, is expressed, is matched only by the weakness of the politico-strategic theory which accompanies it. All theorists of limited nuclear war are in favour of early termination: few, if any, stop to enquire what this might mean. The conventions of type B, as they have been proposed for nuclear war, are left, as it were, in a kind of intellectual limbo, unrelated to any more general analysis of the process of war as a whole. As Foster and Brewer (1976, p. 20) remarked in seizing upon this particular weakness of the theory of limited nuclear war: 'both the counterforce-city avoidance and the limited nuclear options concepts have emphasized limiting the escalatory incentives and ultimate destruction of warfare rather than relating war initiation and conduct to a clear termination concept'. The same authors (p. 20) concede that Schlesinger at least came to recognize this flaw in the intellectual structure of limited options but remain convinced that he failed to resolve the problem. 'Unfortunately, Schlesinger did not indicate,' they comment, 'how or why a limited nuclear war could or should come to a "rapid conclusion" any more than a limited conventional war.'

It is this same objection that lies at the heart of Gray's complaint against those who framed American nuclear strategy. His particular criticism is that even when administration spokesmen have seemed to be serious about generating nuclear war-fighting capacities and doctrines (and Gray insists that efforts in that direction have been only half-hearted), they have lacked any overall theory of victory. However, even without taking up Gray's particular objection, we can see that his more general complaint is consistent with the point presently under discussion – namely, the absence from theoretical treatments of limited nuclear war of any adequate stipulation of the point of termination and of the point of such termination. Gray's diagnosis of the weakness of contemporary strategic theorizing is convincing, even if his prescriptions are more than a little unpalatable. We, therefore, find Gray (1979, p. 64) describing a school of thought which 'has no quarrel whatsoever with the ideas of flexibility, restraint, selectivity, minimal collateral damage and the rest. 'But,' he continues, 'it does have some sizeable quarrel with strategic selectivity ideas that are bereft of a super-ordinate framework for the conduct and favorable termination of the war.' Gray laments specifically that American strategy lacks a theory of victory: more generally, it can be asserted that it lacks a convincing theory of termination.

At the policy level, therefore, there is reason for believing that serious discussion of war-limitation, by means of conventions of termination, has a long way to go. The theory of limited nuclear war insists that such conventions of termination are essential, but tells us little about their nature. The dimensions of this intellectual vacuum are conveyed by placing together two recent official statements issued in general support of a doctrine of limited nuclear war. The first asserted Harold Brown's scepticism about the prevention of nuclear escalation and his fear that a nuclear war would probably go 'all the way':

> In adopting and implementing this policy we have no more illusions than our predecessors that a nuclear war could be closely and surgically controlled . . . I am not at all persuaded that what started as a demonstration, or even a tightly controlled use of the strategic forces for larger purposes, could be kept from escalating to a full-scale thermonuclear exchange . . . (Department of Defense 1980, p. 67).

Brown's intuition was, accordingly, that in the event nuclear war would be unlimited. At the same time, Brown has expressed sentiments which strike at the very heart of nuclear war as a rational strategy. His final report carried the revealing statement, in amplification of his countervailing strategy, that 'nothing in the policy contemplates that nuclear war can be a deliberate instrument for achieving our national security goals because it cannot be' (Department of Defense 1981, p. 43). Taken in conjunction, these two statements make alarming reading. There is, so it is claimed, no rational use of strategic forces in nuclear war and, at the same time, more rather than less of these forces are likely to be employed. It is at this point that the bankruptcy of the theory of limited nuclear war stands revealed for all to see. Without an explicit political theory for the employment of nuclear forces in war, there can be no viable theory as to why these forces should *not* be used. Limitation flows from the concept of war itself; it is not its antithesis. Accordingly, when the theory of war becomes bankrupt, we would expect the theory of limitation to experience a similar fate.

6

The Code of Nuclear Chivalry: A Critique

THE NATURE OF LIMITED NUCLEAR WAR

As has been repeatedly noted, the idea of limits in warfare abounds in paradoxes. According to some accounts, these inner paradoxes must inevitably erode the efficacy of any code of limitation. In fact, it is in precisely these terms that Fair (1971, p. 113) explains the limited impact and final demise of the medieval code of chivalry:

> Of course, at close quarters . . . almost everything went; and quite understandably so, since battles come down to killing, and in that extreme situation, face to face with one's opponent, it becomes difficult to remember, let alone to stick to, any code of decent behavior. This in fact is the paradox of chivalry, that all etiquette or scrupulousness, when it ultimately involves the destruction of someone else or his destruction of oneself, becomes absurd, certainly from a realistic standpoint but not less from a moral one. Chivalric ideals aimed at christianizing or making more decent a form of ancient behavior which is itself indecent and unchristian. Not only was the chivalric idea doomed to peter out in disillusionment and a renewed 'realism': it was also bound to work poorly and inefficiently even in its heyday . . .

Viewed from this perspective, the question to be asked is whether the code of nuclear chivalry is likely to display greater tenacity and effectiveness than its medieval precursor? Or is the judgment of history on medieval chivalry likely to be repeated in the case of the attempted limitation of nuclear war?

Accordingly, the present chapter will examine critically some of the preceding theories and scenarios of limited nuclear warfare. It will attempt to locate these theories in the context of the continuing themes of this study and will also focus upon some of the more prominent difficulties associated with the notion of limited war in a nuclear context.

One point which has to be made immediately is that there is a genuine problem in accepting some theories of limited nuclear war as means by which the totality of war is reduced because, from another point of view, these theories are permissive and allow a degree of nuclear violence that would not otherwise be countenanced. The problem, therefore, is whether we should concentrate upon the nuclear violence which these theories prescribe or whether, alternatively, we should consider the degree of nuclear violence which they tolerate. What from one perspective might be seen as using total nuclear power in a limited fahion, can be seen from another as simply making a limited use of a power that would otherwise be nullified. Viewed in this light, theories of limited nuclear war do not so much hobble an existing power as make effective a latent but unusable power. It is, therefore, a moot point whether they seek to limit nuclear war because it very much depends on whether limited nuclear war is to be compared with nuclear holocaust, on the one hand, or with nuclear stalemate, on the other. Certainly, this is how some of the theorists of limited war perceived the problem. As has been noted of Kissinger's writings on nuclear strategy: 'limited nuclear war should be a substitute not only for all-out nuclear war but also for no nuclear war' (Ball 1975, p. 194). Accordingly, a war which might seem limited in relation to the former situation, does not seem so limited in relation to the latter.

It is also worth repeating that some distinction should be made between conventions which do materially limit warfare and those conventions which prescribe certain modes of warfare but which cannot be said to induce meaningful limitation. For instance, a convention that only civilian targets, and not military ones, would be attacked in a nuclear war should be regarded as a convention of war-fighting, but by no stretch of the imagination could it be deemed a convention of war-limitation.

We might introduce this critical examination of theories of limited nuclear war by outlining the various possible objectives of limitation. Such an exercise is fundamental to any proper understanding of the nature and forms of war-limitation, in as much as restraints can be introduced into warfare in order to secure a number of objectives, not all of which are necessarily consistent with each other. For present purposes, we might suggest that limitations could be introduced into nuclear warfare for purposes of (a) more effective deterrence (b) signalling intent (c) limiting damage in war or (d) winning a nuclear war. The nature and status of the limitations would vary enormously depending upon which, or which combination, of these objectives provided the reason for their adoption.

These sundry objectives, and how they relate to limited-war practices, should be self-evident and can be rapidly reviewed. As to the first, the argument is simply that a threat of retaliation in limited form which is credible, serves as a more effective deterrent than an incredible threat of massive action. Advance preparation is made for a posture of limited war in order that the enemy might more readily believe the seriousness of the preparation. According to this objective, it is asserted that future wars will be fought in a limited fashion largely to convince the opponent that they will be fought at all.

The second objective is similar in inspiration, but simply transposes the deterrence into the actual conduct of the war: limited military actions are designed to signal to the enemy that if he does not desist, more and worse will follow. In this case, therefore, the limitation is contingent upon a reversion to good behaviour on the enemy's part. We should, therefore, make a clear distinction between limited nuclear options as a conscious and decisive alternative to all-out attack, and limited options as a signal of further intent and, conceivably, as part of a slide towards massive action. Limited options might be understood either as an indication that this is as far as we will go or, alternatively, as an indication of how much further we will go, if pressed. Thus Martin (1977, p. 67) has pointed out a confusion in the NATO nuclear strategies of the 1950s in that 'it was not made entirely clear whether the tactical nuclear strategy was intended as a deterrent signal of escalatory prospects or as a way to physically defeat the enemy attack'. In both cases, limitation is prompted by the dictates of deterrence, even though each differs in the manner in which the deterrence is generated. In the first case, war is limited because it is more credible to say that there are some things we will not do; in the second case, war is limited because it is more credible to indicate to the enemy what we have already done and what more we might do if sufficiently provoked.

Thirdly, war can be limited with the objective of limiting resulting damage if war actually breaks out. In this case, a posture for fighting limited war is dictated not by the desire to avoid war altogether, nor by the desire to intimidate the enemy in a war already started, but simply by the utilitarian reasoning that a war with less damage is better for all concerned than a war with more damage.

Fourthly, strategies of limited war might be devised with the primary objective of winning. It is conceivable that states might fight limited nuclear wars because militarily such wars hold out the greater prospects for success. Thus when Gray and Payne (1980) maintain that 'victory is possible', they recommend the acquisition of genuine limited war-fighting capabilities. Arguably, it is a truism that, in the nuclear age, the only form of winnable war is a limited one.

Clearly then the nature of the limitations in a nuclear war, and the effects such limitations will have, will depend largely upon the objectives which underlie them. Although they may share superficial resemblances, a limitation inspired by a policy of war-avoidance is, in principle, quite different from a limitation which signals intent to escalate, and a limitation designed to reduce damage is, in principle, different from a limitation designed to bring military victory closer.

The precise nature of the limitation envisaged by some of the pundits of limited nuclear war can be illuminated by contrasting their variants of limitation with the limitation outlined in the charity model. The selective targeting that was described under the Schlesinger programme was explicitly presented as a means to attaining greater flexibility in options, not as a means of target restriction. The change in targeting policy was effected not by taking some options away (respecting immunities) but by adding additional options to those already in existence: the policy may, in terms of Schelling's analogy, save ducks by sacrificing pipes, but it offers no compelling reason why the ducks themselves may not also become targets.

No statement issued by McNamara, Schlesinger or Harold Brown fits the requirements of the charity model. By way of recapitulation, the essence of that model might be conveyed in the words of a seventeenth century writer: 'Charity and Aequity doth require, that the Warre be so managed as the innocent may be as little damnified as possible' (quoted in Johnson 1975, p. 199). According to the charity model, the innocent constitute an immune category to be 'as little damnified as possible'. By way of contrast, the emphasis throughout all the statements on limited nuclear options over the past two decades, whatever the specific differences amongst them, has been, at most, to allow for a withholding of nuclear forces from city targets — a withholding that cannot be guaranteed to be more than temporary. The charity model requires discrimination between targets and non-targets: the most that the limited nuclear warriors have aspired to is the elaboration of a chronological sequence of attack in accordance with which cities would not be struck *initially*. Schlesinger left a press conference under no illusions on this score:

> The shift in targeting strategy, I should emphasize, does not mean that we are pointing missiles away from city targets to military targets . . . It is also true that we must continue to target cities . . . An assured destruction capability is an essential ingredient in overall deterrence, but it does not have to be, and should not be, the principal option . . . (*Official Text*, US Embassy, London, 25 January 1974, p. 2).

On the other hand, there are strong elements of the city-swapping model in all the forms of limitation that have been prosposed for war in the nuclear age. In fact, as a very general comment, it might be said that the strongest criticism to be made of current theories of limited war, is that they provide no criteria of limitation extrinsic to the bargaining relationship itself. Such limitation as is proposed is, for the most part, provisional and subject to later review. As part of a process by which the belligerents bargain to the limits, war's limitations become mere points in a sequence of hostile exchanges that are likely to continue as long as the nerve holds good. The crucial difference between withholding and immunity — between the city-swapping and charity models — was perfectly captured in Schlesinger's own description of the objectives of the new flexible targeting policy, one aim of which was to endow the United States with the 'ability to withhold an assured destruction reserve for an extended period of time'. Cities were not to become immune: destruction would be withheld from them, for the time being, pending the battle of wills which would terminate at some unforeseeable limit.

Many of the statements explaining the adoption of counterforce, limited options or countervailing strategies show marked similarities with the general structure of the city-swapping model. Although we have reviewed the various instances of convention B that have been suggested in the literature on limited nuclear warfare, the general conclusion must be that these limits have been advanced as chips in a bargaining process, without assurance that they themselves will constitute the limits of the conflict: what the limited nuclear warriors have described is an open-ended process in which the contestants can bargain to the limits. Carlton (1969, p. 129), in discussing a limited form of nuclear war in the shape of 'controlled counter-city teaching strikes', describes it in words that recall our discussion of the city-swapping model and which, despite the author's faith that the limits will hold, betray the essentially unlimited nature of this version of limited war:

> The employment of teaching strikes in any particular conflict would mean that the outcome would not depend on military capacity either on the conventional level ... or on the level of total strategic nuclear capability. Instead the emphasis would be almost exclusively on the rational display of willpower and resolve. Certainly there would appear to be a good chance that the strategy of exchanging teaching strikes would end not in Armageddon but in the restoration of the *status quo ante*. Of course those who decided to make the initial destabilizing move would need to recognize they were testing their opponents' resolve and be prepared ultimately to withdraw if this proved to be adequate. What would constitute an 'adequate' display of resolve is impossible to know in advance.

Even senior American officials, charged with promulgating doctrines of limited nuclear war, have spoken in language reminiscent of the city-swapping model, and have been less than encouraging about the prospects for termination of nuclear exchanges in their early stages. President Carter's Defense Secretary, Harold Brown, may be cited as a sceptic with no great faith in the limits of this kind of limited war. Towards the end of his tenure of office, Brown was to comment candidly on this issue: 'we know that what might start as a supposedly controlled limited strike could well – in my view would very likely – escalate to a full-scale nuclear war' (address reproduced in *Survival* November–December 1980, p. 268). Brown remained a supporter of the limited-war doctrines officially espoused by the Carter Administration and embodied in Presidential Directive 59: he did, however, provide a realistic assessment of the limits of limited war and of what could be expected from them. Nor is it difficult to understand why the sequential limits of a bargaining relationship are so tenuous and precarious. Iklé (1971, p. 42) gives lucid expression to the uncertainties of such a process of escalation:

> . . . the conditions on which both sides can agree for ending the fighting are not independent of the level of fighting. Hence escalation that falls short of defeating the enemy may cut both ways. On the one hand, it may induce one side (or even both) to seek new ways for ending the war since the costs and risks of fighting have become harder to bear. On the other hand, it may raise the ambitions on one or both sides and thus widen the gap between what one side would settle for and what the other demands. It is these opposed effects of escalation that make it so hard to plan for limited wars and to terminate them.

Indeed, in an even more fundamental sense, the trend towards counterforce in American strategic thought in the 1970s can itself be seen as part of that very bargaining process and test of wills with the Soviet Union which would be reproduced, in hot form, were a nuclear conflict to break out. So far were United States' strategists from adopting non-city postures for moral or humanitarian reasons (the immunity of cities), that they publically defended their retargeting doctrines as a reluctant, but militarily necessary, response to

Soviet initiatives. Counterforce was officially justified, not on the grounds that it was a preferable policy, but on the grounds that the Soviet Union was adopting it and must therefore be matched. As press reports of one of Schlesinger's early pronouncements on selective options were to put it 'the possibility was that the Soviet Union might develop the "counterforce" option . . . The United States could not allow the Soviet Union an option that it did not itself possess' (*The Times*, 11 January 1974). If the superpowers are as uncompromising in their actual conduct of hostilities as they are in the adoption of the strategic doctrines which govern such conduct, then the prospects for a restrained war, limited by the dynamics of the bargaining process itself, are none too bright.

The distinction between the charity and city-swapping models as they relate to discussions of limited nuclear war may be conveyed by a revealing and hopefully not too simplistic analogy in terms of types of games. Soccer and tennis, for instance, are structurally different in their internal relationship between the result of the game and its duration in time. In the former case, it is the duration which, in an important sense, determines the result in that it is the side leading after ninety minutes expires that is deemed to be the winner. As regards tennis, the opposite relationship holds in that it is the result which determines the duration, the winner being the player with the necessary total of sets to his credit, at which point in time the game is deemed to be over.

This provides some insight into the differing roles that limits can play in warfare. Just as in games the duration can determine the result, or vice-versa, so in warfare the expenditure of resources and the destruction and suffering determine who the winner is but equally, if less visibly, it can be winning and losing which determine the levels of pain and suffering. Just as games are bounded by various rules of duration or of result, so wars can be bounded by various conventions of limitation. In some cases, the duration of the contest will be determined by levels of suffering. In other cases, levels of suffering will be determined by duration. In terms of this analogy, we might equate soccer with the charity model. There is a finite limitation on the suffering to be endured in that the game ends after ninety minutes irrespective of the result at that stage. City-swapping more closely resembles tennis in that there is no end to the suffering until one of the parties has in fact won: we cannot know in advance how long the ordeal will last.

How, finally, can we begin to compare recent pronouncements on limited nuclear warfare with the structure of that model of war-limitation based on a single combat between champions? This is the most complex stage of the analysis and leads us into a discussion of the most profound issues of war and its limitation.

The adoption of a champion strategy — a combat between single appointed champions — would be deemed patently absurd in contemporary world political circumstances. It is fanciful that nuclear-armed giants could agree to have their disputes settled by such a contrived method. And yet one is left to wonder whether some of the prescriptions for limited nuclear war which the theorists would foist upon us are, in principle, much less fanciful or absurd. The adoption of a champion strategy would depend upon an inordinately high level of mutual self-interest and rational decision making on the part of the contestants. Nonetheless, it is precisely such reciprocity and rationality which seem to be assumed in what are advanced as plausible limited nuclear war scenarios. Thus Halperin (1963, p. 104) appeared to be reasonably optimistic about the prospects for limitation of war even after a direct nuclear strike in a central war between the superpowers:

> . . . if the strategic first blow were clearly limited, if it avoided the destruction of cities and seemed to be aimed at particular strategic targets, and if it should be accompanied by a statement of limited objectives the prospects for limitation might be significant.

Halperin seems to expect considerable rationality, and perception of mutual self-interest, from a party that has already been struck: so much so, he assumes a preoccupation with limitation almost to the exclusion of any notion that the struck party might also want to win. If this is so, that concern with limitation at least matches concern with winning, then we are close to the essentials of a champion strategy because the champion simply trades away greater certainty of victory for the certainty of limitation. If a champion strategy is absurd, are those forms of limitation which assume a perfect balance between the desire to win and the desire not to be hurt, and the rational predication of action upon such an assessment, any less absurd?

However, to understand the nature of the limits proposed for nuclear war, we have to probe more deeply than this and look at the concept of war in its relationship to limitation. In doing so, we find impressive evidence of the intellectual links between limited nuclear options and the classical combat between champions.

The thrust of the following argument can best be presented by reference to an article by Mavrodes (1975) as a convenient demonstration of differing interpretations of war and its limitation. Mavrodes lends himself to this discussion because he is one of very few writers actually to discuss single combat between champions and its relationship to conventions of war-limitation. The main point of Mavrodes' argument is that war confined to counterforce operations approximates, but is not as radical as, the form of single combat. In this sense, noncombatant immunity is but a less extreme version of the champion convention, the armed forces or combatants, collectively, serving as the nation's appointed champion. Mavrodes (p. 125) explains his reasoning as follows:

> . . . consider, on the one hand, warfare which is limited only by the moral requirements that the ends sought should be just and that the means used should be proportionate, and, on the other hand, the convention of single combat *as a substitute for warfare*. Between these extremes there lie a vast number of other possible conventions which might be canvassed in the search for a less costly *substitute for war*. I suggest that the long struggle, in the western world at least, to limit military operations to 'counterforces' strategies, thus sparing civilian populations, is just such an attempt [emphases added].

More succinctly, Mavrodes (p. 127) contends that 'the immunity of noncombatants is best thought of as a convention-dependent obligation related to a convention which *substitutes for warfare a certain form of limited combat*' [emphases added].

What a counterforces posture and the champion have in common, in Mavrodes' account, is the fact that both are departures from war *per se* (to use his own term) in that they are convention-governed forms of combat: each establishes 'a morally desirable alternative to war' (p. 130).

The significance of this position can best be appreciated by contrasting it with the opposing view of which Suarez is a concise exponent. According to Suarez (1944, p. 863) a combat between appointed champions 'has the true character of war', and he further claims that 'the whole business of a war may be reduced to an armed contest among a few combatants'.

There is a clear difference between Mavrodes and Suarez on this issue but is it a difference of semantics only? Mavrodes appears to think so: at least this is the conclusion to be drawn from his indifference whether the distinction 'can be thought of either as dividing wars into two classes, or else as distinguishing wars from certain other international combats' (1975, p. 117). To Mavrodes it matters not whether single combats (and by extension, counterforce combats) have the 'true character of war' or whether they be regarded as convention-governed *substitutes* for war.

How does this relate to the discussion of contemporary theories of limited war? The argument of this study is that it makes all the difference in the world whether we see limits as a necessary part of war or merely as artificial accretions which lead to a bastardized activity, part war and part something else. In agreement with Suarez, we see the champion and all conventions tending towards it as combats having the 'true character of war'. Far from being extraneous adjuncts, limits are an integral part of the very process of warfare.

Mavrodes' perspective is radically different and has important implications. According to him, there is war *per se* and there is combat in accordance with limiting conventions. To quote from him once more: 'the distinction ... is that between warfare *per se* on the one hand, and, on the other hand, international combats which are limited by convention and custom' (p. 131). Mavrodes' error is not in thinking that wars are limited by the conventions that surround them: his error is in thinking that there can be wars without such conventions, wars that are governed only by 'independent moral requirements' (p. 128). But it is not such moral requirements that lend war its essential character; rather it is the conventions without which war becomes a politically-unrecognizable activity.

Specifically, where Mavrodes is led astray is in thinking that the only limitations upon war are those characteristic of convention B. When he speaks of convention-governed combats, it is those conventions of type B which he must have in mind. What he fails to recognize is the existence of those conventions of type A which define the process of war, because in this latter sense it would be a flat contradiction to talk of a form of war which was not convention-governed. In this more fundamental sense, it is the conventions which *are* the war. As Danto (1978, p. 182) has remarked 'there is no war without a convention of war'.

The deficiency of much contemporary theory on limits to war seems to be comparable to the weakness just noted in Mavrodes' argument. In an important sense, limited-war theorists write as if limitations are of type B alone, not a part of war *per se.* What is wrong with limited-war thinking is its tendency to argue in these terms. Limited options are regarded as 'options' in both senses, not just as choices between targets, but as choices about whether those choices need to be made: the limits, or conventions of war, may or may not be opted for. They are not seen as a necessary feature of war, as war.

The root of the problem seems to lie in the disjunction between conventions A and B which exhibits itself in many discussions of limits to war. As a result of this disjunction, we find ourselves listening in upon two separate limited-war dialogues with no communication between the two sets of participants. The charity theorists emphasize the constraint of war by substantive limits and immunities derived from moral-religious-humanitarian premises extrinsic to war itself. The city-swappers speak of limits as a process of bargaining the outcome of which, and the substantive impact of which, cannot be foreseen. If discussion of limits is to make political progress, it can do so only by treating conventions A and B in tandem. In the final analysis it is what we think of war as being, how we define the point of it, that will determine the nature of the limits, or their absence, in any war that we might experience. We might, then, agree with Danto (1978, p. 187):

> War remains the aberration, and the commitment to peace governs the degree of allowable violence in war: which is why victory at any price is disallowed, even victory over those who imply by their conduct of war the belief that war could be the norm. If it were the norm, there would be no war, only slaughter, and anything then would go.

The point may be emphasized in the following way. We have argued repeatedly that the conventions which limit war are of two generic types, those of convention B and those of convention A. We might say that, in the former case, wars embody certain conventions: in the latter case, wars themselves are embodied in certain conventions. Moreover, as between various historical periods and as between different cultures, the extent to which limitations have been practised in warfare has varied enormously. In other words, historically speaking, war has embodied, to a greater or lesser degree, the conventions conducive to substantive limitation in its conduct. However, more important than this fact alone are the changes that have occurred, not as between the conventions embodied in war, but as between the conventions in which war itself is embodied. As the purpose and social function of war has changed, so we can discern a transition in the conventions of type A which define the nature and point of the process. When this occurs, we might almost speak of a paradigm-shift in which one cultural form of war is substituted for another.

How should we describe such paradigms of war and the conventions which lend them their distinctive characteristics? One useful categorization is that suggested by Hans Speier some forty years ago. Speier (1952) distinguished three different social types of war which he referred to as the absolute, the instrumental and the agonistic. Briefly, by the absolute, Speier intended a form of war the point of which was to eliminate physically the enemy and, as such, the conduct of war was without regulation or restriction. 'The opponent,' as Speier phrased it 'is an existential enemy. Absolute war is waged in order to annihilate him' (p. 223). Instrumental war, by way of contrast, is waged 'in order to gain access to values which the enemy controls. Thus it is defeat of the enemy – not necessarily his annihilation – which is desired . . .' p. 225). Finally, there is agonistic war waged 'under conditions of studied equality and under strict observance of rules. Measured in terms of destruction such a fight is highly inefficient and ludicrously ceremonious' (p. 227). Each form of war is based upon an account, in the most general of terms, of why the war is being fought, and the absolute and agonistic forms also depict how the war will be fought. Interestingly, the mode of conduct in an instrumental war is regarded by Speier as unspecifiable as it 'may or may not be restricted, according to considerations of expediency' (p. 223). Instrumental war, we must assume on this account, is distinguished by its motive but not by its conduct, as the conventions surrounding its pursuit may gravitate towards either the absolute or agonistic forms: instrumental war, as a mode of conduct, is not in itself a pure type. We are left, therefore, with two polar conventions in which war may be embodied, the absolute and the agonistic. Intellectually, these are the forerunners of Rapoport's (1960) subsequent distinction between fightlike wars and gamelike wars.

What do such paradigms tell us about war and its limitation? The crucial distinction between absolute and agonistic wars, in Speier's terminology, or between fightlike and gamelike wars, using Rapoport's, is to be discovered in their respective modes of termination and may thus be regarded appropriately as an aspect of the conventions of type A in which the wars are embodied. This takes us into that area of limitation which is most difficult of understanding and most resistant to implementation. As Kecskemeti (1970, p. 111) has commented: 'political rationality as an aspect of the termination of armed conflicts presents more complex problems than the concerted and codified limitation of destruction in wartime'.

How does the mode of termination differ between the two forms of war? In Speier's absolute form, termination is achieved '*without* the enemy' (1952, p. 223). The war is terminated when the enemy is physically eliminated. Nor could it stop short of this condition, since that is the point of the war. Agonistic or gamelike wars are structurally different as to their style of termination. Indeed, it is the mode of termination which sets them apart from absolute wars. As Coser (1961, pp. 347–8) has remarked: 'certain types of highly institutionalized conflicts have built-in termination points. Trials by ordeal, duels and other agonistic struggles are centered upon symbolic endings which give them gamelike features and determine the outcome automatically.'

We live in an age when the only just wars are deemed to be politically-instrumental ones. Absolute wars of extermination would be thought too primitive and agonistic wars would be thought too quaint. National societies engage in war, if at all, to attain or to preserve their vital interests. The problem, then, is to relate the instrumental ends of contemporary warfare to the mode of its conduct. Speier suggested that instrumental war may or may not be regulated. Why is this so? Is instrumental war in the nuclear age embodied in a convention? Or does it only entail its own subsidiary conventions? To put the point more precisely, how do we find a politically-meaningful termination to an instrumental nuclear war that might potentially go all the way? Coser may again be quoted in this context:

> If both victor and vanquished are to make a contribution to the termination of their conflict they must arrive at some agreement ... This applies not only to the conduct but also to the termination of conflicts. In order to end a conflict the parties must agree upon rules and norms allowing them to assess their respective power positions in the struggle ... To the degree that such rules are provided, the conflict is partly institutionalized and acquires some of the features of the agonistic struggle ... (1961, p. 348).

In no situation is such agreement, and the conventions based upon it, more pressing a necessity than in the case of nuclear conflict. What becomes vital is the creation of symbols which might denote the victory of one of the parties or at least the war's termination. Otherwise victory or war's ending would be hopelessly unrecognizable. Nuclear war lacks natural stopping points and natural terminations: if these are to be found, they must first be created. In more traditional military encounters, the contestants had some clues as to the tide of battle and could make rational judgments, based on objectives sought, as to whether the war should be continued or terms solicited. Nuclear war offers no such clues and, as Coser has again suggested: 'when such mutually acceptable symbolic clues are not available the resolution of the conflict will be more difficult' (1961, p. 350). Nuclear war, as an instrumental enterprise, needs symbols of victory, defeat or stalemate and it needs them before it is too late. In the final analysis, given their absence in the natural order of things, such symbols must be created and enshrined in conventions.

We are brought back to Rapoport's account of gamelike assessments of inevitable outcomes which can prevent unnecessary bloodshed by making it unnecessary actually to fight all the way to reach a resolution. Rapoport (1960, p. 148) refers to:

> The common practice among experts to *concede* games or to agree on a draw as a result of insight into the logic of the situation. I submit that this practice is a reflection of a certain moral principle, characteristic of gamelike conflict as opposed to fight-like conflict. The principle has to do with imputing rationality comparable to one's own to the opponent. On the basis of this mutual respect, agreement is possible, even though the interests of the players are diametrically opposed.

The thrust of the argument, therefore, is that as a politically-rational activity, contemporary nuclear warfare must take on features of war that are characteristic of agonistic or gamelike contests. We can indeed say that, in nuclear conditions, the agonistic element becomes a necessary part of any war that is to remain politically-instrumental and especially is this so with regard to its conventions of termination. Without such conventions, without symbols of victory and defeat, there is no way that wars can terminate in a politically-recognizable sense at all: convention-based termination, in the nuclear age is the continuation of war by other means.

This is part of the conclusion of this study. We are led to the realization that an instrumental war can be so *only* if it is embodied within a convention which renders it stylized and quasi-institutionalized. Nuclear war must be approached, in short, as the set combat between appointed champions which has been utilized in the past. But from this conclusion, another might possibly be drawn. Can war still function in such a framework? Does it have any utility as a mode of resolution? Kecskemeti (1970, p. 115) articulates the doubt: 'once the emphasis is put on the avoidance of violence, the problem of conflict termination appears in a changed light. War as a decision mechanism in relation to certain types of political deadlock tends to be regarded as a political phenomenon that has lost any real contemporary relevance.' War can function as a mode of decision in contemporary nuclear conditions only insofar as it approximates the stylized contest of nuclear champions with its own built-in conventions of termination. If a reversion to the champion combat is considered absurd to modern political man, then logically so should the variants of limited nuclear war, because such attractions as they possess derive from their crude approximation to the ideal type of the single set combat. But if this seems to reduce war to frivolity, can war's political purpose be redeemed in mutual extermination? One senses that, as far as instrumental war is concerned, the middle ground between its absolute and agonistic conduct is being eclipsed by technology. The choice left is to accommodate to the latter or to be engulfed by the former. In either case, instrumental war, in its limited nuclear variants, does not appear to have an independent future.

THE PROBLEM OF RECIPROCITY

Perhaps the main objection that is raised against the prospect of successful limitation of nuclear war is the possibility of Soviet non-reciprocation. It does, after all, take two parties to observe a set of ground rules for the conduct of war. The difficulties in keeping a war within limits are, therefore, to be found at two levels: can *either* of the parties successfully limit its own military operations and would *both* do so simultaneously? As has been asked by one writer elsewhere:

> Even accepting the proposition that the US NCA [National Command Authority] can maintain the cool self-discipline and organizational control necessary to implement a strategy of

> limited reprisal and fine-tuned diplomatic coercion under the
> heavy stresses of a deep nuclear crisis . . . to what end can such a
> strategy be put if the Soviet adversary has declared in advance
> that he will not be a party to any such doctrinal contrivance
> (Lambeth 1977, p. 81)?

There is some reason to have doubts about the likelihood of
Soviet reciprocity. As one RAND Corporation study was to
point out: 'if there is little convergence in Soviet and American writings on deterrence, there is even less complementarity
in their statements on limited strategic war' (quoted in
Kolkowicz 1980, p. 28).

It is not possible to resolve in this study the issue of likely
Soviet conduct in a future war. Experts on Soviet military
doctrine and strategy are divided on most of the major issues
raised by the debate, as they are on the rules of evidence by
means of which it might be resolved. Some analysts are
happy to cite Soviet military authorities as evidence of a lack
of Soviet interest in limiting war; others maintain that Soviet
declaratory policy is only part of the total picture, and that
even if no Soviet statement can be found in support of
limited options and slow-motion warfare, in the event the
Soviet Union would have reasons for seeking to limit war
equally as strong as those of the United States.

The standard Soviet line has been that the introduction of
rules of restraint into contemporary warfare is, at best,
wholly impracticable and, at worst, an insidious Western
ploy. The noted specialist Thomas Wolfe pointed out in the
mid-1960s the negative Soviet assessment of limited-war
possibilities:

> The main body of Soviet writing on the conduct of theater war-
> fare begins with the assumption that both tactical and strategic
> nuclear weapons will be used in any major theater campaigns that
> develop as part of a general war. In the same way, most Soviet
> writers still advance the standard argument that introduction of
> tactical nuclear weapons in local war situations would mean
> escalation into world war (Wolfe 1966, p. 62).

Moreover, analysts who present this as a depiction of the
Soviet attitude can make use of some very explicit Soviet
statements in support of their argument. Thus G. Arbatov,
the top Soviet academic adviser on the United States, wrote

at the time of the Schlesinger counterforce statements in the following critical vein:

> The idea of introducing rules and games and artificial restrictions by agreement seems illusory and untenable. It is difficult to visualize that a nuclear war, if unleashed, could be kept within the framework of rules and would not develop into an all-out war. In fact such proposals are a demagogic trick designed to re-assure the public opinion (quoted in Kolkowicz 1980, p. 13).

Another review of the Soviet literature conveys the same impression of uncompromising Soviet lack of interest in schemes for conducting war in accordance with agreed rules of limitation:

> Once the nuclear threshold is crossed, Soviet military doctrine continues to posit — as it has throughout the past decade — that the role of nuclear weapons is the simple and unambiguous attain-ment of military victory, a task to be achieved not by slow-motion counterforce targeting, selective attacks on vital military or economic resources of the enemy, or any other limited schemes to influence his strategic behavior, but rather through the massive application of nuclear force on all targets necessary to destroy his war-waging ability and his capacity for collective strategic action (Lambeth 1977, pp. 87—8).

One can only speculate as to the reason why the Soviet authorities adhere to this attitude: it may be no more than military propaganda, it may reflect unwillingness to fight wars on Western-derived rules, or it may be a straightforward Soviet calculation that the political and technological diffi-culties in the path of limitation are simply insurmountable. There are further possibilities. On the one hand, as one com-mentator has observed, Soviet ideology insists that the wars actually fought by the Soviet Union are necessary and there-fore just wars: with such an underpinning of moral and ideological fervour, the rationale for restricting the military effort must inevitably be obscured. As has been said: 'im-plicit in Soviet writing is the recognition that it is extremely difficult to explain to one's soldiers and civilians that a war can be both just and limited at the same time' (Jones 1975, p. 59).

Other writers have drawn attention to strong military reasons why the Soviet Union should not comply with

Western prescriptions for the conduct of limited wars. A recent article suggests that the Soviet Union would deliberately move its ground forces in Western Europe in such a way that selectivity and city-avoidance strategies would be rendered inoperable. It would do so, according to this argument, to inhibit NATO forces from making use of their tactical nuclear weaponry:

> By *intentionally* operating some of its forces near West German urban zones, the Warsaw Pact would be manipulating the threat of massive collateral damage . . . In fact, a Pact use of suburban hugging tactics would exploit NATO's attempt to engage in a controlled battlefield nuclear war, for if nuclear weapons were used in this scenario, NATO would be forced to fire on its own cities and population (Bracken 1980, p. 205).

According to this argument, the Soviet Union would not permit NATO the option of conducting a counterforce war in Europe because it would not allow a physical possibility of target discrimination. This writer concluded therefore that 'the projection of Western hopes about collateral damage minimization on to Soviet doctrine is a misleading foundation for building theatre forces' (p. 206).

Nevertheless, there can be no certainty that the Soviet authorities are as unenamoured of limited-war strategies as the foregoing account would suggest. Some writers have indeed indicated that the Soviet position on this matter has moderated with the years. As long ago as the mid-1960s, Wolfe contended that there were indications of an increasing Soviet receptivity to the idea that local wars, at least, might be contained within limits and not necessarily lead to all out superpower conflict. Wolfe (1966, p. 70) cited an article by Col I. Korotkov, published in April 1964, in support of this contention:

> It must be admitted that our military thought, while having duly worked out problems of missile-nuclear war, has devoted insufficient attention to the study of limited (local) wars, although the imperialist powers repeatedly throughout the post-war period have resorted to them . . . *Only recently have we begun to correct this shortcoming.*

Others have insisted that, regardless of the tenor of Soviet statements, we should not expect Soviet operational practice to be bound by doctrinaire orthodoxies, and that the lack of a body of civilian strategic literature in any way comparable with that found in the United States does not mean that Soviet military authorities are either unfamiliar with, nor necessarily unsympathetic towards, ideas of the limited conduct of war. The argument has been expressed by Lambeth (1977, p. 97) in the following way:

> ... notwithstanding the heavy-handed themes enunciated in open-Soviet military writings, there are valid reasons for suspecting that in their private thinking and planning, Soviet political and military leaders are closely attuned to the issue of strategic targeting selectivity and are fully prepared, both intellectually and operationally, to wage less than insensate strategic offensive warfare should they conclude that the exigencies of the moment warranted it as a preferred course of action.

NUCLEAR WAR AND UNCERTAIN LIMITS

Apart from this entire issue of the likelihood of Soviet reciprocity in limiting a nuclear war, the main point of contention in discussions of limited nuclear warfare has been the technical one of determining whether, even if a war were fought by agreed conventions of limitation, its effects could in any meaningful sense be considered to be limited (*see* Drell and Hippel 1976). The present author does not have the technical competence to pass judgment on these arguments. Nonetheless, one thing is abundantly clear. While it is one of the main premises of all the theories of limited nuclear war that such wars can be sufficiently contained to produce specific effects and to reduce other effects substantially, the fact remains that the most impressive characteristic of all the scientific study of the impact of nuclear war, is its marked uncertainty about the extent of the resulting damage. The main finding of the Office of Technology Assessment's report on *The Effects of Nuclear War,* published in 1979, was accordingly that 'the effects of a nuclear war that cannot be calculated are at least as important as those for which calculations are attempted' (p. 3). The report also suggested that the 'impact of even a "small" or "limited" nuclear attack would be enormous' (p. 4). The report was based on a series of studies of various cases ranging from an attack on a single city, through an attack on oil refineries, to a counterforce attack on ICBM silos and large-scale attack on military and economic targets. The number of immediate deaths ranged from 200,000 to 160,000,000 depending on the individual case but for *each* case, the report produced a range of immediate deaths that varied by a factor of five as a minimum and twenty as a maximum. This fact alone bears eloquent testimony to the committee's insistence on the unpredictability of the effects in a nuclear war. Thus one well-informed observer, in reviewing the OTA report, concluded that the certitudes of limited nuclear option programmes were based on dangerously shifting foundations:

> The effects of any nuclear operation are therefore essentially unpredictable . . . And all the limited and selective options that have now been incorporated in the SIOP notwithstanding, the possibility of conducting limited and controlled nuclear exchanges in which damage is a matter only of policy choice remains no less unreal than it was before the re-thinking of the mid-1970s (Ball 1980b, p. 234).

Above all, one cannot fail to gain an impression that many of the forms of limitation proposed in these theories are, in principle, as quaint as many of the ancient and medieval practices which would, no doubt, be dismissed as irrelevant to the conditions of contemporary warfare. Codes of military etiquette and chivalry which depend for their sustenance upon cosmopolitan norms, perceived mutuality and co-ordination with the enemy would be thought inapplicable to present-day conditions. Nonetheless, in their place, the theorists of limited nuclear war have attempted to create a new code of nuclear chivalry, every bit as colourful and fanciful as the medieval chivalric displays. Could there be anything more quixotic than the following scenario, recommended by Halperin (1963, p. 107), for American conduct during a nuclear confrontation:

> . . . limiting a central war may depend on both sides' believing that limitation is possible and that the other is likely to reciprocate restraint. The United States should continue to emphasize that the changes it is making in its strategic posture are relevant to the limitation of central war: for example, its increased control

over its strategic forces, the location of these forces away from
population centres, and its programme for the construction of
fallout shelters. The United States might also suggest that the
Soviets take similar action . . . The United States might spell out
even more explicitly its commitment to particular kinds of limitations by stating more clearly than was done in the McNamara
speech that we would not target cities unless the Soviets did so,
and we might privately suggest to the Soviets that they separate
these two types of targets so that city destruction would not
become necessary.

Of all the stylized conflicts that can be found in history, this
is surely as contrived and theatrical as any.

Even more so is the case where the theorists envisage a
negotiated termination of the war after a few limited nuclear
exchanges between the parties. Again we might ask whether
there is any fundamental difference between artificial limitations before the event, as in the form of an agreement to hold
a single combat, and premature termination of the war after
it has begun? Is there not a deficiency in the logic which
argues that it is absurd to do before the outbreak of war what
it is reasonable to do — indeed is the *only* objective — once
war has broken out? It is surely naive to believe that the
mutuality of interests necessary for war-limitation is unattainable before war but to expect it to emerge when the
positions of the antagonists are, *a fortiori,* polarized by hostilities?

Apart from these general observations, there are a number
of specific criticisms, or requests for greater clarification,
which might be addressed to the contemporary theorists of
limited nuclear war. The remainder of this chapter will outline a number of these issues.

Firstly, as to that most intractable of all arguments about
limits to war, whether a diminution of its horrors increases
the likelihood of its occurrence, the recent official pronouncements on limited nuclear war have little of value to
contribute. Carter's Defense Secretary, Harold Brown, resolved the problem to his own satisfaction by insisting that it
simply did not exist. 'There is no contradiction,' Brown
reiterated, 'between this focus on how a war would be fought
and what its results would be, and our purpose of insuring
continued peace through mutual deterrence' (address repro-

duced in *Survival,* November–December 1980, p. 268). The claim, however, was patently disingenuous and less than respectful to those critics who had deployed the argument. For instance, on 17 August 1980, only a few days before Brown's remarks, the *New York Times* had quoted the opinion of P. Warnke, former Director of the Arms Control and Disarmament Agency, to the effect that 'deterrence is always weakened by any strategy that seems to contemplate a limited nuclear war'. It was less than charitable to respond to the argument by simply denying that there was anything to it.

Not only was it uncharitable, it was logically perverse, because in a very fundamental sense all strategies of deterrence are predicated upon the intentional manipulation of the risk of war. An editorial in *The Times* of 4 September 1980 was perfectly correct when it commented upon criticisms of Presidential Directive 59 that 'the most familiar one is that by making the United States' nuclear force easier to use it makes it more likely to be used. But it is just this likelihood that is the essence of deterrence.' Viewed in this light, the conclusion that limited nuclear war doctrines strive to increase the threat of war breaking out is undeniable, as otherwise the argument that they possess greater deterrent power would be equally invalid. We might, therefore, observe with greater precision that selective nuclear options, as presented in recent American programmes, are designed to reduce the *risk* of war by increasing the *threat* of it: whether that greater threat is sufficient to deter war's occurrence is the central dilemma of all deterrence theory and, accordingly, to assert that the dilemma does not exist is completely untenable.

Secondly, it deserves to be repeated that whatever selectivity the new doctrines intend to introduce into nuclear targeting, the revisions do not entail any conscious and irreversible decision to switch the nuclear threat away from civilian populations. Schlesinger was unequivocal on this point in one of his early press conferences on the topic of counterforce. 'The shift in targeting strategy,' he clarified, '. . . does not mean that we are pointing missiles away from city targets to military targets . . . we must continue to target cities . . .' (*Official Text,* US Embassy, London, 25 January 1974, p. 2).

The question asked by Bruce Russett was, therefore, a moot one. Reserving judgment on the 1974 revisions of strategic targeting, Russett wanted to know 'to what degree will the targeting of Soviet military installations replace, rather than merely supplement, the targeting of cities?' (Letter to *The Times,* 15 January 1974).

In this context, Schlesinger's clarifications in testimony before the Senate Armed Services Committee on 5 February 1974 are of interest. Schlesinger's remarks were as follows:

> . . . if a nuclear clash should occur . . . in order to protect American cities and the cities of our allies, we shall rely into the war-time period, upon our assured destruction force and persuading through intra-war deterrence any potential foe not to attack cities (*Official Text,* US Embassy, London, 15 February 1974, p. 2).

The statement is highly revealing: it indicates not the abandonment of mutual assured destruction, but its displacement in time. What Schlesinger's new strategy seems to do, on his own description of it, is to postpone MAD and to reinstate it as the orthodoxy of a war-time rather than of a peace-time strategy. From being the reprisal held in reserve to preserve the peace, MAD under the Schlesinger innovations would become the reprisal held in reserve to preserve nuclear war's limitations.

Thirdly, in any listing of the pressures to devise new strategic policies in the 1970s and 1980s, it would be remiss not to highlight the momentum of technological development and the brute facts of weapon system acquisition. As a consequence of MIRV technology and the acquisition of large numbers of theatre nuclear devices, the actual number of available nuclear warheads expanded dramatically in the course of the 1970s. This fact alone impinged upon targeting policy because, to put it in its crudest terms, there simply were not enough soft civilian targets to go round. As G. Treverton had suggested: 'with more and more nuclear warheads, the United States reached the point in 1974 where even the all-out "assured destruction" retaliation would have sent some 70 per cent of the war heads against military, not civilian or economic targets' (*Observer News Service,* 5 September 1980). Similarly, it was not the quantity alone of nuclear weapons, but also their improving quality, which was to precipitate new thinking on their use. It was suggested above that limited-war theory has, to some extent, been prisoner to a technological imperative, as a consequence of which strategic doctrine has followed design achievements as much as it has dictated them. The force of this argument had in no way diminished during the 1970s. There is, therefore, unconscious irony in the defence, put forward by Robert Ellsworth, of the Schlesinger proposals of 1974. Taking exception to an earlier *New York Times'* editorial, Ellsworth contended that 'it is not a "new Nixon strategy" which . . . requires enormous numbers of new, highly accurate warheads. The contrary is the case: it is the enormous numbers of new, highly accurate warheads which require a new strategy' (letter to *New York Times,* 25 January 1974). Ellsworth was right but for the wrong reasons. As an explanation of the pressures leading to a reassessment of strategic targeting, Ellsworth's analysis had much to commend it: as a vindication of that new policy, it was less than persuasive, because surely no administration could claim virtue for a strategic policy seen to be hostage to technological fortune.

Fourthly, and following from the previous account of Soviet attitudes to limited nuclear war, it is necessary to record the uniformly hostile Soviet response to Carter's Presidential Directive 59. What we are to conclude from this negative response as to future Soviet intentions is far from clear, but at the very least it is necessary to recognize ostensible Soviet opposition to the content of the strategic doctrine given official sanction in the United States in July 1980. While public Soviet declarations on this issue may not reflect the totality of Soviet thinking, nor even its dominant features, they must at least be acknowledged and efforts made to come to terms with them. We can distinguish at least three grounds on which Soviet spokesmen took exception to the enunciated American policy. The first was the articulation, as in *Pravda* of 7 August 1980, of fears that the underlying American intention was to develop a first-strike capability. Secondly, Soviet commentaries alluded to the theme of the increased likelihood of war concomitant with erroneous thinking about the possibilities of fighting limited wars. A

Tass report by A. Krasikov on 8 August 1980 developed this objection:

> The White House is trying to instill in Americans and people of other countries the idea that it is possible to wage a nuclear-missile war dealing blows only against troops and command posts while the civilian population escapes suffering or suffers only minimally. This is a very dangerous doctrine whose aim is to lull the people's vigilance and to bring closer the destruction of civilization.

The final theme was an assertion of Soviet autonomy and a refusal to be seen to be bound by American-devised prescriptions for the conduct of nuclear war. This might be thought the least serious of the Soviet objections, centring as it does upon Soviet *amour propre* rather than upon the actual substance of the American policy. At any rate, G. Trofimenko of the USSR's Institute for the Study of the USA and Canada, rebutted the expectations of US policy makers that they 'could hope to impose upon the other side their own "rules of the game" in a military conflict' (*New York Times*, 22 September 1980).

Fifthly, we need to be aware that scepticism about the new posture was not confined to the Soviet Union but was expressed also within Carter's own administration. Defense Secretary Harold Brown, during his Senate confirmation hearings, had said he thought it unlikely that a limited nuclear exchange would remain limited and, while he was to defend the posture affirmed in PD 59, he continued to express reservations about the prospects for successful limitation. During an interview on an ABC news programme on 17 August 1980, Brown maintained his belief that 'nuclear strikes, a nuclear strike on the United States, even though we retaliated initially in a limited way, would probably escalate ultimately to an all-out nuclear war' (*Official Text*, US Embassy, London, 19 August 1980). The replacement Secretary of State, Edmund Muskie, was similarly to tell a Senate hearing on Carter's directive that 'I do not want anyone to wrongly conclude that we suddenly have become confident about our ability to orchestrate nuclear exchanges and control escalation . . .' (*Official Text*, US Embassy, London, 17 September 1980).

Sixthly, although there are general similarities between Schlesinger's selective options and Brown's countervailing strategy, there are nonetheless some apparent differences that must not be allowed to escape our notice. Curiously, the public relations' claims made on behalf of the two strategic postures to some extent belie the novelty of their respective substances. On the one hand, during the Ford administration, Schlesinger was happy to draw attention to the new look of his strategic offerings whereas, as previously illustrated, there were marked continuities between the 1960s and early 1970s: limited counterforce options were part of American strategic practice long before they became part of declared strategic policy. As regards PD 59, we can perhaps arrive at the reverse judgment, that the administration's emphasis upon continuity distracts attention from some original features. Whilst the Schlesinger doctrine might fairly be regarded as old wine in new bottles, there is a specific sense in which Carter's strategic decisions represent new wine in old bottles.

What are the reasons for this claim? Ostensibly, as administration spokesmen were at pains to demonstrate, PD 59 is no more than the culmination of a decade's strategic development. '. . . PD 59 is not,' in Brown's words, 'a new strategic doctrine; it is not a radical departure from US strategic policy over the past decade or so' (address reproduced in *Survival,* November–December 1980, p. 268). Nonetheless, some of the emphases of PD 59 had not been as apparent in earlier policy statements. Above all, one feature of PD 59 which had not previously been given prominence, if stated at all, was the one pertaining to the targeting of the enemy's political and military control centres. Numerous official and background statements suggested that such Soviet centres featured high on the list of target priorities. One official, for instance, argued that the emphasis in the new policy would be upon threatening the targets most valued by the Soviet leadership amongst which he included 'its own ability to maintain control after a war starts' (*New York Times,* 6 August 1980). Brown, himself, cited as a more credible deterrent one which threatened 'the military and political command systems' (*Official Text,* US Embassy, London, 19 August 1980).

Various analysts noted this new emphasis of PD 59 and

were puzzled as to its implications, and one inspired *New York Times* report of 17 August 1980 suggested that the puzzlement was felt also in official circles. It quoted a spokesman as saying that: 'this policy seems to assume that both sides could engage in selective nuclear strikes without blowing each other up . . . But how will the Soviet leaders be able to control what their generals do during war if the Kremlin is going to be the first place that's taken out?' Flora Lewis likewise drew attention to both the novelty and the dangers of this aspect of the recently stated nuclear strategy:

> A policy question raised by the latest White House directive is the inclusion of 'command and control' targets. One constant of nuclear strategy has been the understanding that contrary to conventional doctrine, the enemy's command should be left intact so that there is still someone capable of stopping action with whom to negotiate before escalation becomes automatic and unconditional for humankind. Is this axiom being abandoned? Some American officials say not necessarily, that the US President should have the choice of liquidating the enemy's leadership if he thinks there is someone more amenable around to take charge. That is an intensely risky notion (*New York Times*, 15 August 1980).

What added to the seeming inappropriateness of such a measure in the context of the conduct of a limited nuclear war, was the almost simultaneous issuance of Presidential Directive 58, a series of measures designed to ensure greater survivability for America's own command structure in event of war. Such measures accorded well with the requirements of a limited nuclear strategy, but made the targeting of the enemy control systems seem even more out of phase with the general tenor of the new doctrine.

A seventh point which can be made refers to the crucial question of termination of a war that has begun. Regrettably, on this score, PD 59 and its accompanying exegeses offer no enlightenment. In a discussion of the ingredients of a countervailing strategy, Harold Brown remarked that 'in our planning we have not ignored the problem of ending the war, nor would we ignore it in the event of war' (*New York Times*, 21 August 1980). However, he did not elaborate on the nature of these plans for terminating the war. We are left to ponder, as with the city-swapping model, at which limit it would all end. When we recall Brown's other cautions that a limited nuclear war is likely to go all the way, the precise content of such plans for ending a war becomes even more elusive and our faith in its efficacy cannot but be shaken. If the Secretary of Defense knew the details of these plans for terminating war but could still fear that limited war in the beginning would become all-out war in the end, we can be forgiven for harbouring an occasional doubt.

An eighth and final observation is in order. What underlies the various strategic rethinkings of the 1970s, and is articulated in PD 59, is the need to think through, in a serious and comprehensive fashion, the realities of preparing for and, if need be, of actually conducting a nuclear engagement. It is this which the limited nuclear warriors of the past decade claim to have achieved — that they have faced up to, and come to terms with, the conduct of nuclear war in a limited form. Given this context, it is more than a little confusing to have the authors of the programme tell us also that 'nothing in PD 59 contemplates that nuclear war can be a deliberate instrument for achieving our national security goals, because it cannot be' (*Official Text,* US Embassy, London, 19 September 1980). How realistic has been the rethink about fighting a limited nuclear war is called fundamentally into question by this statement. Either fighting a nuclear war cannot serve strategic interests, or the administration is not serious in its intention to acquire the capacity to fight such a war. In the light of Brown's statement, the limited nuclear warriors cannot have it both ways.

One summary and general point remains to be made. This study has been concerned with conventions mitigating warfare, but the recurrent question has been how far war can be convention-governed without alteration to its fundamental nature. In other words, we are back to the possibility that rules governing the character of war may be such as to transmute warfare into some game-like activity. Paskins and Dockrill (1979 pp. 105–6) make this point obliquely by reference to an extreme convention designed to prevent fatality:

> . . . it makes sense to think of wrestling matches and even duels as surrounded with rules designed to guard against fatalities. With

war it is different. There are many instances in military history of the evolution of practices aimed to limit fatalities, but fighting whose rules were aimed to preclude fatality would not be war.

Let us examine this proposition in the light of one famous wartime suggestion — the proposal that, instead of employing the atomic bomb against Japanese cities, the surrender of Japan be induced by a harmless demonstration of the bomb's military capabilities. Would such a course of action, intended to terminate the war without fatalities, have been a normal act of war, or must it be dismissed as a frivolity inconsistent with war's deadly serious purpose? Certainly the scientific committee charged with the task of examining the technical feasibility of such a demonstration claimed to have taken the proposal seriously and to have carefully examined its possibilities. 'We were determined,' Arthur Compton, a senior scientific adviser, was to record, 'to find, if we could, some effective way of demonstrating the power of an atomic bomb without loss of life that would impress Japan's warlords' (Compton 1956, p. 239). Even Edward Teller was subsequently to regret that such a demonstration was not attempted:

> I believe that we should have demonstrated it to the Japanese before using it. Had we succeeded, had the Japanese surrendered after such a demonstration, then a new age would have started in which the power of human knowledge had stopped a war without killing a single individual (quoted in Giovannitti and Freed 1967, p. 329).

Would such a contrived and artificial termination of the war have been a humane limitation on war? Or would it have been a social nicety in complete contradiction to the stated aims for which the United States was engaged in war with Japan?

The capacity of stylized conventions to limit killing in war could not be thought encouraging in the light of earlier precedents in the course of the Second World War. As is well known, the precision bombing with which Britain prepared to conduct the war rapidly took the form of indiscriminate area bombardment as Bomber Command groped for an operational policy which was consistent with its role as an independent force and with the technical limitations of its bomber fleet. It is difficult to conceive that the very Bomber Command which was to devise the saturation bombings of Berlin, Hamburg and of Dresden had but a few short years before prevented its aircraft from bombing German naval vessels at Wilhelmshaven, as they were considered too close to the shore to be attacked without collateral civilian damage (Hastings 1981, p. 28). The conventions of aerial bombardment were, therefore, to be the most spectacular casualties of the war. Likewise, although the United States Air Force had a slightly cleaner record in its offensive against Germany, by early 1945 it was heavily engaged in fire-bombing of Japan with massive civilian loss of life.

It was against this background that the decision on use of the new atomic weapon had to be taken. The politico-strategic problem was how to end the war while minimizing loss of life in securing that objective and, of course, it is history that the view which prevailed was the one which argued that these objectives could best be realized by military employment of the atomic bomb, without warning, against Japanese cities.

What, then, are we to make of the abortive proposal to demonstrate the bomb's destructive potential? It has been argued above that, as a result of a set combat between champions, a conventional or artificial notion of victory is substituted for victory as a brute physical fact: the enemy, although defeated, is still in existence as a military force. The champion is accordingly the supremely stylized form of resolution of conflict by military encounter. From this perspective, if in a less extreme form, the proposal that the United States demonstrate the bomb, rather than employ it as a weapon of war, can be seen as a suggestion for an equally stylized termination of the conflict with Japan. War is thought to require killing, and yet this was a proposal to conduct the final stages of the war in such a manner that any further killing could be averted. As with the champion, the intent of the proposal was that a conventional notion of victory (based on the awe of a demonstrated effect) be substituted for the bloody but 'real' victory which would flow from invasion, or from repeated poundings of Japan by atomic weapons. In other words, if adopted, this initiative would have led to a convention of limitation whereby the United States agreed not to destroy Japan (actually) if Japan agreed not to resist further. The demonstrated detonation of the nuclear device would constitute a symbolic victory for the Americans, just as if their appointed champion had carried the day: the Japanese would be defeated (symbolically) although still capable of resistance (physically).

The proposal to demonstrate the bomb never gained much support in the highest échelons of the American decision-making apparatus. The writings of Truman, Stimson and Byrnes convey the impression that no decision was needed to use the bomb in a military capacity: it would have required a decision *not* to use it, and this possibility was not seriously entertained. This conforms with Compton's impression of the discussions at the decisive Interim Committee meeting of 31 May 1945 to the effect that 'it seemed to be a foregone conclusion that the bomb would be used' (1956, p. 238) and with Oppenheimer's intuitive judgment that 'the decision was implicit in the project. I don't know whether it could have been stopped' (quoted in Giovannitti and Freed 1967, p. 328). Nonetheless, the proposal for a demonstration was repeatedly made and was persistent over time even if most of its adherents were to be found within the scientific community, rather than amongst those in political authority (*see* Smith 1965, p. 26). Scientific advisers Bush and Conant had made a suggestion for a demonstration of the bomb in a memorandum to Stimson on 30 September 1944, and Alexander Sachs had reported that President Roosevelt was favourably impressed by a similar suggestion made by him in December 1944 (Schoenberger 1969, p. 45). The proposal was reiterated in the Franck report of June 1945 which favoured a 'demonstration in an appropriately selected uninhabited area' (Smith 1965, p. 45). The possibilities of a demonstration had already, by this time, been mooted during a lunch-time discussion at the 31 May meeting of the Interim Committee.

Perhaps the fullest, and most colourful, suggestion for a demonstration of the bomb, as an alternative to its direct employment against Japanese cities, was that put forward by Lewis Strauss, Special Assistant to Navy Secretary, Forrestal:

> . . . I proposed to Secretary Forrestal that the weapon should be demonstrated before it was used. Primarily it was because it was clear to a number of people, myself among them, that the war was very nearly over . . . My proposal to the Secretary was that the weapon should be demonstrated over some area accessible to Japanese observers and where its effects would be dramatic. I remember suggesting that a satisfactory place for such a demonstration would be a large forest of cryptomeria trees not far from Tokyo . . . I anticipated that a bomb detonated at a suitable height above such a forest . . . would lay the trees out in windrows from the center of the explosion in all directions as though they were matchsticks, and, of course, set them afire in the center . . . (quoted in Giovannitti and Freed 1967, p. 145).

In fact, Ralph Bard, Under Secretary of the Navy, was to resign over the issue. He argued that the Japanese should at least be given some preliminary warning of the dropping of the bomb and, in support of this, appealed to the humanitarianism and the 'fair play attitude' of the United States (p. 146).

Many reasons were given for the non-adoption of the demonstration proposal. Interestingly, however, they all related to the technicalities of the operation or to other practical difficulties. Oppenheimer recalled that 'we did say that we did not think exploding one of these things as a firecracker over a desert was likely to be very impressive' (quoted in Feis 1966, p. 55), and fears of malfunction, or Japanese interference, were widely expressed. At any rate, the scientific committee reported that 'we can propose no technical demonstration likely to bring an end to the war; we can see no acceptable alternative to direct military use' (Schoenberger 1969, p. 143). No one seemed to question, in principle, whether this was a proper thing to do *in time of war* when American lives were at stake. Or, perhaps, the judgment that such gentlemanly etiquette had no place in war did not have to be expressed: it was already embodied in the irresistibility with which the use of the bomb became policy, and in the unspoken consensus that employment of the bomb was a legitimate act of war requiring no particular justification nor special gestures of chivalry towards the enemy.

Mercifully, we have very little experience of the manner of employment of nuclear weapons in war. The bombings of

Hiroshima and Nagasaki constitute the totality of our direct experience. While it would be rash to draw general conclusions, or to base prescriptions, on that single experience in what might have been a unique situation (if for no other reason than that possession of the bomb was unilateral), we can at least make the comment that the saving of lives by the adoption of stylized conventions of combat has no firm precedent in the nuclear age. Whether the demonstrations of intent, outlined in the recent theories of limited nuclear war, will have more appeal than did the idea of an atomic demonstration in 1945, or whether symbolic acts of war will have a greater capacity for inducing limitation now than then, remains to be seen.

Conclusion

This study has been concerned with two different types of convention for the limitation of warfare, one of which limits war by stipulating the very nature of its process and the other limiting war by introducing into it substantive restraints. At one level, as has been indicated, there is potential tension between the two conventions, as each places an inverse priority upon the process of resolution and the substantive limitation to which the process is subjected. On the other hand, it is the argument of this study that limitations in war, if they are to make political sense, must be located within a convincing political description of the nature and purpose of war itself.

The relationship is similar to that between the *ius ad bellum* and the *ius in bello*. It was earlier argued that some writers assume an inherent antagonism between the two, it being thought illogical at best, or unfair at worst, both to discriminate between belligerent parties as to their respective causes, and to treat them identically as to their conduct. As Claude (1980, pp. 90–1) has commented: 'the early modern statesmen of the European system seemed to believe, and they had some basis for believing, that they had to choose between *jus ad bellum* and *jus in bello,* between restricting the right to go to war and limiting the manner of fighting . . . Moreover if it seems illogical to attempt to regulate the conduct of the unjust half of a war, there may be a psychological barrier to the regulation of the conduct of the just half.'

This is so, however, only insofar as the relationship between *ius ad bellum* and *ius in bello* is perceived to be an antagonistic one. Once again, the argument of this study would be that we require a return to those gross limitations which the

238

medievalists saw as deriving from the very purposes of warfare itself. In other words, the *ad bellum* and *in bello* were never as completely opposed as Claude suggests, various constraints on the conduct of war being understood as an irreducible component of the cause which lent war its justice. As has been said elsewhere in a similar context: 'exactly because the political quality of life can give a moral reason for going to war, those for whom it is a reason cannot be indifferent to the moral boundaries of war and cannot consistently *pursue victory at any price*' (Danto 1978, p. 179). Accordingly, in the nuclear age, the substantive limitations of convention B have to find their vitality in the very process of war.

Conventions of type A are predicated upon particular conceptions of the nature of war: they limit war by stipulating the form of settlement and this form finds its meaning in the wider social definition of the purpose of war. To claim, therefore, as is done in this study, that war can be limited by describing its essential function, is to make a very general claim which in no way prejudices any particular concept of war. On the contrary, such a formulation has the virtue that it is compatible with each and every conception of war as a purposeful social or political activity. For instance, the limitations deriving from the nature of war itself are as compelling in a politically-necessary war as they are in one deemed morally just. Indeed, it is this idea of a spillover from the purpose of war to the mode of its substantive conduct, that provides a point of identity as between the doctrine of just war and the theory of *raison d'état*: in both cases, war is limited by the ends for which the war is fought.

It is from this perspective that the limitations upon nuclear war are to be most fully appreciated. The theorists of limited nuclear war, as has been seen, have suggested a variety of conventions in accordance with which a nuclear war might be conducted with restraint on both sides. And yet such a conception of limited nuclear war remains fearsomely inadequate as long as it is unattached to a convincing political account of the purpose of a war of this kind. Limitation in nuclear war requires that usage of nuclear weapons be permitted only when supported by a sustained political theory of the nature and purposes of the war in which they will serve. As things stand, this requirement must place overwhelming restrictions on *any* resort to nuclear weaponry, because the theorists have fallen far short of providing us with any such theory.

What should be emphasized, then, are the necessary macro-restraints upon the conduct of nuclear war as opposed to the equally worthwhile, but less potent, micro-restraints. While it is fit and proper that war's moral universe be fully explored, and the various just and unjust forms of conduct be argued about, and while the international jurists provide valuable service in creating, and recreating afresh, a body of positive law for armed conflict, in the final analysis there can be no substitute for that limitation which must derive — if it is to derive at all — from a politically-meaningful description of the nature and purpose of war's very enterprise. Until such time as a persuasive account is offered of the relationship between war's political ends and its nuclear means, the conclusion that must inescapably be drawn is that, as a matter of political theory, the macro-limitations inherent in war itself must serve as a prohibition upon resort to this particular means.

Contemporary warfare encounters yet another special difficulty in terms of its effective limitation: not only do we have to construct a meaningful relationship between *ius ad bello* (pre-war) and *ius in bello* (intra-war) considerations, but also there is need for clarity on the relationship between *ius in bello* (intra-war) and *ius post bellum* (post-war) considerations. Any over-arching doctrine of limits to war must encompass these three areas, and ensure consistency in their interrelationship: effective limitation can occur in each of these three phases provided only that preoccupation with one phase does not nullify the objectives of another. The peculiar problem of contemporary warfare, in nuclear conditions, is that, in contrast with traditional warfare, the latter two phases may inadvertently be collapsed into one. In traditional discussions of the law of war, legal theorists have generally distinguished between the requirements of behaviour in relation to the enemy during war, and required behaviour after the war. Unfortunately, nuclear weaponry does not respect such fine chronological distinctions. As nuclear deterrence

CONCLUSION241

theorists, and Schelling specifically, have long since demonstrated, nuclear weapons allow during the war that infliction
of punishment on the enemy civilian population which
traditionally could only be wrought after the war, and after
the clash of arms had rendered vulnerable the homeland of
one of the contestants. It is the very essence of the 'diplomacy
of violence' that the more gory fruits of victory, in the form
of a capacity to slaughter the enemy population, are bestowed during the war and not as a consequence of its
successful prosecution. Moreover, the fruits are mutually
bestowed.

In other words, in an all-out nuclear exchange the *in bello*
and *post bellum* phases may be collapsed. It follows that, just
as a *ius in bello* may be read back into, and indeed may
undermine, the original *ius ad bellum*, so the rules for the
proper treatment of the vanquished, if they are to be respected at all, have to be read back into, and become a part of,
the *ius in bello* which prescribes the actual conduct of
hostilities. A *ius post bellum* can no longer be respected in its
own right as, by then, it may aready be too late.

Figuratively speaking, we can now see that substantive
limitation in war can be effective only by reaching both backwards and forwards: the substantive limitation of war must
reach backwards and become a necessary part of the reasoning for the initiation of war; likewise it must reach forward
and become a necessary part of the reasoning for its termination. Only in this way can conventions A and B be effectively
combined and meaningful limitation of war ensured.

Does this review of contemporary thinking on limits to
war provide us with any sense of the direction in which we
are travelling? How, as regards the limitation of war, are we
currently performing in comparison with generations and
centuries past?

Two characteristics of recent attitudes towards warfare are
pre-eminent. The first is the virtual disappearance of those
conventions of warfare that have their origins in a cosmopolitan military *esprit de corps*. To a large extent, previous
periods of restraint in warfare have owed much to transnational social values rooted deeply in the domestic social
structures of the various states. As was written, with more

than a trace of nostalgia, back in the 1930s: 'restricted warfare was one of the loftiest achievements of the eighteenth century. It belongs to a class of hot-house plants which can only thrive in an aristocratic and qualitative civilization. We are no longer capable of it . . .' (quoted in Fuller 1972, p. 25). Such restraints as were practised in the age of chivalry were prompted by comparable social forces.

The other feature is the prevalence of military resort to the terror principle. We are experiencing now the full realization of the Platonic restriction in accordance with which 'the guilty are compelled by the innocent sufferers to give satisfaction'. This theme, that the innocent may suffer as a means of putting pressure on the guilty, has surfaced as a major characteristic of modern warfare and with it, as has been frequently pointed out, the claim to immunity on the part of noncombatants has been called into serious question. The terror principle is expressed in the area and fire bombings of the Second World War, in the nuclear assaults on Hiroshima and Nagasaki, in the entire structure of nuclear deterrence and in the activities of various domestic and transnational dissidents in furtherance of their political goals. However, the principle, in its starkest form, had long since been enunciated. General Sherman, for instance, during the American Civil War had vindicated his own military conduct in precisely these terms. 'If the people raise a howl against my barbarity and cruelty,' he argued, 'I will answer that war is war . . . If they want peace they and their relatives must stop the war' (quoted in Fuller 1972, p. 107). The civilian hostage, on a mass scale, has in consequence become a typical means of contemporary warfare.

The road to total war is a journey often made by military historians and there is no need to retrace it in this study. We might note at the most general level that changes in the practice of war can largely be attributed to changing conceptions of its nature and purpose, and to the broadening of political goals associated with the development of the modern nation-state. The transition has been one from fighting just or chivalrous wars to fighting politically-necessary wars and the constraints of the former seemed to make little sense in relation to the latter.

The tendency is still in this direction, with the qualification that there has been some confluence of two streams of thought, the just war and *raison d'état* traditions. Whereas the nineteenth century was content to make the state judge of its own recourse to war, the twentieth century has sought to add the ideological sanction of justness, conferred by the international community, to a resort to war primarily determined by political calculations. There is then more than a grain of truth in the rueful judgment that Bismarck fought necessary wars and killed thousands, whereas we have fought just wars and killed millions.

There is no reason to expect this trend to abate: on the contrary, following Claude's argument, there is every likelihood that the tendency is gaining in strength:

> The recent refurbishment of the old just war doctrine owes a good deal to the intensification of the ideological factor in both domestic and international politics. It perhaps owes even more to the lessening of anxiety about war and to the growth of confidence that war can be controlled and prevented from assuming the proportions of global catastrophe. Just as the earlier subordination of justice to peace indicated acute anxiety about the danger of World War III, the current subordination of peace to justice reflects relaxation about the danger. A growing sense of security, warranted or not, underlies the conviction that mankind can afford to indulge in warfare for the sake of promoting justice. ... For better or for worse, we are back to the position that it is legitimate for states to resort to war as an instrument of policy, if that policy is just (Claude 1980, p. 96).

This takes us little closer to making the stark choice presented by any contemplation of limits to war in the nuclear age. We have every reason to believe that limited war would be preferable to all-out war: simultaneously, we have every reason to believe that no war is preferable to a limited war which is likely, in any case, to get out of hand. How this particular circle can be squared resists all philosophical analysis. On the one hand, limitation of war, in a nuclear context, has considerable human appeal. To be able to think about war as other societies and earlier ages have been able to do, has much to commend it. One historian of warfare recounts the following instance:

The effect of a declaration of war as it occurs among the Inland Negroes and the Ba- Mbala is to render the encounter less severe, so much so that a special name, *Kutara* or small war, is given by the latter people to this kind of warfare. A day and place are appointed for the battle, the bush is cleared to give a fair and open field, and the kind of weapons and mode of fighting so regulated that rarely are any of the combatants killed (Davie 1929, p. 292).

It is scarcely conceivable that a nuclear equivalent of this *Kutara* would pass as genuine warfare. But, at the other extreme, is a nuclear exchange involving possibly some 250 million prompt deaths any closer to the concept of war? This is pointless slaughter, and pointless slaughter is not what we understand war to be. If we must have war, then it should be war, not slaughter, and we can move in this direction only by accepting intrinsic limits as a necessary part of war, and not as frivolous follies which undermine war's dignity and deadly serious purpose. At this level, and in comparison with the alternative, limited nuclear war has its attraction. Iklé (1977, pp. 130—1) explains why it is proper to think in these terms:

It is a tragic paradox of our age that the highly humane objective of preventing nuclear war is served by a military doctrine and engines of destruction whose very purpose is to inflict genocide . . . It is crucial, of course, that this contingency be blocked. But should nuclear war nonetheless break out, the desperate logic of the Great Deterrent offers not the slightest mercy for humanity.

The danger, of course, is that a little war can be more easily contemplated. Ian Smart, in a letter to *The Times* of 17 January 1974, resisted the attractions of limitation by placing all his moral eggs in the one deterrence basket. 'The only humane policy,' he maintained, '. . . is the one which reduces to a minimum the chance of anyone being killed . . .' Could the chance of war breaking out be reduced to zero, we might be content to back Smart's judgment, but the question that has to be asked as far as the reduction of the chances of war breaking out is concerned, is how little is enough? What is the room for doubt on the probability of war? In the last analysis, political philosophy provides no adequate chart for selecting a course between the Scylla of limited war and the Charybdis of nuclear holocaust.

Bibliography

Adcock, F. and Mosley, D. J. (1975) *Diplomacy in Ancient Greece,* London, Thames and Hudson.

Åkerman, N. (1972) *On the Doctrine of Limited War,* Lund, Berlingska Boktryckeriet.

Alexander, L. A. (1976) 'Self-defense and the killing of noncombatants: a reply to Fullinwider', *Philosophy and Public Affairs,* Vol. 5, No. 4, Summer.

Amdur, R. (1977) 'Rawls' theory of justice: domestic and international perspectives', *World Politics,* April.

Anscombe, E. (1970) 'War and murder' in R. Wasserstrom (ed.) *War and Morality,* Belmont California, Wadsworth.

Armour, W. S. (1923) 'Customs of warfare in ancient India', *Transactions of Grotius Society,* Vol. 8.

Arnett, R. L. (1979) 'Soviet attitudes towards nuclear war: do they really think they can win?' *Journal of Strategic Studies,* Vol. 2, No. 2, September.

Aron, R. (1956) 'A half-century of limited war', *Bulletin of the Atomic Scientists,* Vol. xii, April.

Aron, R. (1958) *On War,* London, Secker and Warburg.

Augustine St (1972) *The City of God,* Harmondsworth, Penguin.

Ayala, B. (1912) *De Jure et Officiis Bellicis et Disciplina Militari Libri III,* Washington, Carnegie Institution.

Bailey, S. D. (1972) *Prohibitions and Restraints in War,* London, Oxford University Press.

Bainton, R. H. (1960) *Christian Attitudes Towards War and Peace,* Nashville, Tennessee, Abingdon Press.

Baldwin, H. W. (1959) 'Limited war', *The Atlantic,* May.

Ball, D. (1975) 'Déja vu: the return to counterforce in the Nixon administration' in R. J. O'Neill (ed.) *The Strategic Nuclear Balance,* Canberra, Strategic and Defence Studies Centre, Australian National University.

Ball, D. (1977) 'The counterforce potential of American SLBM systems' *Journal of Peace Research,* Vol. xiv, No. 1.

245

Ball, D. (1980a) *Developments in US Strategic Nuclear Policy under the Carter Administration*, ACIS Working Paper No. 21, Los Angeles, Center for International and Strategic Affairs, University of California.

Ball, D. (1980b) 'Review of "The effects of nuclear war"' *Survival*, September–October.

Ballis, W. B. (1937) *The Legal Position of War: Changes in its Practice and Theory from Plato to Vattel*, The Hague, Nijhoff.

Barnett, R. W. (1975) 'Trans-SALT: Soviet strategic doctrine' *Orbis*, Vol. xix, No. 2, Summer.

Barnie, J. (1974) *War in Medieval Society: Social Values and the Hundred Years War 1337–99*, London, Weidenfeld and Nicolson.

Baylis, J., Booth, K., Garnett, J. and Williams, P. (1975) *Contemporary Strategy*, London, Croom Helm.

Beeler, J. (1971) *Warfare in Feudal Europe 730–1200*, Ithaca, Cornell University Press.

Bennett, B. (1977) *Fatality Uncertainties in Limited Nuclear War*, R-2218-AF, Santa Monica, Rand Corporation.

Bennett, J. C. (ed.) (1962) *Nuclear Weapons and the Conflict of Conscience*, London, Lutterworth Press.

Beres, L. R. (1980) *Apocalypse: Nuclear Catastrophe in World Politics*, Chicago, University of Chicago Press.

Bernal, J. D. (1958) 'Disarmament and limited nuclear war', *New World Review*, Vol. xxvi, January.

Best, G. (1976) 'How right is might? some aspects of the international debate about how to fight wars and how to win them' in G. Best and A. Wheatcroft (eds) *War, Economy and the Military Mind*, London, Croom Helm.

Best, G. (1980) *Humanity in Warfare*, London, Weidenfeld and Nicolson.

Best, G. (1981) 'World War Two and the law of war' *Review of International Studies*, Vol. 7, No. 2, April.

Betts, R. K. (1979) 'Nuclear peace: mythology and futurology', *Journal of Strategic Studies*, Vol. 2, No. 1, May.

Bhatia, H. S. (ed.) (1977) *International Law and Practice in Ancient India*, New Delhi, Deep and Deep Publications.

Bialer, U. (1980) *The Shadow of the Bomber*, London, Royal Historical Society.

Blackett, P. M. S. (1956) *Atomic Weapons and East–West Relations*, London, Cambridge University Press.

Bohannan, P. (ed.) (1967) *Law and Warfare*, New York, American Museum.

Booth, K. and Wright, M. (eds) (1978) *American Thinking About Peace and War*, Sussex, Harvester Press.

Bracken, P. (1980) 'Collateral damage and theatre warfare', *Survival*, September—October.

Bramson, L. and Goethals, G. (eds) (1964) *War: Studies from Psychology, Sociology and Anthropology*, New York, Basic Books.

Brandt, R. (1974) 'Utilitarianism and the rules of war' in M. Cohen *et al.* (eds) *War and Moral Responsibility*, Princeton, Princeton University Press.

Brazier-Creagh, K. R. (1957) 'Limited war', *Brassey's Annual.*

Brennan, D. G. (ed.) (1975) *The Implications of Precision Weapons for American Strategic Interests*, New York, Hudson Institute.

Brenner, M. J. (1975) 'Tactical nuclear strategy and European defence: a critical reappraisal', *International Affairs*, Vol. 51, No. 1, January.

Brodie, B. (1954a) 'Nuclear weapons: strategic or tactical', *Foreign Affairs*, Vol. xxxii, January.

Brodie, B. (1954b) 'Unlimited weapons and limited war', *The Reporter*, 18 November.

Brodie, B. (1957) 'More about limited war', *World Politics*, Vol. x, October.

Brodie, B. (1959) *Strategy in the Missile Age*, Princeton, Princeton University Press.

Brodie, B. (1973) *War and Politics*, London, Cassell.

Brodie, B. (1978) 'The development of nuclear strategy', *International Security*, Vol. 2, No. 4, Spring.

Brower, M. (1962) 'Controlled thermonuclear war', *The New Republic*, 30 July.

Brown, E. J. (1968) *Chemical Warfare: A Study in Restraints*, Princeton, Princeton University Press.

Brundage, J. A. (1969) *Medieval Canon Law and the Crusader*, Madison, University of Wisconsin Press.

Bull, H. (1979) 'Recapturing the just war for political theory', *World Politics*, July.

Burns, A. L. (1970) *Ethics and Deterrence: A Nuclear Balance Without Hostage Cities?*, Adelphi Paper No. 69, London, Institute for Strategic Studies.

Buzzard, A. (1956a) 'Massive retaliation and graduated deterrence' *World Politics*, Vol. vii, January.

Buzzard, A. *et al.* (1956b) *On Limiting Atomic War*, London, Royal Institute of International Affairs.

Buzzard, A. *et al.* (1957) 'On limiting atomic war', *Bulletin of the Atomic Scientists*, Vol. xiii, June.

Cane, J. W. (1978) 'The technology of modern weapons for limited military use', *Orbis*, Vol. 22, No. 1, Spring.

Carey, J. (ed.) (1971) *When Battle Rages, How Can Law Protect?* New York, Oceana Publications.

Carlton, D. (1969) 'Anti-ballistic missile deployment and the doctrine of limited strategic nuclear war' in C. F. Barnaby and A. Boserup (eds) *Implications of Anti-Ballistic Missile Systems,* London, Souvenir Press.

Carlton, D. and Schaerf, C. (eds) (1977) *Arms Control and Technological Innovation,* London, Croom Helm.

Carroll, B. (1970) 'War termination and conflict theory: value premises, theories and policies', *The Annals of the American Academy of Politcal and Social Science,* November.

Carter, B. (1974) 'Nuclear strategy and nuclear weapons', *Scientific American,* May.

Cassesse, A. (ed.) (1979) *The New Humanitarian Law of Armed Conflict,* Naples, Editoriale Scientifica.

Chakravarti, P. C. (no date) *The Art of War in Ancient India,* Dacca, University of Dacca.

Cheminant, P. le (1961) 'Tactical deterrence or limited war', *Brassey's Annual.*

Cicero, M. T. (1913) *De Officiis,* London, Heinemann.

Clark, G. (1958) *War and Society in the Seventeenth Century,* London, Cambridge University Press.

Clark, I. (1980) *Reform and Resistance in the International Order,* Cambridge, Cambridge University Press.

Clarke, H. B. (1902) *The Cid Campeador and the Waning of the Crescent in the West,* New York, Putnam's.

Claude, I. (1980) 'Just wars: doctrines and institutions', *Political Science Quarterly,* Vol. 95, No. 1, Spring.

Clausewitz, K. von (1976) *On War* (ed. by M. Howard and P. Paret), Princeton, Princeton University Press.

Cohen, M., Nagel, T. and Scanlon, R. (1974) *War and Moral Responsibility,* Princeton, Princeton University Press.

Compton, A. H. (1956) *Atomic Quest,* London, Oxford University Press.

Corvisier, A. (1979) *Armies and Societies in Europe 1494–1789,* Bloomington, Indiana University Press.

Coser, L. (1961) 'The termination of conflict', *Journal of Conflict Resolution,* Vol. 5, No. 4.

Cox, R. H. (1960) *Locke on War and Peace,* Oxford, Oxford University Press.

Craig, G. A. (1958) 'The problem of limited war', *Commentary* Vol. xxv, February.

Creveld, M. van (1977) *Supplying War: Logistics from Wallenstein to Patton,* Cambridge, Cambridge University Press.

Danto, A. C. (1978) 'On moral codes and modern war', *Social Research,* Vol. 45, No. 1, Spring.

Davie, M. R. (1929) *The Evolution of War,* New Haven, Yale University Press.

Davis, L. E. (1975–6) *Limited Nuclear Options: Deterrence and the New American Doctrine,* Adelphi Paper No. 21, London, International Institute for Strategic Studies.

Deane, H. A. (1963) *The Political and Social Ideas of St. Augustine,* New York, Columbia University Press.

Department of Defense *Annual Report,* Washington, USGPO.

Doppelt, G. (1978) 'Walzer's theory of morality in international relations', *Philosophy and Public Affairs,* Vol. 8, No. 1, Fall.

Draper, G. I. A. D. (1958) 'The idea of the just war', *The Listener,* 14 August.

Draper, G. I. A. D. (1972) 'International law and armed conflicts', *International Affairs,* Vol. 48, No. 1, January.

Draper, G. I. A. D. (1973) *The Implementation of the Modern Law of Armed Conflicts,* Jerusalem, Hebrew University Press.

Drell, S. D. and Hippel, F. von (1976) 'Limited nuclear war', *Scientific American,* November.

Dupuy, T. N. (1961) 'Can America fight a limited nuclear war?', *Orbis,* Vol. 5, No. 1, Spring.

Dyer, P. W. (1973) 'Will tactical nuclear weapons ever be used?', *Political Science Quarterly,* Vol. 88, No. 2, June.

Dyer, P. W. (1977) 'Tactical nuclear weapons and deterrence in Europe', *Political Science Quarterly,* Vol. 92, No. 2, Summer.

Earle, E. M. (ed.) (1944) *Makers of Modern Strategy,* Princeton, Princeton University Press.

Elbe, J. von (1939) 'The evolution of the concept of the just war in international law', *The American Journal of International Law,* Vol. 33, October.

Entreves, A. P. D' (ed.) (1948) *Aquinas: Selected Political Writings,* Oxford, Blackwell.

Fair, C. (1971) *From the Jaws of Victory,* London, Weidenfeld and Nicolson.

Fairbanks, C. (1976) 'War-limiting' in K. Knorr (ed.) *Historical Dimensions of National Security Problems,* Lawrence, University Press of Kansas.

Falk, R. (1975) 'Methods and means of warfare' in P. Trooboff (ed.) *Law and Responsibility in Warfare,* Chapel Hill, University of North Carolina Press.

Farer, T. J. (1971) 'The laws of war 25 years after Nuremberg', *International Conciliation,* May.

Farrar, L. L. (ed.) (1978) *War: A Historical, Political and Social Study,* Santa Barbara, ABC-CLIO.

Feis, H. (1966) *The Atomic Bomb and the End of World War II,* Princeton, Princeton University Press.

Fernández-Santamaria, J. A. (1977) *The State, War and Peace: Spanish Political Thought in the Renaissance,* Cambridge, Cambridge University Press.

Forsyth, M. G. *et al.* (eds) (1970) *The Theory of International Relations,* London, Allen & Unwin.

Forsythe, D. P. (1976) 'Law, morality and war after Vietnam', *World Politics,* April.

Foster, J. and Brewer, G. (1976) *And the Clocks Were Striking Thirteen: The Termination of War,* P-559, Santa Monica, RAND Corporation.

Fox, W. T. R. (1970) 'The causes of peace and conditions of war', *The Annals of the American Academy of Political and Social Science,* November.

Frankland, N. (1965) *Bombing Offensive Against Germany,* London, Faber and Faber.

Freedman, L. (1980) *Britain and Nuclear Weapons* London, Macmillan for Royal Institute of International Affairs.

Frei, D. (1974) 'The regulation of warfare', *Journal of Conflict Resolution,* Vol. 18, December.

Friedman, L. (ed.) (1972) *The Law of War: A Documentary History* (2 Vols), New York, Random House.

Friedrich, C. J. (1948) *Inevitable Peace,* Cambridge, Harvard University Press.

Froissart, J. (1839) *Chronicles of England, France, Spain, and the Adjoining Countries,* London, William Smith.

Fuller, J. F. C. (1946) *Armament and History,* London, Eyre and Spottiswood.

Fuller, J. F. C. (1972) *The Conduct of War 1789–1961,* London, Methuen.

Fullinwider, R. K. (1975) 'War and innocence', *Philosophy and Public Affairs,* Vol. 5, No. 1, Fall.

Gallie, W. B. (1978) *Philosophers of Peace and War,* Cambridge, Cambridge University Press.

Garlan, Y. (1975) *War in the Ancient World,* London, Chatto and Windus.

Garnett, J. (1979) 'Limited "conventional" war in the nuclear age' in M. Howard (ed.) *Restraints on War,* Oxford, Oxford University Press.

Gentili, A. (1933) *De Iure Belli Libri Tres,* London, Oxford for Carnegie Endowment for International Peace.

Gilbert, F. (1944) 'Machiavelli: the Renaissance of the art of war' in M. E. Earle (ed.) *Makers of Modern Strategy,* Princeton, Princeton University Press.

Gilpin, R. (1962) *American Scientists and Nuclear Weapons Policy,* Princeton, Princeton University Press.

Giovannitti, L. and Freed, F. (1967) *The Decision to Drop the Bomb*, London, Methuen.

Glasstone, S. (ed.) (1962) *The Effects of Nuclear Weapons* (rev. edn) Washington, USGPO.

Gray, C. S. (1979) 'Nuclear strategy: the case for a theory of victory', *International Security,* Vol. 4, No. 1, Summer.

Gray, C. and Payne, K. (1980) 'Victory is possible', *Foreign Policy,* No. 39, Summer.

Green, P. (1966) *Deadly Logic: The Theory of Nuclear Deterrence,* Ohio, Ohio State University Press.

Greenwood, T. and Nacht, M. (1974) 'The new nuclear debate: sense or nonsense', *Foreign Affairs,* July.

Griffiths, F. and Polanyi, J. (eds) (1979) *The Dangers of Nuclear War,* Toronto, Toronto University Press.

Groom, A. J. R. (1974) *British Thinking About Nuclear Weapons,* London, Frances Pinter.

Grotius, H. (1925) *De Jure Belli Ac Pacis Libri Tres,* London, Oxford for Carnegie Endowment for International Peace.

Halperin, M. H. (1962) 'The "no-cities" doctrine' *New Republic,* 8 October.

Halperin, M. H. (1963) *Limited War in the Nuclear Age,* New York, Wiley and Sons.

Halperin, M. H. (1968) *Contemporary Military Strategy,* London, Faber and Faber.

Hamilton, B. (1963) *Political Thought in Sixteenth-Century Spain,* Oxford, Oxford University Press.

Handel, M. (1978) 'The study of war termination', *The Journal of Strategic Studies,* Vol. 1, No. 1, May.

Hartigan, R. S. (1965) 'Noncombatant immunity: its scope and development', *Continuum,* August.

Hartigan, R. S. (1966) 'Saint Augustine on war and killing: the problem of the innocent', *Journal of the History of Ideas,* Vol. xxvii, No. 2, April–June.

Hartigan, R. S. (1967) 'Noncombatant immunity: reflections on its origins and present status', *Review of Politics,* April.

Hartigan, R. S. (1974) 'War and its normative justification', *Review of Politics,* October.

Hastings, M. (1981) *Bomber Command,* London, Pan Books.

Held, V., Morgenbesser, S. and Nagel, T. (eds) (1974) *Philosophy, Morality and International Affairs,* New York, Oxford University Press.

Hendel, C. W. (1934) *Jean-Jaques Rousseau: Moralist,* New York, Bobbs-Merrill.

Hobbes, T. (no date) *Leviathan* (ed. by M. Oakshott) Oxford, Blackwell.

Holst, J. J. and Nerlich, U. (1977) *Beyond Nuclear Deterrence,* New York, Crane, Russak and Co.

Holst, J. J. and Schneider, W. (eds) (1969) *Why ABM?* New York, Pergamon Press.

Howard, M. (1970) *Studies in War and Peace,* London, Temple Smith.

Howard, M. (1976) *War in European History,* Oxford, Oxford University Press.

Howard, M. (1978) *War and the Liberal Conscience,* London, Temple Smith.

Howard, M. (ed.) (1979) *Restraints on War,* Oxford, Oxford University Press.

Huizinga, J. (1949) *Homo Ludens,* London, Routledge and Kegan Paul.

Huizinga, J. (1954) *The Waning of the Middle Ages,* New York, Double-day.

Huizinga, J. (1959) *Men and Ideas,* New York, Meridian Books.

Iklé, F. C. (1971) *Every War Must End,* New York, Columbia University Press.

Iklé, F. C. (1977) 'Can nuclear deterrence last out the century' in R. Pranger and R. Labrie (eds) *Nuclear Strategy and National Security: Points of View,* Washington, American Enterprise Institute.

Institute for Strategic Studies (1970) *Problems of Modern Strategy,* London, Chatto and Windus.

International Institute for Strategic Studies (1980) *The Future of Strategic Deterrence,* Adelphi Papers Nos. 160, 161, London.

Irving, D. (1980) *The Destruction of Dresden,* London, Futura Edition.

Jessup, P. C. (1957) 'Political and humanitarian approaches to limitation of warfare', *American Journal of International Law,* Vol. 51.

Johansen, R. C. (1974) 'Countercombatant strategy: a new balance of terror?' *Worldview,* July.

Johnson, J. T. (1975) *Ideology, Reason and the Limitation of War: Religious and Secular Concepts 1200–1740,* Princeton, Princeton University Press.

Jones, C. D. (1975) 'Just wars and limited wars: restraints on the use of Soviet armed forces', *World Politics,* Vol. xxviii, No. 1, October.

Josephson, M. (1957) 'Fantasy of limited war', *The Nation,* 31 August.

Joyce, J. A. (ed.) (no date) *Three Peace Classics,* London, Peace Book Club.

Kadt, E. J. de (1964) *British Defence Policy and Nuclear War,* London, Frank Cass and Company.

Kahn, H. (1960) *On Thermonuclear War,* Princeton, Princeton University Press.

Kahn, H. (1962) *Thinking About the Unthinkable,* London, Weidenfeld and Nicolson.

Kahn, H. (1965) *On Escalation: Metaphors and Scenarios,* London, Pall Mall.

Kahn, H. (1970) 'Issues of thermonuclear war termination', *Annals of the American Academy of Political and Social Science,* November.

Kann, R. (1944) 'The law of nations and the conduct of war in the early times of the standing army', *Journal of Politics,* Vol. vi.

Karber, P. A. (1970) 'Nuclear weapons and flexible response', *Orbis,* Vol. 14, No. 2, Summer.

Karsten, P. (1978) *Law, Soldiers, and Combat,* Westport, Greenwood Press.

Kaufmann, W. W. (ed.) (1956) *Military Policy and National Security,* Princeton, Princeton University Press.

Kaufmann, W. W. (1964) *The McNamara Strategy,* New York, Harper and Row.

Kecskemeti, P. (1970) 'Political rationality in ending war', *Annals of the American Academy of Political and Social Science,* November.

Keegan, J. (1978) *The Face of Battle,* Harmondsworth, Penguin Books.

Keen, M. H. (1965) *The Laws of War in the Late Middle Ages,* London, Routledge and Kegan Paul.

Khadduri, M. (1955) *War and Peace in the Law of Islam,* Baltimore, Johns Hopkins.

Kierman, F. A. (1974) 'Phases and modes of combat in early China' in F. Kierman and J. Fairbank (eds) *Chinese Ways in Warfare,* Cambridge, Harvard University Press.

King, J. E. (1957) 'Nuclear plenty and limited war', *Foreign Affairs,* Vol. xxxv, January.

King, P. (1975) 'The new American nuclear debate: flexible madness or inflexible sanity?' *Australian Outlook,* August.

Kissinger, H. A. (1957) *Nuclear Weapons and Foreign Policy,* New York, Harper for Council on Foreign Relations.

Kissinger, H. A. (1960) 'Limited war: nuclear or conventional?' *Daedalus,* Fall.

Kissinger, H. A. (1965) *The Troubled Partnership,* New York, McGraw-Hill.

Kissinger, H. A. (1979) *The White House Years,* London, Weidenfeld and Nicolson, Michael Joseph.

Knorr, K. and Read, T. (eds) (1962) *Limited Strategic War,* London, Pall Mall.

Knorr, K. (ed.) (1976) *Historical Dimensions of National Security Problems,* Lawrence, University Press of Kansas.

Kolkowicz, R. (1980) 'On limited war: Soviet and American doctrines', unpublished conference paper, Australian National University, July.

Kotzsch, L. (1956) *The Concept of War in Contemporary History and International Law,* Geneva, Librairie E. Droz.

Lambeth, B. S. (1975) *Selective Nuclear Operations and Soviet Strategy*, P-5506, Santa Monica, RAND Corporation.

Lambeth, B. S. (1977) 'Selective nuclear operations and Soviet strategy' in J. J. Holst and U. Nerlich (eds) *Beyond Nuclear Deterrence*, New York, Crane, Russak and Company.

Levinson, R. B. (1953) *In Defense of Plato*, Cambridge, Harvard University Press.

Liddell-Hart, B. H. (1946) 'War, limited' *Harper's Magazine*, March 1946.

Liddell-Hart, B. H. (1960) *Deterrent or Defence*, London, Stevens and Sons.

Lider, J. (1977) *On the Nature of War*, Farnborough, Saxon House.

Lider, J. (1979) *The Political and Military Laws of War: An Analysis of Marxist–Leninist Concepts*, Farnborough, Saxon House.

Locke, J. (1963) *Two Treatises of Government* (ed. by P. Laslett) Cambridge, Cambridge University Press.

Lofgren, C. A. (1967) 'How new is limited war', *Military Review*, July.

Machiavelli, N. (1883) *Discourses on the First Decade of Titus Livius*, London, Kegan Paul, Trench and Company.

Machiavelli, N. (1965) 'The art of war' in A. Gilbert *Machiavelli: The Chief Works and Others*, Durham, Duke University Press, Vol. 2, pp. 561–726.

McClintock, R. (1967) *The Meaning of Limited War*, Boston, Houghton Mifflin.

Martin, L. (1974) 'Changes in American strategic doctrine – an initial interpretation', *Survival*, Vol. xv, No. 4, July–August.

Martin, L. (1977) 'Limited options in European strategic thought' in J. Holst and U. Nerlich (eds) *Beyond Nuclear Deterrence*, New York, Crane, Russak and Company.

Martin, L. (ed.) (1979a) *Strategy in the Nuclear Age*, London, Heinemann.

Martin, L. (1979b) 'Limited nuclear war' in M. Howard (ed.) *Restraints on War*, Oxford, Oxford University Press.

Mattingly, G. (1962) *Renaissance Diplomacy*, London, Jonathan Cape.

Mavrodes, G. I. (1975) 'Conventions and the morality of war', *Philosophy and Public Affairs*, Vol. 4, No. 2, Winter.

May, M. (1970) 'Some advantages of a counterforce deterrence', *Orbis*, Vol. xiv, Summer.

Melzer, Y. (1975) *Concepts of Just War*, Leyden, Sijthoff.

Midgley, E. B. F. (1975) *The Natural Law Tradition and the Theory of International Relations*, London, Elek.

Miller, L. (1964) 'The contemporary significance of the doctrine of just war', *World Politics*, Vol. 16, No. 2, January.

Montesquieu (1949) *The Spirit of the Laws,* New York, Hafner Press.

Moore, J. N. (ed.) (1974) *Law and Civil War in the Modern World,* Baltimore, Johns Hopkins University Press.

More, St T. (1964) *Utopia* (ed. by E. Surtz) Newhaven, Yale University Press.

Morgenthau, H. (1977) 'The fallacy of thinking conventionally about nuclear weapons' in D. Carlton and C. Schaerf (eds) *Arms Control and Technological Innovation,* London, Croom Helm.

Morton, L. (1961) 'The twin essentials of limited war', *Survival,* May–June.

Moulton, H. B. (1973) *From Superiority to Parity: The United States and the Strategic Arms Race 1961–71,* Westport, Greenwood Press.

Mukherjee, T. B. (1967) *Inter-State Relations in Ancient India,* Meerut, Meenakshi Prakashan.

Myrdal, A. (1980) 'The super powers' game over Europe' in E. P. Thompson and D. Smith (eds) *Protest and Survive,* Harmondsworth, Penguin.

Nagel, T. (1974) 'War and massacre' in M. Cohen *et al.* (eds) *War and Moral Responsibility,* Princeton, Princeton University Press.

Nardin, T. (1976) 'Philosophy and international violence', *American Political Science Review,* Vol. 70, September.

Nash, H. T. (1975) *Nuclear Weapons and International Behaviour,* Leyden, Sijthoff.

Nef, J. U. (1950) *War and Human Progress,* London, Routledge and Kegan Paul.

Nettleship, M. A. *et al.* (eds) (1975) *War, Its Causes and Correlates,* The Hague, Mouton.

Nickerson, H. (1973) *Can We Limit War?* New York, Kennikat Press.

Nisbet, R. (1976) *The Social Philosophers,* St Albans, Paladin.

O'Brien, W. (1967) *Nuclear War, Deterrence and Morality,* New York, Newman Press.

O'Connell, D. P. (1975) *The Influence of Law on Sea Power,* Manchester, Manchester University Press.

Office of Technology Assessment (1979) *The Effects of Nuclear War,* Washington, USGPO.

Oman, C. W. C. (1953) *The Art of War in the Middle Ages* (rev. edn), Ithaca, Cornell University Press.

Oppenheim, L. (1921) *International Law: Vol. II War and Neutrality,* London, Longmans, Green and Company.

Osgood, R. (1957) *Limited War: The Challenge to American Strategy,* Chicago, University of Chicago Press.

Osgood, R. (1962) 'Nuclear arms: uses and limits', *The New Republic,* 10 September.

Osgood, R. (1970) 'The reappraisal of limited war' in Institute for Strategic Studies *Problems of Modern Strategy*, London, Chatto and Windus.

Osgood, R. (1979) *Limited War Revisited*, Boulder, Westview Press.

Osgood, R. and Tucker, R. W. (1967) *Force, Order and Justice*, Baltimore, Johns Hopkins University Press.

Otterbein, K. (1973) 'Anthropology of war' in J. J. Honigmann (ed.) *Handbook of Social and Cultural Anthropology*, New York, Rand McNally.

Paret, P. (1976) *Clausewitz and the State*, Oxford, Oxford University Press.

Paskins, B. and Dockrill, M. (1979) *The Ethics of War*, London, Duckworth.

Phillipson, C. (1911) *The International Law and Custom of Ancient Greece and Rome* (2 Vols) London, Macmillan.

Plato (1934) *The Laws*, London, Dent and Sons.

Plato (1941) *The Republic*, London, Oxford University Press.

Pocock, J. G. A. (1975) *The Machiavellian Moment*, Princeton, Princeton University Press.

Potter, R. (1969) *War and Moral Discourse*, Richmond, John Knox Press.

Potter, R. (1973) 'The moral logic of war' in C. R. Beitz and T. Herman (eds) *Peace and War*, San Francisco, Freeman and Company.

Pranger, R. J. and Labrie, R. P. (eds) (1977) *Nuclear Strategy and National Security: Points of View*, Washington, American Enterprise Institute for Public Policy Research.

Preston, R., Wise, S. and Werner, H. (1956) *Men in Arms*, London, Atlantic Press.

Pritchett, W. K. (1974) *The Greek State at War* (2 Vols), Berkeley, University of California Press.

Proctor, J. H. (ed.) (1965) *Islam and International Relations*, London, Pall Mall.

Pufendorf, S. (1934) *De Jure Naturae et Gentium Libri Octo*, London, Oxford for Carnegie Endowment for International Peace.

Purtill, R. (1971) 'On the just war', *Social Theory and Practice*, Fall.

Quester, G. (1966) *Deterrence Before Hiroshima: The Airpower Background of Modern Strategy*, New York, John Wiley and Sons.

Ramsey, P. (1961) *War and the Christian Conscience*, Durham, Duke University Press.

Ramsey, P. (1963) *The Limits of Nuclear War*, New York, Council on Religion and International Affairs.

Ramsey, P. (1968) *The Just War*, New York, Scribner's.

Rapoport, A. (1960) *Fights, Games and Debates*, Ann Arbor, University of Michigan Press.

Rathjens, G. (1974) 'Flexible response options', *Orbis* Vol. xviii, No. 3, Fall.

Reiss, H. (ed.) (1971) *Kant's Political Writings*, Cambridge, Cambridge University Press.

Richelson, J. T. (1979) 'Soviet strategic doctrine and limited nuclear operations: a metagame analysis', *Journal of Conflict Resolution*, Vol. 23, No. 2, June.

Rosecrance, R. N. (1959) 'Can we limit nuclear war?' *Military Review*, Vol. xxxviii, March.

Roszak, T. (1963) 'A just war analysis of two types of deterrence', *Ethics*, Vol. xxiii, No. 2, January.

Rousseau, J. J. (1973) *The Social Contract*, London, Dent and Sons.

Ruede, E. (1972) *The Morality of War: The Just War Theory and the Problem of Nuclear Deterrence in R. Paul Ramsey*, New York, Conventual Franciscan.

Russell, F. H. (1975) *The Just War in the Middle Ages*, Cambridge, Cambridge University Press.

Russell, F. M. (1936) *Theories of International Relations*, New York, D. Appleton-Century.

Russett, B. (1972) 'A countercombatant deterrent? Feasibility, morality and arms control' in S. Sarkesian (ed.) *The Military-Industrial Complex: A Reassessment*, Beverly Hills, Sage Publications.

Schelling, T. (1960) *The Strategy of Conflict*, Cambridge, Harvard University Press.

Schelling, T. (1966) *Arms and Influence*, New Haven, Yale University Press.

Schneider, H. W. (ed.) (1948) *Adam Smith's Moral and Political Philosophy*, New York, Hafner Publications.

Schoenberger, W. S. (1969) *Decision of Destiny*, Ohio, Ohio University Press.

Schwarzenberger, G. (1968) *International Law: Vol. II The Law of Armed Conflict*, London, Stevens and Sons.

Scott, J. B. (1934) *The Spanish Origin of International Law. Part I: Francisco De Vitoria and His Law of Nations*, London, Oxford for Carnegie Endowment for International Peace.

Scoville, H. (1974) 'Flexible madness', *Foreign Policy*, Spring.

Seabury, P. (1970) 'Provisionality and finality', *Annals of the American Academy of Political and Social Science*, November.

Sealey, R. (1976) *A History of the Greek City States circa 700–338 B.C.*, Berkeley, University of California Press.

Singh, S. D. (1965) *Ancient Indian Warfare With Special Reference to the Vedic Period*, Leyden, E. J. Brill.

Skinner, Q. (1981) *Machiavelli*, Oxford, Oxford University Press.

Slessor, Sir J. (1957) *The Great Deterrent*, London, Cassell.

Smith, A. K. (1965) *A Peril and a Hope: The Scientists' Movement in America 1945–7*, Chicago, University of Chicago Press.

Smoke, R. (1977) *War: Controlling Escalation*, Cambridge, Harvard University Press.

Snow, D. M. (1981) *Nuclear Strategy in a Dynamic World*, Alabama, University of Alabama Press.

Snyder, J. L. (1977) *The Soviet Strategic Culture: Implications for Limited Nuclear Operations*, R-2154-AF, Santa Monica, RAND Corporation.

Spaight, J. M. (1947) *Air Power and War Rights* (3rd edn), London, Longmans, Green and Company.

Speier, H. (1952) *Social Order and the Risks of War*, Cambridge, MIT Press.

Spellman, J. W. (1964) *Political Theory of Ancient India*, Oxford, Oxford University Press.

Stawell, F. M. (1929) *The Growth of International Thought*, London, Thornton Butterworth.

Steinbruner, J. (1976) 'Beyond rational deterrence: the struggle for new conceptions', *World Politics*, Vol. xxviii, No. 2, January.

Stillman, E. O. (1970) 'Civilian sanctuary and target avoidance policy in thermonuclear war', *Annals of the American Academy of Political and Social Science*, November.

Stockholm International Peace Research Institute (1976a) *The Law of War and Dubious Weapons*, Stockholm, Almquist and Wiksell.

Stockholm International Peace Research Institute (1976b) *Armaments and Disarmament in the Nuclear Age*, New Jersey, Humanities Press.

Stockholm International Peace Research Institute (1978a) *Tactical Nuclear Weapons: European Perspectives*, London, Taylor and Francis.

Stockholm International Peace Research Institute (1978b) *Anti-Personnel Weapons*, London, Taylor and Francis.

Strausz-Hupé, R. (1957) 'Limits of limited war', *The Reporter*, Vol. xvii, 28 November.

Sturzo, L. (1929) *The International Community and the Right of War*, London, Allen & Unwin.

Suarez, F. (1944) *Selections from Three Works* (ed. by J. B. Scott) Oxford for Carnegie Endowment for International Peace.

Talbot, S. (1979) *Endgame: The Inside Story of SALT II*, New York, Harper and Row.

Teller, E. and Brown, A. (1962) *The Legacy of Hiroshima*, London, Macmillan.

Thomas, A. V. W. and Thomas, A. J. (1970) *Legal Limits on the Use of Chemical and Biological Weapons*, Dallas, Southern Methodist University Press.

Thomas, J. R. (1966) 'Limited nuclear war in Soviet strategic thinking', *Orbis*, Spring.

Thompson, E. P. and Smith, D. (eds) (1980) *Protest and Survive*, Harmondsworth, Penguin Books.

Thucydides (1954) *History of the Peloponnesian War*, Harmondsworth, Penguin Books.

Tooke, J. (1965) *The Just War in Aquinas and Grotius*, London, SPCK.

Toynbee, A. J. (1951) *War and Civilization*, London, Oxford University Press.

Trooboff, P. D. (ed.) (1975) *Law and Responsibility in Warfare*, Chapel Hill, University of North Carolina Press.

Tucker, R. W. (1960) *The Just War: A Study in Contemporary American Doctrine*, Baltimore, Johns Hopkins.

Tucker, R. W. (1975) 'Weapons of warfare' in P. D. Trooboff (ed.) *Law and Responsibility in Warfare*, Chapel Hill, University of North Carolina Press.

Turner, G. and Challener, R. (eds) (1960) *National Security in the Nuclear Age*, London, Stevens and Sons.

Turney-High, H. H. (1949) *Primitive War: Its Practice and Concepts*, Columbia, University of South Carolina Press.

United States Senate (1975) *Briefing on Counterforce Attacks* (Hearings before the Subcommittee on Arms Control, International Law and Organization of the Committee on Foreign Relations, 11 September 1974) Washington, USGPO.

United States Senate (1976) *Effects of Limited Nuclear Warfare* (Hearings before the Subcommittee on Arms Control, International Organization and Security Agreements of the Committee on Foreign Relations, 18 September 1975), Washington, USGPO.

United States War College (1977) *Strategies, Alliances, and Military Power: Changing Roles*, Leyden, Sijthoff.

Van Cleave, W. R. and Barnett, R. W. (1974) 'Strategic adaptability', *Orbis*, Vol. 18, No. 3, Fall.

Van Cleave, W. R. and Cohen, S. T. (1978) *Tactical Nuclear Weapons: An Examination of the Issues*, London, MacDonald and Jane's.

Vattel, E. de (1916) *The Law of Nations or the Principles of Natural Law*, Washington, Carnegie Institution.

Vaughan, C. E. (ed.) (1962) *The Political Writings of Jean Jacques Rousseau*, Oxford, Basil Blackwell.

Veale, F. J. P. (1968) *Advance to Barbarism: The Development of Total Warfare from Sarajevo to Hiroshima*, London, Mitre Press.

Verbruggen, J. F. (1977) *The Art of Warfare in Western Europe During the Middle Ages*, Amsterdam, North Holland.

Wakin, M. (ed.) (1979) *War, Morality and the Military Profession*, Boulder, Westview Press.

Walzer, M. (1977) *Just and Unjust Wars,* New York, Basic Books.

Walzer, M. (1980) 'The moral standing of states: a response to four critics', *Philosophy and Public Affairs,* Vol. 9, No. 3.

Wasserstrom, R. (ed.) (1970) *War and Morality,* Belmont, Wadsworth.

Watkins, F. (ed.) (1951) *Hume: Theory of Politics,* Edinburgh, Nelson.

Weisacker, C. F. von (1978) *The Politics of Peril,* New York, Seabury Press.

Wells, D. A. (1969) 'How much can the "just war" justify?' *Journal of Philosophy,* Vol. lxvi, No. 23, 4 December.

Wernham, A. G. (ed.) (1958) *Benedict de Spinoza: The Political Works,* Oxford, Oxford University Press.

Wesson, R. G. (1978) *State Systems: International Pluralism, Politics and Culture,* New York, Free Press.

Wharton, M. (1955) *A Nation's Security: The Case of Dr J. Robert Oppenheimer,* London, Secker and Warburg.

Wilborn, T. L. (1977) 'The new flexible strategic response doctrine: insights from critics of mutual assured destruction' in United States War College *Strategies, Alliances and Military Power,* Leyden, Sijthoff.

Wohlstetter, A. (1974) 'Threats and promises of peace: Europe and America in the new era', *Orbis,* Winter.

Wolfe, T. W. (1966) 'Trends in Soviet thinking on theatre warfare and limited war' in J. Erickson *et al.* (eds) *The Military-Technical Revolution,* London, Pall Mall.

Wolfers, A. and Martin, L. (eds) (1956a) *The Anglo-American Tradition in Foreign Affairs,* New Haven, Yale University Press.

Wolfers, A. (1956b) 'Could a war in Europe be limited?' *Yale Review,* Winter.

Wolff, C. (1934) *Ius Gentium Methodo Scientifica Pertractatum,* London, Oxford for Carnegie Endowment for International Peace.

Wolin, S. S. (1961) *Politics and Vision: Continuity and Innovation in Western Political Thought,* London, Allen & Unwin.

Wright, J. W. (1934) 'Sieges and customs of war at the opening of the eighteenth century', *American Historical Review,* July.

Wright, N. A. R. (1976) 'The tree of battles of Honoré Bouvet and the laws of war' in C. T. Allmand (ed.) *War, Literature and Politics in the Late Middle Ages,* Liverpool, Liverpool University Press.

Wright, Q. (1942) *A Study of War* (2 Vols), Chicago, University of Chicago Press.

Wright, R. F. (1930) *Medieval Internationalism: The Contribution of the Medieval Church to International Law and Peace,* London, Williams and Norgate.

Yadin, Y. (1963) *The Art of Warfare in Biblical Lands,* London, Weidenfeld and Nicholson.

York, H. (1976) *The Advisors: Oppenheimer, Teller and the Superbomb,* San Francisco, Freeman and Company.

Index